STANDING TALL
Together

JACQUI TAM

STANDING TALL
Together

JACQUI TAM

ICEBERG

Published in Canada by Iceberg Publishing, Edmonton

Library and Archives Canada Cataloguing in Publication

Title: Standing tall : together / Jacqui Tam.
Names: Tam, Jacqui, 1960- author. | Container of (work): Tam, Jacqui, 1960-
    Standing tall. | Container of (work): Tam, Jacqui, 1960- Twenty-one days in
    May.
Identifiers: Canadiana (print) 20220470065 | Canadiana (ebook) 2022047012X |
    ISBN 9781989815076 (hardcover) | ISBN 9781989815083 (EPUB)
Subjects: LCSH: Tam, Jacqui, 1960- | LCSH: Cancer—Patients—Family
    relationships—Newfoundland and Labrador. | LCSH: Mothers and daughters—
    Canada—Biography. | LCSH: Children of cancer patients—Canada—
    Biography. | LCSH: Alzheimer's disease—Patients—Canada—Biography. |
    LCSH: Alzheimer's   disease—Patients—Family relationships—Canada. | LCSH:
    Fathers and daughters—Canada—Biography. | LCGFT: Biographies.
Classification: LCC RC523.2 .T343 2023 | DDC 362.1968/310092—dc23

Standing Tall: A Daughter's Gift
First trade paperback edition: August 2002
First pocket paperback edition: January 2006
Special international edition: January 2010
Tenth anniversary edition: August 2012

Standing Tall: Twenty-One Days in May
First edition: September 2016

Standing Tall Together
First edition: October 2022

Cover Design: Kenneth Tam

Iceberg Publishing
301-14032 23 Ave NW
Edmonton, AB Canada T6R 3L6
icebergpublishing.com

For my parents
Richard Joseph Barron and Mary Louise Barron (nee Morry)

Introduction

My father would have been 100 years old on August 8th this year, and my mother 94 on September 8th. I can't help but smile when I remember how she liked to remind him of their age difference and tease him about the fact that she was the younger woman in his life.

When he died on October 30, 1994 after his decade long battle with Alzheimer's, he was just 72; I was 34. Looking back, I really had no concept of how young we both were.

When she died on May 25, 2006, three weeks after a cancer diagnosis, she was just 77; I was two days shy of 46. I remember vividly that the first thing I did on the morning of my birthday was read my mother's obituary in the newspaper, the one I'd written two nights before.

When I find myself wishing that they were with us still, I remind myself that it is unlikely either would have made it to 90 or beyond.

Life was hard during their younger years.

My mother was a 1940s tuberculosis survivor, the significance of which I didn't fully appreciate until her weakened lungs became one of the key factors in her inability to recover from surgery to remove the cancer in her abdomen.

My father had health issues of one sort or another all throughout my childhood. Every three years or so for pretty much as long as I can remember, he'd end up in hospital. He'd lost two-thirds of his stomach, a lobe of one lung, and much more before Alzheimer's held him in its grip. My mother would say it was good that he'd married a nurse, because he really needed one.

Logically, I know that unless I could somehow have given them both the gift of almost-perfect health, wanting them here today is a kind of selfishness. Their quality of life would have been less than either wanted or deserved. I could never want to see my father's suffering through Alzheimer's extended. I could never want my mother to be the person she never wanted to be — an invalid who depended on others for her most basic needs.

But that still doesn't stop me from wishing — especially on those days that etch themselves on our hearts and souls — that they were with us still. That I could pick up the phone, knowing my mother would say the perfect thing, or hear my father tell me, "Don't worry, duck, everything will be alright."

Then something happens that reminds me I am utterly foolish, because of course they are here with us still, and I allow myself to feel their presence, almost as if they were standing beside me.

Like the day on the side of the mountain where my son, Kenneth, married the beautiful Jeannine.

It was 2021, the world was still dealing with COVID-19, but the planning of the event was going smoothly. There was just one detail that was proving to be problematic: the groom's necktie. Few retail outlets were stocking them in a work-from-home world, and though we had dozens between us — including all the ones I'd collected during my own suit-and-tie phase — it didn't seem quite right that a tie worn so often to one of our respective offices should join us on the mountain on such a momentous day. But all efforts, online and otherwise, to locate the perfect tie, were proving unsuccessful.

Don't worry, I told Kenneth — because I totally believed it — the right tie will come along.

Unrelated to wedding preparations, my husband Peter and I

decided it was time, after seven years, to start sorting through the bins that were occupying a rented storage locker where we'd quickly stashed things after relocating from a big house in one province to a smaller house in another.

It was a warm, sunny summer day, and I was sitting in our garage surrounded by dark blue and light grey bins. When I lifted the lid off one, I looked at Peter, told him it contained keepsakes from mom and dad. My heart broke a little, even as it filled — the past, with all its joys and heartbreaks, suddenly filling me.

Slowly I began to remove the items at the top. Don't ask me to tell you what was there because I can't remember. Everything faded from my mind when I saw a box with a plastic, see-through cover, a box that contained one of my father's neckties — one he would have worn when he was still able to dress up in his grey flannel pants, navy or black blazer, and take my mother to a work dinner that would be followed by dancing. I had kept it because it had been one of his favourites. I hadn't realized it would be a gift he gave to his grandson and his new granddaughter-in-law, across time and space.

The right colours. The kind of paisley pattern that was one of my mother's favorites.

Dad, I thought, I should have known there was no way you were going to miss Kenneth's wedding. And if there was a tear or two in my eye, or if the world began to spin a little as connections across time and space and lives made themselves felt, Peter and I will never tell.

There was the little detail, of course, of making sure the tie really did match Kenneth's suit and both he and Jeannine liked it. So I admit to holding my breath while it was collected and the suit brought out. But of course, it was perfect. And the little man, now grown, who so adored his grandfather, had 'Dick' with him on the side of the mountain when, eyes full of tears, he said his vows.

And my mother? Well, since I had legally been appointed the

marriage commissioner for that day — it being COVID and there only being four of us plus the photographer at the wedding — she was standing there too, captivated by the beautiful Jeannine, marveling at how she could look so stunning after hiking up the side of a mountain, and I swear, trying to fix my windblown hair, even as she fretted about whether or not the marriage was actually real and legal if I was conducting it.

I felt them there that day... I feel them here with me right now as I write this.

• • •

Much has happened in the 28 years since my father died and the 20 since *A Daughter's Gift* was first released. Much has happened in the 16 years since my mother passed away, and the six since *Twenty-one Days in May* came out.

My father's story is set in a time before today's level of awareness about Alzheimer's — before current diagnosis practices, before there were any drugs that might help slow the progression of the disease, before Alzheimer's support groups had the funds for robust awareness campaigns and programs. Had the story been set in more recent times, many of the questions we had, especially in the early stages, would have been answered, and the experience different — at least in some ways — because of that.

But what isn't different, and what is at the core of *A Daughter's Gift*, is the impact of the disease on both the individual and loved ones — how it can ravage people and change their relationships with one another.

What isn't different is the importance of holding onto the fact that your loved one still exists, albeit within a now tortured mind and body, and as impossible as it seems, love will find a way to break through for moments of connection and knowing if you are present for them.

What isn't different is the value of and need to appreciate the good days and the special, surprising moments, and never let the disease become the definition of a person's life, never let it erase them.

What isn't different is the impact of that person's life, despite the disease.

A few years after *A Daughter's Gift* was released, when I was still regularly delivering presentations to Alzheimer's groups, Kenneth accompanied me to an event that was scheduled on a particularly stormy night. He'd be both my company for the drive and my tech support at a venue that was expected to cause some challenges in that regard. It was the first time he would have seen me deliver the presentation, and when it was over and we were slowly driving home on icy, snowy roads, he told me there was another message he thought people should hear.

As I sat listening to the stories you told and looking at the photos of Dick up on the screen, it occurred to me that I only ever knew my grandfather when he had Alzheimer's. I never knew Dick when he was well. I only knew the "sick" Dick, not the "healthy" Dick. And despite that, my grandfather was one of the three most powerful and positive influences on my life. People need to know that. People need to know how important they still are, to know that Alzheimer's doesn't take that away. Alzheimer's is incredibly cruel, and a journey that no one should have to endure, but it doesn't end a person's importance or significance or influence.

I included that message in future presentations. As time went on, and not just family members but people who were in the early stages of Alzheimer's themselves increasingly came to my talks, I was so very grateful to see how much this observation meant to them as they inevitably came up to me afterwards to thank me, tears in their eyes.

My mother's story was a sharp contrast to my father's in so many ways, and this bears out in its telling.

She retained her mental sharpness until the very end, acutely aware of all that was happening and determined that her final days be on her terms. Her battle against what I have since learned was a particularly aggressive and rare form of cancer, in combination with the tuberculosis-caused damage to her lungs, could never have been won, even the medium term.

Before *Twenty-one Days* first came out, Kenneth offered to write a Foreword for the short volume, an offer I gratefully accepted.

This story comes from a different place, he wrote. *Instead of crossing time and space, it holds its counsel within a three-week window. Though it touches on the certainties of my mother's relationship with my grandmother, it is rooted in the daily reality of a proud woman and her daughter, quietly approaching an end neither is naive about.*

The differences between this story and A Daughter's Gift *were inevitable. My grandmother's death affected my mother very differently than my grandfather's had. This was not just because the circumstances were so distinct — abrupt and unexpected, instead of protracted and inevitable — but because Jacqui Tam's relationship with Mary Louise Barron was truly different than her relationship with Richard Joseph Barron.*

So much of what my mother holds dearest and consciously chooses to be part of her identity came from my grandfather's quiet strength and trust. He gave her courage and belief in herself, as any father should do — must do — for his children. He was her rock and inspiration. Mary Barron was her drive.

My grandmother was the sort of nurse who would see darkness and move towards it. Her calling was to help those in pain, and that dedication shaped both the way she treated others, and the expectations she placed on her daughter.

She always impressed upon my mother the need for steel, determination, and toughness, but also kindness. She expected her only daughter to set the same example that she herself strived to embody. She gave her daughter love, but tested her always. This was, I think, as important to my mother's life, and my life, and even the creation of Iceberg Publishing, as everything my grandfather shared with us.

Instead of trying to capture it all, my mother has chosen this final chapter — this fragment that brings everything that mattered between her and her mother into sharp focus. Paired with A Daughter's Gift, *these twenty-one days will show you how two very different parents together managed to forge one of the most formidable people I know.*

I thought a long time about those words after I first read them. My father was my rock, my inspiration — that was a certainty. Was my mother my drive? Yes, I think she largely was, though she was not only that.

For years I watched her toil late into the night working out the schedules for her nursing students' clinical rotations, even when she was dealing with the most raging migraines, then get up the next morning, still with the migraine, fix her hair and make-up, put on her crisp white uniform and head to the hospital.

For years I watched her push and push — in both her professional and personal life — doing what she believed was needed or expected of her. Rarely asking for help. Keeping up appearances. Trying to never let anyone down.

• • •

My father was a remarkable man, my mother a remarkable woman. I am forever grateful to have been their daughter and every day, I still draw on the gifts they gave me, the foundation they laid, the lessons they taught, the examples they set, their strength and love.

Which is why, to mark the 20th anniversary of the publishing company that was born with my father's story, we have created *Standing Tall: Together*, and brought their two stories together under the same cover in an Iceberg Publishing special edition omnibus.

I can't help but feel this is the way it was always meant to be.

In celebration of two incredibly special people.

In recognition of their enduring impact.

And most of all, in the deepest gratitude and love.

STANDING TALL

A Daughter's Gift

The mind forgets. The soul remembers.

JACQUI TAM

Richard Joseph Barron

1
Looking for Stars

I remember the moment as if it had happened yesterday. My father was near the end of his struggle with Alzheimer's and though physically weak, he would refuse to sit or lie for any length of time, choosing instead to shuffle painfully, slowly, and unsteadily from one end of his house to the other. Sometimes he would allow my mother or me to walk with him, holding his hand or arm for support; mostly, we had to remain a step or two behind, ready to catch him if he stumbled but knowing that if he did, the best we could do was slow his fall to the hardwood floor.

But on this particular night, he was content to clutch my hand as we walked. There was no conversation for he had long since lost his ability to effectively communicate with words. Nor was there any recognition, since his children and grandchildren had all but ceased to exist for him a couple of years before. In fact, his periods of lucidity were now so infrequent and so brief, I no longer really hoped for them. So we simply walked back and forth through the living room and dining room of my mother and father's house, past the windows from which he'd hung Christmas lights through all the years of my childhood; past the antique piano I had struggled on through seven years of music lessons; past the couch where we would sit for birthday and anniversary photos. Back and forth. Back and forth. Past memories that filled my heart and mind, even as I wondered what was filling his.

Back and forth. Shuffling. Walking. Going nowhere.

At some point in the evening's journey, the straight path we'd been following changed. Veering to the left, as if choosing some fork in an invisible road, my father led me to the dining room window. His left hand still gripped mine as his right hand awkwardly pushed aside the edge of the heavy lace curtain. Still grasping my hand with his left and the curtain with his right, he looked upwards to the sky, lifted our joined hands and said: *Look. The stars. Look for the stars.* Clearly. Articulately. Peacefully. My father's voice as it would have sounded years ago. My father's smile as it would have looked. My father's eyes when he looked into mine, as alive as they had been in the past, before Alzheimer's had turned them from a lively and mischievous grey-green to the dull, non-existent colour of emptiness.

I don't remember what I said to him. I only remember that at that particular moment, I knew this man was speaking to his daughter, that my father was speaking to me — the married woman who still counted him as one of her very best friends; the little girl he'd loved and protected.

Seconds later he let the curtain fall and we went back to our walking. He slipped back into his world and I slipped into mine, wondering where these brief moments of recognition come from and thinking back to the stories he'd told me about sailing, about using the stars to find his way through uncertain and uncharted waters. His eyes became vacant; his body fought unsuccessfully to stay erect; his walk again became the anguished, slow-motion struggle to move one foot in front of the other on legs that were ready to collapse.

My father died some weeks later. I honestly can't remember the exact period of time that passed between his reference to the stars and his early morning death on October 30th — the final weeks were a blur marked only by heartbreaking images, unshed tears and an agonizing helplessness, not the calendars or clocks of normal times.

After he died, my mother and I visited the funeral home to take care of the 'arrangements'. I had never before made the arrangements to bury someone, and so had no experience with this type of session. The funeral director led us carefully through the steps and listened patiently while we talked about how special a man my father had been, how much he'd suffered, how we wanted our farewell to him to be as perfect as we could make it. When a book filled with photographs of flower arrangements was passed to me, I wondered silently how I could possibly find flowers beautiful enough for my father. I knew he must have red roses, because red roses had been particularly special to him. But roses alone didn't seem to be enough.

I slowly turned the pages of the binder, only half aware of the conversation continuing in the background and returning always to a single page and a particular arrangement of red roses, white carnations and another type of flower I didn't remember seeing before. *What are these flowers?* I interrupted. *They're beautiful.*

I turned the book back towards the funeral director and slid it across the desk.

They're lilies, he answered, *stargazer lilies.*

I believe moments like this prove that the people who love us and the people we love, never really leave us; that messages across time and space and lives are not just figments of over-ambitious imaginations, but realities of everyday existence; that if the bond between two souls is strong enough and loving enough, communication is possible, even in circumstances where logic tells us it is impossible. And I believe, in that moment, my father completed a message he had somehow found the strength and awareness to begin on the nameless night of weeks before.

I told my mother and the funeral director that this was the arrangement — these were my father's flowers. And exquisite stargazer lilies and rich red roses adorned my father's casket. A precious gift to him; a precious gift to me. *Look for the stars,* he'd told me, and without even knowing where or when to look, I'd found them — at the moment I needed them most.

My father died of Alzheimer's, but I haven't lost the man who had been such a powerful and positive influence in my life. He is still with me, his stars and his lilies are with me.

This is the story of my father, as I remember him. This is the story of his struggle with a devastating disease, and the struggle of those who suffered beside him. This is the story of his presence still in my life and my own journey through his stars. And it is a tribute to a profoundly honourable man who lived his life not for glory or fame and not for wealth, but to be a good man, to be a good father, and above all, to make a difference.

Never doubt that love is the

most powerful force in the universe.

Not fame. Not glory. Not wealth.

Love.

2

A Solitary Search for Answers

My father was the only person who knew about his earliest Alzheimer's symptoms, and even he could not have known where they were leading. He would be driving home from work, or travelling to a well-known location in the city — St. John's, Newfoundland — where he'd lived for more than thirty years, and all knowledge of where he was would suddenly disappear.

When he eventually spoke to me of these episodes, almost five years after they had started, he described them as 'blackouts' that would force him to pull over to the side of the road and sit for an undetermined number of minutes. Eventually, the blackout would end, he would pull back onto the road and ultimately reach his destination. Initially he said nothing about them, and initially the 'attacks' (as they became known in our family) were short enough and infrequent enough that during normal times, he could almost ignore their existence.

For my part, I have more questions than answers about the early stages of his illness. I don't know how long and how much he hid from all of us. I don't know when the first episode occurred, how long it was until the second, or when it became impossible for him to believe his forgetfulness was simply the result of being preoccupied by some work or family problem. I don't know what he thought or felt the first time all that he knew vanished from his awareness. I don't know what he felt for days afterwards. And I can only begin to imagine the feelings of panic and terror that must have rushed through his entire being when he became totally and completely lost, still knowing this should not be so, when he became aware that something was terribly wrong.

He must have sat behind the steering wheel of his four-wheel drive vehicle, with his heart racing, his eyes darting, his fingers clutching and thumbs drumming the steering wheel. He must have stayed awake at night, wondering what was happening — when and where it would happen again.

If I'd known what was going on, perhaps I would have understood more fully, why he increasingly refused to do things he had always loved to do and go places he had always loved to go. Perhaps I would have looked beyond the physical for explanations when he would begin to feel ill just before a planned outing. I knew he wasn't well, that physically he had less energy than usual; I knew he was increasingly nervous about not being well; I knew he sometimes seemed preoccupied and on occasion asked the same question more than once. But I didn't know, or I didn't want to know, what was really happening. The signs weren't invisible, but for a time I didn't understand them.

In the early stages of Alzheimer's there is both denial and hope. The physical and mental symptoms you witness could be caused by any number of conditions and the conviction is the cause will be found and treated and life will return to normal. The reality and the tragedy is that the symptoms do not stop.

A diagnosis of hypoglycemia and the related diet adjustments offered the first hope for my father. An identified Vitamin B^{12} deficiency and resulting supplements offered the second. A controversial treatment called Chelation therapy, designed to remove harmful chemicals from the bloodstream, offered the third. And each contributed to some apparent, albeit small physical improvement. But my father's overall condition continued to deteriorate, his memories continued to fade and he became more and more afraid.

I have many memories of his wild-eyed, frightened look. I have many memories of him driving with me, sitting in the passenger seat in the front of my car, twirling his thumbs constantly, eyes fixed straight ahead with such intensity that I would wonder what he feared would happen if he looked at the scenes passing on the left or the right. I have many memories of his fingers clutching his legs with such strength that the knuckles straining against the weathered skin were white. Holding tightly to something, anything … though I never really knew what.

My father taught me to drive and I had always enjoyed it when he drove places with me, keeping me company when there were errands to be run or people to be picked up from school or work. But I came to dread the inevitable twirling thumbs and clutching fingers. The repetitious questions. And the aura of fear that seemed to radiate from him and then envelope me as he locked his gaze forward.

The fear that clung like an increasingly heavy and uncomfortable cloak on my father's shoulders and the associated physical habits weren't the only warning signs. My father's self-control had been a keystone of his character and when it came to illness, even extremely serious surgeries, he gathered the will to force recovery much more quickly than was considered normal. Within forty-eight hours of having part of a lung removed he was out of bed and forcing himself to stand erect, beginning his own battle to ensure the shoulder the doctors warned him would now droop, remained as straight and square as the unaffected one. And that's just one example.

But he wasn't able to control or beat his Alzheimer's symptoms. He tried. He'd always been an avid reader, and his reading tastes began to change. Books and magazines on illness prevention, aging, memory, alternative medicines, and the brain began filling the spaces on his bedside table. He had always been organized and knew where every tool in his garage and every item in his desk could be found, but he became obsessed with the arrangements and placements — regrouping with elastic bands and cases, reorganizing things into drawers and carefully labeling them. Regrouping, reorganizing, regrouping, reorganizing. It was as if he was willing himself to remember where he was putting things, and when he failed, going back to the same task over and over again, as if the repetition was the answer.

In these early stages, my father was increasingly afraid, increasingly frustrated, increasingly angry. He conducted a private search for answers while demanding a level of self-control that ensured many of his failures and emotions were hidden from us. But I still remember the haggard look on his face, the strand of hair that would so uncharacteristically fall into his eyes, the muttering over something forgotten when he thought no one was close enough to hear, and the days he would spend in his bed after the most recent 'attack'. The slow, insidious change, the immeasurable suffering and the inevitable loss of control.

The intense challenge when you love someone who suffers from a disease like Alzheimer's is to remember that whether in the first days or the last, the disease can not be allowed to become the definition of the person's life. People with Alzheimer's, like people with other diseases, are not their illnesses. They are individuals, with stories to tell, knowledge to share, contributions to make. They are sons and daughters, mothers and fathers, lovers and friends. But they are not their illnesses and we cannot allow them to become so, even when their illnesses seem all-consuming. Even when they are all consuming. When we can hardly bear to watch what is happening. When we sometimes cannot admit to ourselves what we see.

This man who sat beside me in my car and twirled his thumbs

around and around and around was still the father I had always adored. This man whose hair fell into his eyes unnoticed as he frantically fought with his own mind was still my greatest teacher. He was not his illness and I will be forever thankful that I somehow always knew that.

An estimated decade after the blackouts began, when my father no longer knew me, when he'd become a shell that still held enough awareness to try desperately to appear normal, someone I worked with confided that as a mother, her greatest fear was that she would become desperately ill and that the ill or crippled mother was the only person her daughter would remember. Not the young mother; not the happy mother; not the mother who had been her friend. She didn't actually ask whether or not that was how it was with me — if I could remember my father before his illness or if the illness had become so all-encompassing that it had somehow erased the man, replaced who he was — but I saw the question in her eyes and felt it in her heart.

I told her that I saw more clearly than perhaps I wanted to the physical and mental ravages of my father's illness, and that my greatest pain and my tremendous confusion was that such a wonderful man must suffer so... but in my eyes he was the man he had always been, in my heart and soul he was my father, and everything we had shared was no less important, no less significant, no less real because of his condition. Everything he had been, he still was.

When youth becomes age and joy becomes pain,

see with your heart, remember with your soul

and treasure the person within the transformation.

He is still there. She is still there. And your love will be recognized.

3

War and Wisdom

My father and mother married when he was thirty and she was twenty-four. At that point in his life, he was six feet two inches tall, a muscled 180 pounds. His black hair, which he wore brushed straight back and cut fashionably short, had just begun to grey around the temples. He walked with confidence and pride; he had a mischievous twinkle in his grey-green eyes and a chuckle in his heart. He'd already spent more than a dozen years travelling the world — in the merchant navy during the second world war; in the army during the Korean war; and as a ship's engineer between the wars.

He had met my mother less than a year before he left for Korea while she was suffering from tuberculosis. Confined to bed in her room in her parent's home in the picturesque community of Ferryland, Newfoundland, she maintains she was much more interested in reading her book than meeting the visitor her sister's boyfriend was bringing. As the story goes, he fell in love with her that first night and visited four times before he left for the war. When he asked if he could write to her and if she would write to him, she agreed, thinking his request was based on the need of a lonely soldier to have a 'girl' at home. She received the first letter from him on the same day she received the news that she must be admitted to the hospital for what would, at best, be a long-term stay.

For the next two years, my mother fought her battle with

tuberculosis and my father fought his battles in Korea. By the time he returned home to Newfoundland, some three years after he'd left, she'd recovered from the disease, completed her nursing studies and was working. They'd also been out of contact for six months and she was engaged to be married to someone else.

In the last months of my father's life, my mother frequently relived her decision to break off the Korean contact so many years before. As she watched the suffering and isolation caused by his illness, she would wonder at the suffering and isolation he experienced during a war forty years in the past and feel tremendous guilt that she may have then added to a despair she really hadn't understood.

The story of my mother and father could have ended in 1951, but it didn't. When friends and relatives encouraged my father to contact her, he did, and the dashing Dick Barron and vivacious Mary Morry were married six months later.

Even though I didn't share this period of time with my father, my mother spoke so often of their whirlwind romance that it became an integral part of my own memories, and I have no problem picturing the man he was when they married. Just as I have no problem picturing at least some aspects of his earlier years, because his talent as a storyteller provided a collection of diverse images from his late teens and early twenties.

He was shipwrecked in the North Atlantic when his ship was torpedoed and he told me, as often as I asked, how he'd spent nine hours clinging to the sides of the survival raft, his legs freezing in the icy water as he talked continuously to the only other person to reach the raft with him — a shipmate who'd died shortly after they'd entered the water. He said he couldn't let himself think about the death of his friend and the only way not to think about it was to talk to him as if he was still alive. So he talked and drank the rum that was part of the emergency supplies, and he survived. He didn't focus on the pain of those hours in the telling of his story; nor did he try to protect me by hiding it. In fact, he often joked about the antifreeze, as he called the rum. But the terror of the seas was one of the horrors that revisited him in the late stages of his life.

He was part of the cleanup crew for Hiroshima, one of the many young men who wore masks and gloves to enter an area of devastation and destruction — an area filled with invisible and unknown dangers. He told me, as often as I asked, about the camera he carried with him that day, the roll of film that was completely blank despite the fact that he'd taken a number of photos, and the ultimate confiscation of that film and the mementos he'd collected. He believed the radiation had erased the images on the film, the same images that were forever etched on his heart and soul, and which perhaps led to his later refusal to eat anything prepared in a microwave. A paranoia which, had we realized it, was one of the earliest manifestations of the disease that was taking control of him.

My mother says my father could not bear to hear a child cry, that he could handle almost anything except a child's tears and pain. This sometimes made things difficult when my two brothers (Steve who was six years older than me and Rik who was three years older) and I were young, but my mother understood that his reaction was rooted in his war-ridden past where he'd heard screams of pain, fear and despair from too many emaciated, starving, suffering and dying children. And she did what she could to help him move beyond the nightmares of his past.

When my father spoke to me of the children of Korea, he talked about the little boy he and some other members of his troop had rescued and hidden in their camp. The small boy's home had been destroyed and his only remaining family, his two sisters, were missing. They'd found the boy alone and crying and brought him to their camp where he would sleep in the foot of my dad's sleeping bag. They made sure he was well-fed, well-clothed and well-cared for. The plan was to either locate his family or find a way to bring the child back to Canada. It took some time and more than a little effort, but they eventually found his sisters and reunited the family. That little boy stayed in my father's heart.

He told me other things about Korea — of days and nights spent building bridges and blowing them up, of using chemicals to stay awake for seventy-two or 100 hours because even a moment's rest would have meant death. He talked of sleeping under the snow — of how he used the snow as his only blanket while breathing through a snorkel that broke the surface and provided an air path, of how his main concern was the enemy finding them during the night and filling the holes with snow. He told me about the painstaking and intense task of clearing mine fields, about how mines were tricky and sometimes they were placed on top of one another so the removal of the top mine would activate the bottom. His eyes filled with pain, he told me about the day he watched a man, who refused to listen to his cautions, lift a deactivated mine out of a field and be blown apart by the one that lay beneath.

What is perhaps most amazing in all of this is that there was no hatred or animosity in his stories and so I did not think to hate the people who'd been labeled enemies. He did not even seem to judge them, so I never thought to either.

Of course, not all his stories were tragic. Some were exciting or funny. Some were so far-fetched and told with such a mischievous twinkle that we never really knew where fact ended and extreme exaggeration began.

My father had been travelling for some fifteen years before he returned from Korea. He'd sailed the oceans, walked and run through jungles. He'd flown in airplanes and even parachuted from them. He would chuckle over the fact that he'd managed to spend more hours on or in the ocean than most other people without ever having learned how to swim. He would speak with a mixture of sadness, amusement and self-derision about the fact that shortly before his release from the army, he'd trusted most of his possessions to an acquaintance who was returning home before him. (The acquaintance disappeared with my father's suitcases — shoes, suits, photos, mementos, everything.) And he would chuckle whenever he put on a pair of sandals because open-toed shoes carried the memory of a little boy's startled reaction to the first pair of sandals my father wore after he'd returned from the West Indies. The little boy, astonished by my father's attire as he strode down a city street, came to an abrupt stop and proclaimed loudly to his mother and everyone else within hearing range — *Look Mommy! Look! That man's wearing lady's shoes!*

I never really saw my dad as a wanderer, but in retrospect, I guess that's how he could have been described. Maybe he was searching for something or someone. Maybe he was searching for himself. Whatever he may or may not have been seeking, I believe he simply set his own path from his very early days. He accepted the world as his school and its peoples as his teachers. He found his own questions, his own answers and became a powerful teacher in his own right.

In each life there is joy and there is despair.

There are roads to be traveled

and worlds to be explored.

But we choose what we will see, we choose what we will learn

and perhaps most important of all

we choose what we will teach.

4

Phantoms in the Night

I was about ten years old before I really believed my father slept through the night, that he did more than lie in the dark listening and resting. Honestly.

I had a terrible habit of waking when the house was dark and quiet, usually because of terrifying dreams — nightmares that would leave me shaking and so paralyzed with fear that I was incapable of leaving my bed. My parents' room was located down a short hallway from mine, but I'd be too frightened to walk even that distance, imagining that the object of my dream-induced terror (the witch, ghost or monster) was waiting just inside the living room entrance, ready to kidnap or attack me as I passed the doorway. So I would lie in my bed and because I didn't want to awaken my older brothers (afraid I'd be teased the next day) or alert the 'monsters' lurking just beyond my vision, I would quietly, very quietly, call to my father... *Daddy... Daddy*. And he would immediately answer me. *What is it, duck?*

When I told him I was scared, he'd get out of bed and come to me, sit by my side until I went back to sleep or lead the terrified, sleepy-eyed girl back to his room, where I'd take up more space than I should have in my mom and dad's double bed.

I believed (as illogical as it now seems) that anyone who could answer such a quiet call so quickly, couldn't possibly have been sleeping. Also, since he never looked groggy, never complained that I had woken him or said anything at all the next day about being tired, since he always went to bed much later than I and was always up long in advance, with breakfast prepared and sitting on the table when he called me, I simply accepted, at face value, the evidence that indicated he stayed awake most of the night.

This belief was likely intensified by the fact that until I was seven years old, I actually slept on a small cot-style bed in my parent's room. My paternal grandmother had moved in with us when I was two, and the three-bedroom house accommodated my two brothers in one room, my grandmother in the second, and my parents and I in the third. I don't remember waking up in the night as much during this period... except for when I developed a habit of rolling off the mattress and falling with an unpleasant thud onto the floor... but this was quickly solved when my father made and installed a guard rail for my bed. In essence, my childlike eyes had no evidence to support the fact that my father slept through the night, so I simply believed he didn't.

There was one other reason I awoke frequently as a child — pain in my knees that was so severe it would wake me up and keep me from going back to sleep. On these occasions, I'd walk to the room myself and stand in the doorway, usually getting a response even before I uttered a word. Those nights must have been even more disturbing for my parents, because the pains were harder to ease than the aftermaths of the nightmares and because they would know, even if I didn't, that the pains held much more real threats than the nightmares.

As an adult looking back over those years, I'm both amazed and ashamed that it never even occurred to me how my seven-year presence in my parent's bedroom might have been a terrible inconvenience, or that continual cries for help in the middle of the night, because I was unable to cope with the phantoms that found release in my imagination, might have caused either my father or mother any discomfort.

Was I an incredibly self-centered child? Was it simply that my father never gave me any reason to believe I was a bother to him? Or was it both?

It took me a long time to realize that my father's war experiences had taught him to sleep so lightly that even, or perhaps especially, my frightened whispers would bring him to complete alertness. While he had eventually readjusted to sleeping in a bed and not on the hard, cold ground (something he had found very difficult when he and my mother were first married) the lightness of his sleep never really changed. My brothers and I benefited greatly, not just from his readiness to meet our nighttime needs, but his signals that meeting those needs was never a burden to him.

My father saved me from countless nighttime phantoms, rescued me when the wind that gusted outside my bedroom sent shivers down my spine, and gave me the confidence to sleep when I could not find it within myself. He did this without ever making me feel as though I was being absurd or a nuisance, and without ever expecting or asking for anything in return. The quiet, unhurried word, the gentle hand resting on the head or shoulder, the gentle eyes so deep with wisdom… these created childhood peace. And I thank him, from the very depths of my soul, for these unconditional gifts.

How immense the heart

and how courageous the soul

that loves unconditionally

that gives without expectation,

and what an extraordinary gift

is that love.

5

Ladies Before Gentlemen

My father frequently said, mischief dominating his face, that if they put back all the parts they'd taken out of him over the years, he'd weigh exactly the same as he did when he was twenty. Then he'd start the list — his tonsils, his appendix, two-thirds of his stomach, part of a knee, part of a lung...

Physical illness wasn't new to my father; experience had taught him (and us) that he'd spend more than a few days in hospital approximately every three years. My mother, for her part, would joke that he was awfully lucky he'd married a nurse because he really needed one.

Most of the conditions for which he received treatment had some degree of lasting impact on his life and by association, ours. For instance, when I was two or three, he had most of his stomach removed because of severe bleeding ulcers. He lost a great deal of weight afterwards which he never fully regained and there were many things he couldn't eat. Most desserts were avoided and ice cream in particular was completely indigestible. People who weren't aware of the reasons would have described him as an extremely picky eater, but it wasn't that he didn't like most foods, *they simply didn't like him,* as he was fond of saying with a particularly frank and somewhat innocent expression.

Whether or not the gastrectomy in any way increased the likelihood that he would develop Alzheimer's is a question that will always sit in the back of my mind, unless or until research provides definite answers about the factors that increase a person's tendencies to contract the disease. What we do know (in retrospect) is that at the same time the early symptoms of Alzheimer's were becoming more and more apparent, my father was suffering from a severe B^{12} deficiency. This deficiency, we were told by doctors, had been caused by the fact that with most of his stomach gone, his body had been unable to process this particular nutrient properly or in sufficient quantities for more than twenty years.

B^{12} deficiencies, if severe enough, can lead to nerve damage which in turn can cause memory problems. If the condition is treated early enough, there's a chance the damage can be reversed or at least halted, which is why the discovery of his extreme deficiency offered some very real hope when it was first made. But intense B^{12} supplements, while they seemed to cause a slight physical improvement, at least for a short time, didn't reverse the mental deterioration. Whether they slowed it is something we can only speculate about.

Another 'part' my father lost due to surgical procedure was the cartilage in his knee which was removed at a time when this kind of procedure required a two-week stay in hospital. He and my brothers had been fishing (or trouting as it was called where I grew up) and arrived home earlier than expected. My father came limping into the house across the hardwood floor of the dining room, using a knotty old tree branch for a crutch and still wearing hip rubbers plastered with mud and bits and pieces of the bog he'd limped through. Neither my mother nor I believed anything was wrong, thinking instead that he was teasing us until, that is, we realized in one of those *how did I miss that* moments, that if he was going to tease, the joke wouldn't have included muddy boots (which were absolutely forbidden on the hardwood floor) and a knotty tree branch. So we stopped laughing at

his antics, helped him to a chair and a short time later, delivered him
to the hospital.

Like the stomach surgery, the knee surgery was successful, but
the joint did continue to give him trouble as the years passed. Long
car trips required regular stops so he could stretch his leg. Movies,
plays, concerts and other activities or outings that required sitting for
a number of hours were increasingly uncomfortable, became few and
far between, and eventually all but stopped. It would be unfair to
say my father's discomforts hampered family activities significantly
however; they didn't. We simply worked around them.

The impact of Alzheimer's was different. As I've already explained,
there was a period when my father's symptoms were known only to
him and while there must have been subtle shifts in his behavior, I
can't say I was conscious of them.

To put this in perspective, I should perhaps provide the context
for this period in our lives. I lived at home while I completed my
undergraduate degree. At the end of my third year of studies, I met
the man who would become my husband — Peter — and he and my
father developed a special closeness. They often puttered, as I called
it, around the garage and backyard fixing this and chuckling over that.
Peter had grown up in Trinidad, one of the islands my father had
visited frequently, and they were fond of swapping and comparing
stories. When I left home to complete a twelve-month graduate degree
program, Peter returned to the West Indies to apply for Canadian
landed immigrant status.

My dad seemed fine when we left, but his physical condition
weakened as the year progressed. My mother says she believed that
this was a result of all his children being gone, of a loneliness that he
would not admit since he fully recognized and believed we must go
wherever necessary to be happy. She cites a lack of energy, no real
interest in going places, tiredness and headaches. Hers was a perfectly

logical and reasonable explanation. However, when the symptoms continued after first Peter and I moved back, then Rik (who'd been living near Steve in Vancouver), the empty nest syndrome couldn't be used as an explanation. Indeed, within a year of our return, it became undeniable that there was more going on than anyone even wanted to consider.

Peter and I returned to Newfoundland in May, exactly one year after we'd left, and were married the following fall on October 1st. We were aware that my father hadn't been well, and as the months passed, witnessed ourselves the attacks of dizziness, disorientation, consternation and greyness. Our son, Kenneth, was born the following July, much to my father's intense delight. By this time Rik had also moved back and was living with our parents.

My oldest brother Steve, who had lived in British Columbia for approximately a decade since he'd moved there to complete his medical internship, and his fiance Glenna, visited during the last days of my pregnancy, though they weren't present for the birth. Steve and Glenna were planning to marry in September, and while we wanted to be with them for this occasion as much as they'd wanted to be with us for Kenneth's birth, we couldn't attend because of jobs and our new family situation. Everyone was especially pleased that my parents would be making the trip, however, and that helped ease any disappointment they or we felt.

In keeping with the difficulties my father was beginning to consistently demonstrate leading up to any particularly noteworthy occasion, he appeared quite ill in the days leading up to their flight to Vancouver. The symptoms, we were told by one physician who was a friend of the family, were not unlike those experienced by someone suffering from malaria, something my father had indeed contracted at a young age. Despite his discomfort, however, my parents managed to endure the lengthy flight and the various airport changes.

The wedding day marks the first occasion when my mother truly recognized (or perhaps first understood) the seriousness of what was happening to her husband. In fact, she's never been able to recall the day without re-experiencing the pain associated with my father's complete inability to remember the wedding, and the disorientation, confusion and panic she felt pervading the whole occasion.

First, my father did not look or feel well physically. This may not have been apparent to most of the guests, since they did not know him. Nor was it as obvious to Steve as it might have been had they lived closer together. But it worried my mother and she questioned my dad's ability to get through the day.

She says she will never forget the feeling when my father turned to her before they left for the church and asked repeatedly whether or not she'd packed his overnight case. (He'd need it because they were staying somewhere different the coming night.) It was the repetition of this question as well as the manner in which it was asked that sent fear as sharp as a dagger through her confidence and into her heart.

She says she will never forget a second incident in the church where the wedding was being held. After my mother and father had returned from communion, he walked ahead of her into the pew. Such an invisible action to anyone who didn't know my father, this was frighteningly significant to my mother. In more than thirty years of marriage he had always, without exception, stepped aside to let my mother precede him into a pew, or through a door. *Ladies before gentlemen.*

My mom had told me that when someone had asked her a number of years after her marriage what kind of man her husband was, she'd paused, thought for a moment and said — *my husband is a gentle man.* He was a 'gentle man' and a 'gentleman', and the fact that this simple action was so totally out of character was absolutely terrifying for her.

My parents made it through this day, alone in their awareness of the shadow that hung over them, my mother with increasing fear, my father with his own growing panic and confusion. Reputed to be a quiet man, my father conversed a little less than usual, while my mother watched over him and began a process she would continue for years, of filling in gaps in conversations, answering questions he would have answered had he been able to, easing the awkwardness of the situation, watching, always watching, and listening.

At one point he slipped away from her unnoticed. When she realized he was missing, she searched until she found him wandering alone in a garden outside the home where the wedding reception was taking place. He looked intense. Totally focused. Worried. Puzzled. As if he was analyzing some terribly difficult problem, but not knowing where or how to start to deal with it. She asked if anything was wrong. He said no. She asked what he was doing. He said *just thinking.*

One of the first things Alzheimer's can remove from the people who suffer from the condition is enjoyment of the sometimes momentous, sometimes simple events in the lives of their families, first for the Alzheimer's victims and increasingly for those who love them. The marriage of his eldest son was an occasion of great celebration and happiness for my father — for the most part. Steve recalls that he acted in a totally characteristic manner for virtually the entire visit. He says our father knew exactly what was going on and what the occasion was — he recognized and conversed normally with people; he continued to nurture and enjoy a special relationship with his future daughter-in-law; he shared the exceptional friendship with his son that was and still is a source of deep joy for Steve; he did most of the things he would normally have done in the way he would have always done them.

But in retrospect we were able to see that the weeks leading up to the wedding had filled him with anxiety. And the marriage ceremony and festivities that followed immediately afterwards never became a memory for him. In fact his only memory of that segment of time was the painful absence of the mental pictures he knew he should have had. You see, the one thing he did remember for a long time afterwards was that while he knew he'd been present at my brother's wedding, he couldn't find even a hint of a memory of being there.

I sometimes wonder who suffered most as a result of my father's confusion on that day in late September, though I suspect it was my mother. Both Steve and Glenna could still appreciate and hold tightly to the myriad of memories my parent's visit and my father's presence provided, the togetherness all the more important because of its infrequency. I was insulated from the reality of that day by the thousands of miles that separated us and don't even remember anymore how I felt when I was told about it. I suspect I buried whatever emotions I experienced into some well-insulated place so I could, if not completely convince myself things were normal, then at least behave as if they were. And while my father had lost what could be considered the most crucial sections of the event, he did know that Steve and Glenna had been married. But for my mother, this period filled her with a fear she would carry for years to come, a fear that would colour her impressions of even the happiest of events, as she witnessed her husband's departure from our lives.

Two years later my parents made a second trip to Vancouver. Steve and Glenna had moved into a new home and Steve waited for dad to arrive so they could build together the steps leading from the back door. He was looking forward to working beside his father as he would have done through his childhood and early adult years. My father had been the leader and teacher in those days, always certain about how to proceed, always meticulous about the quality of task. On this occasion, however, as they gathered the needed tools and materials, and then moved to position the string that would guide the placement of rails, my father hesitated. He turned to his son with an air of puzzlement that was subtle but very real, and his role switched from leader to follower, from instructor to pupil. It was the first time Steve had personally witnessed this loss of something once so second-nature in our father, and it both surprised and deeply pained him. Of course he didn't reveal this — he simply played the role required of him — just as we all did.

The two years between the wedding and the building of the steps had seen many changes in my father — changes that we coped with by wrapping protective insulation around our hearts and souls. The inability to do the things he'd always done, the uncharacteristic behaviors, the repetitive questions, the worried, puzzled and intense looks, the vacant stares and long silences as he removed himself from our company and wandered alone — these now shaped my father's reality and had become our constant sadness.

> Change is often felt before it is spoken,
>
> signaled by an uncharacteristic gesture
>
> sparked by an uncommon silence.
>
> Sometimes it is the
>
> last thing we would want
>
> and the only reason we cope
>
> is because we must.

6

Beachcombing for Dreams

Every summer while I was growing up, we would spend two weeks at the most beautiful beach in the world. It wasn't sandy, and the waves that crashed into the shore to awaken me every morning as I lay in my dark green sleeping bag were far too cold to surf or swim through. Sometimes the sun shone and it was hot. Other times the beach was shrouded in a cold, bone-chilling fog that all but hid the nearby rugged cliffs. Sometimes there was even cold, driving rain, the kind that comes at you sideways and makes it impossible to stay dry.

It didn't matter. This beach called Bellevue on the rugged island of Newfoundland was, to me, the most beautiful place in the world.

Whether the sun was shining or fog swirling through the campsite, I would awaken in the early morning to the sound of waves rushing to shore, the smell of bacon being cooked on a black cast-iron frying pan. The days were spent combing the beach; splashing in the water; seeing if we could walk further along the shore than we ever had before; trying to get back around rocky cliffs before the tide came in and trapped us.

I was fascinated by the shapes and sizes of the rocks that covered the beach, and every summer I would search for those that looked most like chocolate candy, toffee or mints. I'd trudge slowly across the beach gathering as many as I could as my partner in the search found room in his pockets to carry whatever I chose. If he sometimes told me I should leave some of them behind, I don't remember. I just know that every summer for as long as I wanted, I left the beach with new rocks so that throughout the fall and winter, my playmates and I could sort them into tiny jars of candy that we would sell for pennies in our play store. *Oh yes sir, we have mint candies and wonderful toffees. How many would you like?*

My dad would also build boats for us. He would sit, take out his small, sharpened pocket knife and patiently turn odd-shaped pieces of driftwood into sleek sailboats, while I searched the nearby rocks for any stray feathers left behind by seagulls. The best ones for sailing were tall, straight and full, and when I found one, I'd run gleefully back to my father, shouting with excitement, so he could finish the boat.

How wonderful it was to be that small, wispy-haired girl, holding a perfect little sailboat in my hands. To walk to the edge of the water with my father, bend down and send our boat gently and lovingly on its adventures. Everything magical could happen to that boat, and we'd stand there watching until the tiny feather sail could no longer be seen bobbing against the horizon.

The beach was rarely littered in the days of my childhood, but once in a while we'd find an empty bottle. On these occasions, pieces of paper would be scrounged from the bottom of a pocket or beach bag, a pencil or pen would materialize from somewhere and we'd scribble a message. One of us would pitch the message-filled bottle into the water and we'd stand and watch, speculating on who would find it or where it would go, until it too, was out of sight.

There was also an annual rescue by my father and older brothers. The cliffs that sheltered the beach beckoned climbers. Young women or men, convinced they were able to climb from the rocky shore to the wooded areas above, would pick a place that looked safe and start their ascent. Screams for help would inevitably reach my family's ears, as the climbers reached a spot where they realized they could go neither up nor down. My mother and I would run to take our places at the base of the cliff to watch, along with anyone else who was on the beach, as the drama unfolded and the climbers were somehow brought to safety.

On days when the combination of wind and tide was exactly right, we'd all sit on one particular rock near the edge of the ocean. Facing the cliff, we'd pretend we didn't hear the waves come rushing towards us and then scream with utter delight when the freezing water splashed up and over our backs, shoulders and heads. The wetter we got, the more we screamed. Often my brothers and I perched on the rock while our parents stood dry and laughing on the shore, my dad leaning close to my mom to say something to her. Sometimes we all huddled together on a rock that we called our own.

There were plenty of fish in the cold waters of the Atlantic ocean in those days, and seagulls rarely came to shore. Except for early evening, then they would settle in an area unsheltered by the walls of cliffs that were so characteristic of most of the area. I wanted to get close to them so badly that we spent evening after evening creeping as quietly as we could in their direction. There must have been hundreds nestled together on the beach and I suspect they knew we were approaching long before they gave any indication. And then, just when I thought that tonight I would get close to them, they would rise almost as one from the beach, the sound of their wings and their cries echoing for miles, and fly away over the ocean towards the setting sun. We'd turn back towards the path to our campsite, and I'd fall asleep knowing that at some point after we'd left, they'd probably returned to their place and were sleeping too.

Sometimes we'd leave the beach for a day and head outside the park to fish or pick berries. I didn't much like the flies that seemed to swarm towards me as soon as I sat anywhere with a fishing pole, and I had recurring bad luck when it came to stepping in black holes in a bog that seemed to suck my boot right off my foot, leaving me balanced absurdly on one leg and trying to keep the other sock clean while I figured out a way to get my boot back. The berries were always turned into delicious jam that was spread on crackers and paired with cocoa around the evening campfire. The trout we caught were roasted over an open fire. And my socks and boots were always cleaned.

As the years passed, we moved out of the tent that had first been our summertime home and into a tent camper. Then we moved up to truck campers, first a homemade camper and then a factory built one. Sometimes the weather was warm and sunny for fourteen days straight; often there were periods of rain and sometimes intense thunderstorms that would see us huddled in our car on the beach — my brothers and father watching the lightning flash across the sky while my mother and I moved our hands from our eyes to our ears, trying to block out the terrifying flashes of light and booming crashes of thunder. Sometimes friends would camp nearby for a few days; sometimes, uncles, aunts and cousins would arrive and spend the day; sometimes our neighbors and friends would come to walk the beach with us. But even on the weekends, when there were more people than usual at the park, the beach was never really crowded. And that was one of the reasons I loved it. I didn't find the open spaces empty and I wasn't lonely, despite the absence of people.

By the time I was fourteen, my mother, father and I were camping alone — my brothers by then were working or away at cadet camp. That was an unusual summer. For the first time that I could remember, the ocean was filled with icebergs and the wind that whispered across the water had the feel of September or October. Large icebergs could be seen in the distance; smaller pieces seemed to be heading slowly towards shore. It was a magical sight. But it was also the first year I was unable to find the peace of mind that Bellevue had always given me.

I have already mentioned the knee pains I experienced as a child, the ones that worried my parents even as I settled back to sleep after waking them with my discomfort. I had finished Grade 8 that year and because my class was moving to a new school for Grade 9, we held graduation celebrations — a Mass followed by a dance in late June. The next day was sunny and bright, and I have a memory of doing something for my dad in the garage, though I don't remember what. I was wearing my shorts and noticed, as I squat down, that my left knee looked swollen. I stood up and moved around, studied it from different positions trying to convince myself it was normal. I finally had to admit that it was bigger than it should be and with an unreasonable kind of panic in my heart, went to find my mother. Perhaps I'd danced too much the night before, we said, and the swelling would simply go down. It didn't.

I learned later that both my parents were quite distressed from the first moment I approached them with the problem, a reaction that was partially based on years of concern over nighttime pains. By the time we reached Bellevue that summer, we had been through a series of x-rays and knew there was some issue, probably a cartilage problem, but it was too soon to tell. We would have to watch and wait to see if anything changed.

I didn't realize, but was told later, that I had begun walking more slowly than usual. My mother says she lived with increasing anxiety every time I would ask her why she was walking so fast when it was I who could no longer keep up. Their deepest concerns were hidden from me as they held a silent vigil. And that summer we walked a little slower and avoided the muddy black holes of the bogs.

For me, the icebergs became a focus. Each day we would analyze their movement just as each evening we would check to see whether or not the swelling in my knee had changed. Then one afternoon, as my father and I stood on the beach looking towards the left and the right, we realized that one of the bergs appeared to be sitting right on the beach, well beyond the spot where the seagulls gathered each evening and farther than I'd ever walked before.

Can we please see if we can reach them? It can't be that far, can it?

And so we began to walk towards the blue-white structure at the water's edge to see if we could actually touch this majestic piece of nature.

For almost two hours we walked, our complete attention given over to whether or not the iceberg was actually close enough to touch once we got there. I remember our feet getting sore — we hadn't been prepared for such a long trek across the beach — but we refused to turn back. As we grew closer we realized the largest piece of the iceberg would be too far out into the water to reach, but smaller pieces, which we hadn't been able to see from a distance, had broken off and were riding in on the waves.

I ran across the beach to retrieve a piece that would have been about eight inches long and perhaps four or five inches in diameter. To me, it was as if we were touching gold, and my father didn't hesitate for even a second when I asked if we could bring it back to the camper and keep it in our small freezer. He simply wrapped it in something (a cap, a shirt, I don't remember) and we took turns holding it as we walked as quickly as I could manage back across the rocks. The cold chunk slowly got smaller as we walked, melting in the unfamiliar surroundings, so the piece that we placed carefully in the freezer was smaller than the one I had first touched.

I don't know what touching that piece of iceberg meant to my father — he never said and I never asked. I know that for me it was like touching a star or a sunset, something I never thought I'd be able to touch. If my dad didn't feel as I did, however, he seemed to instinctively understand and accept its significance to me. He could have told me we shouldn't try to walk that far because of my knee.

He could have encouraged me to turn back when we realized how far away the iceberg really was. He could have told me the iceberg would just melt and drip all the way back, or be too cold to carry, or take up too much room in a tiny freezer. He could have told me my need to keep it was illogical or just plain silly. But he did none of these things; he simply walked beside me, talking about anything and nothing, and helped me carry my dream.

After we displayed our treasure back at the campsite, we wrapped it in a piece of foil and placed it in the freezer. Then we checked my knee and smiled at one another, since the swelling was no better, but no worse than it had been at the start of the journey.

I kept that piece of iceberg in the freezer at my parents' home for years and years, until it literally evaporated into nothingness and we threw away the foil wrap that had protected it. We kept it because it was a dream I could occasionally pick up and hold. Because, increasingly, it became symbolic of a journey my father and I would travel in the months that followed.

My father's last trip to Bellevue took place a few summers before he died. He strolled along the beach in a khaki shirt, long khaki pants, socks and shoes, despite the heat of the day. My husband was a little ahead of us with Vulcan, our German Shepherd puppy. My son would skip along with his granddad for a time... chattering on as only small children can, as I once did... then run to the edge of the surf and scream in glee as the cold water rushed up to cover his beach shoes. For a time I walked slowly behind, filled with sensations and memories from the past and present, wondering if my father would ever again walk this particular shore. When my son ran off to catch up with his dad and his dog, I strode up alongside my father and walked next to him, stopping when he did to look out over the ocean, helping him find beach rocks he could send skipping over the waves, talking to him as he used to talk to me. After a time we reached the others; my dad found a piece of driftwood and sat on the beach to carve his sailboat as my son searched for the feather.

At this stage in my father's illness, there were many things he could no longer do and many places he would no longer go. It was growing harder to convince him we actually wanted his company, harder to ease his anxieties as he traveled on roads that were no longer familiar, harder to convince my mother he would be fine with us and she needed some time to herself. When he walked along the beach on this summer afternoon, his pace was slower than it had ever been, his walk less certain, his words fewer. My heart broke, not for the first time, as I watched him — his strength diminished, mixed with a growing weakness, his joy measured, mixed with a silent despair. But I didn't cry at the time; you learn not to.

My dad finished that last sailboat, his last sailboat, and set it on a wave with his grandson. He found some rocks for me (I now use them for paperweights and bookends) and helped carry them back to the car. Perhaps he also said his own goodbyes to the sea he had sailed upon, to countries he had visited, to memories of years past, and to a future Iceberg he would inspire, but never touch with his own hands.

If a child comes to you

with a piece of the world in her hand

and asks you to help her carry it home,

know that she is trusting you

with her heart and soul

and carry it gently and with love.

Just as my father did.

7

Follow the Leader

My father bought a new car about six years before he died — a fully loaded, four-door, midnight blue Ford Taurus sedan. That would have been perfectly normal if it hadn't been for the fact that long before they became popular, my father preferred... actually, it would be more accurate to say he had an absolute passion for... four-wheel drive vehicles. For as long as I could remember, 'his car' had been a green Land Rover, then a full-size Blazer, then a brown Jeep, followed by a maroon Bronco, and finally a navy blue Bronco.

I'm not sure I can accurately describe how it felt to see him sitting behind the wheel of that car, or to slide in next to him as opposed to stepping up into a high riding four-wheel drive vehicle, except to say that it seemed and felt wrong. While my father looked totally right in a Land Rover or Bronco, he looked totally wrong in a four-door sedan; it was almost as if he had been somehow diminished, as if someone had taken something important from him.

How he came to purchase this particular vehicle is less of a puzzle now than it was then. My mother says they decided to buy a car because they wanted a vehicle with four doors. Her recollection is that it would be easier for my son to get in and out of a car than the four-wheel drive — he would have been almost four years old at the time, and my dad was still able to pick him up from day care a couple of days each week and take him home.

There was another issue my husband was aware of (though I don't recall hearing about it at the time) and one that likely had even more of an impact on the decision. My mother had always been nervous about driving dad's vehicles. When we were growing up, she usually had her own, and it was always a car. Apparently, my father would look at the car he'd bought and shaking his head with some disgust and disdain, admit to Peter he didn't know why he'd bought 'that thing'. However, his other comments led Peter to believe he bought a car at least partly because he knew my mother would soon need something to drive.

As I write this I'm torn between believing this was all very logical and believing it was all very illogical. Throughout my entire childhood we had always felt safe through even the stormiest of winters because we knew that the vehicle my father drove and maintained could get us safely through even the worst conditions. Had he been analyzing things with his normal ability, he would never, ever have accepted that my mother — who didn't like to drive in the winter under any circumstances — could be comfortable driving in the winter in the car they'd purchased. And instead of going to the dealership he chose mainly because it was the closest to his house, he would have gone the extra ten minutes across town to purchase one of the four-wheel drive cars that were now on the market. Problem solved — a car, so my mother would be comfortable driving it and my son would be able to clamor in and out with no assistance; a four-wheel drive so she would be safe whatever the season.

My mother never drove this vehicle after all, however, because about two months after they pulled out of the dealership in their new car, they pulled back in and traded it in on the Bronco that under normal circumstances, they would have bought in the first place. She told me she'd stepped out of the house and into the driveway one morning, and seeing my father sitting behind the wheel of a car, realized that it *simply wasn't right*. When she suggested they go back and trade it in, he took her there without question.

I was with them the evening they were closing the somewhat unusual deal (unusual because it had taken more than a little flexibility on the part of the salesperson to refinance everything after just two months and because my mother had done all the negotiating) and I remember well the difficulty my father was having following what was going on. Perhaps it was because we were so close that I could feel his discomfort escalate to fear and then to nervous panic as the explanations were made and paper after paper given to him to sign. But it was his reaction to the completion of the deal that was particularly heart-wrenching for me.

As we stood in the cramped little office where the papers had been signed and the deal finalized, absolute relief flooded my father's face and he began to chuckle in a chuckle that wasn't his, laugh with a laugh that wasn't his, and then turned to the tall, pretty, young, female assistant who'd helped him through the process, put his arms out and hugged and kissed her. The action was totally out of character for him, and totally inappropriate for the situation. Just as my father stepping into a church pew in front of my mother had been a moment of revelation for her, this was a moment of revelation for me. This particular action, while normal for some individuals, wasn't consistent with my father's personality. And for a split second, the enormity of what was happening engulfed me as I had a glimpse of a terrifying future.

As often seems to be the case as I write this, it's necessary to put the timing of this particular incident in context. My father had not been diagnosed as having Alzheimer's and at least for me, Alzheimer's wasn't even something that seemed either widespread or was generally understood or talked about at the time. The focus was on the continuing physical difficulties. He would awaken in the morning drenched in sweat, skin sallow and ashen looking, and be so weak he would spend the day in bed, drifting in and out of sleep, sweating his way through sets of sheets. He would be somewhat disoriented for the few days the episode lasted, but no more than could be attributed to his feverish state. He was being treated for hypoglycemia and we adjusted to the necessary diet changes and eating habits. I believe now that we were also adapting to the subtle changes that were occurring in his behavior and condition without realizing many of them were taking place. In many ways, my father was perfectly capable of acting normally and would often hide his increasing anxiety at his inability to understand and cope with things he had always done. When the occasion was too stressful, the effort too great, his behavior would take one of its bizarre twists. His brow would furrow and he would become impatient as he suspected his every action and word were being studied. He was generally able to recover quickly enough, though, so that within a very short period of time, he was himself again — just physically not feeling well and often more preoccupied than usual. For our part, we believed his anxiety was mostly a result of his concern over his physical well-being; we were also told that his intermittent forgetfulness was entirely consistent with his B^{12} deficiency, the other condition that had, as already noted, been discovered.

I suspect most people who have watched the insidious spread of Alzheimer's as it claims a loved one's life experience the same kind of confusion and helplessness that first began to churn within me at this time. There was so much about our lives that was unchanged, but so many other things that were completely out of rhythm. There was so much about my relationship with my father that was exactly as it had always been, and yet there were subtle, almost undefinable and definitely unacknowledged shifts in roles. There was also an unconscious sense, a growing knowledge that everything was not fine, that we carried with us the weight of something not entirely understood.

My father was retired by now — had been for almost three years. I believed the retirement route was chosen because physically he was no longer able to cope, and that was true, at least partially. However, I didn't know at the time that he had been having a great deal of difficulty coping mentally as well. My mother was still working, and for the time that would remain before she retired early to care for her husband full time, my father was still able to drive her to and from work — from his house to the hospital and home again, or from his house to our apartment and our apartment to the hospital.

The days and nights during this period developed a routine of their own, a slow motion pattern of days flowing to evenings, often with little or nothing to mark the passage of time. My dad would drive my mother to work and she would call him numerous times a day to make sure he was physically okay until he picked her up at 4:30 or 5:00 p.m. Sometimes the phone would go unanswered because he was vacuuming or doing something in the garage or yard. This created a growing concern, so telephone jacks became even more numerous than they had been and eventually a portable phone was added to the collection. When she worked evenings, as frequently happened, he'd spend the hours with us.

During this time, I was working days from Monday to Friday and Peter was working primarily evenings and weekends, so that one of us could be home with Kenneth. On the couple of days each week Peter worked afternoons instead of evenings, my dad would pick Kenneth up after day care and take him back to our apartment. I didn't worry that he would forget my son; as I've already pointed out, the physical deterioration was the focus at this stage. Some days he would be physically too ill to follow the normal routine and alternate arrangements would be made; sometimes my mother would even stay at home with him; but most of the time he was quite capable of caring for his grandson and they both looked forward to their hours together.

My mother, now an Assistant Director at a children's hospital, was required because of cutbacks and organizational changes, to work weekends. Peter frequently worked Saturdays and Sundays as well, and on the weekends when they both worked, my dad and I would spend the days together — picking up groceries, shopping, running errands, playing with Kenneth. My father had become nervous about staying at home alone. However, even though he didn't like to be alone, he rarely admitted this and he certainly wouldn't foist himself on anyone — so I'd call him and ask whether or not he could come spend the day with me because I needed his help. And it was true, I did. However, I also wanted his company as much as I wanted to give him the same care he'd always given me, to be there when he needed me without making him feel he was a burden.

He would arrive at my apartment at the agreed upon time and we'd plan the day. I'd be the driver — nothing unusual about that, I generally had been since I'd gotten my license about ten years before — and we'd take care of whatever needed to be done. We'd prepare something for lunch that wouldn't upset his stomach — chunky chicken soup and a ham and cheese sandwich. He helped in every and any way he could, with everything and anything I asked. He spent these days puttering around my apartment, being the best father and grandfather he could.

Every so often something would happen to disturb the growing predictability of these days and weeks. Early on a fall evening, for instance, my father left our apartment to return home for supper. It wasn't a weekend, and he'd already picked my mother up from work and taken her home, so I don't recall why he would have been back at our home. In any event, by the time he left, it was already dark.

The drive to his own home lasted a maximum of ten minutes, and when my mother called to ask if he'd left yet because his supper was getting cold, we had to tell her he'd been gone for more than forty-five minutes. No, he hadn't said he was stopping anywhere. No, there didn't seem to be anything wrong when he left. No, he hadn't been confused when he was with us.

I remember standing by the phone after we hung up trying to think what we should do — sounds silly perhaps, but it was almost as if my mind couldn't or perhaps didn't want to process the implications. Peter was preparing to leave to trace the route between our homes when the phone rang. It was my mother reporting that my father had called. He'd taken a wrong turn, ended up at the airport (which was about halfway between our homes), couldn't figure out how he'd gotten there or how to get home. So he sat there and waited until the fog of his confusion cleared enough for him to realize he should call home. Rik, who'd been preparing to leave my parent's house to search for him, left to meet him at the airport and lead him home.

I remember the relief being so intense that I sat, suddenly, as the emotional surge that flooded through me took an almost physical form. However, emotionally and analytically I knew this was a route my father had traveled thousands of times — the darkness of the early fall evening could not be used as a legitimate excuse for the confusion. So the relief changed to another emotion as the realization took hold that even things most familiar to him were becoming unfamiliar.

A second completely unrelated incident from those months also stands out. My father had taken my mother to have her hair done, promising to return to pick her up a couple of hours later. Almost an hour after the appointed time, she was still waiting for him to arrive. My father was rarely late; in fact, he was usually the person doing the waiting and she says the experience of standing there waiting for him was unforgettable. She called the house and received no answer, which wasn't a surprise because she knew in her heart and soul he was out there — somewhere.

She was right; he was 'out there'. He'd returned to pick her up and gone to the wrong place, where, as far as we know, he sat in the parking lot waiting for her. He was actually quite close, in a hotel parking lot where he picked her up many times before from various conferences and meetings, and which just happened to be a couple of buildings away from the hair salon.

As her worry escalated into panic, she decided to go look for him. She didn't really have a search plan; she knew only that she had to find him. And as she headed in the direction of the hotel, she saw him driving towards her. She doesn't know where he was going, if he'd realized he was in the wrong place, or if he'd just begun driving aimlessly; and she was never able to find out. For the period of time after that until he moved permanently from the driver's to the passenger's seat, he didn't leave while she had her hair done. Instead he'd bring a book and wait in the Bronco.

Growing periods of intermittent forgetfulness were being replaced by increasingly frequent episodes of a dementia that weren't improved by B^{12} supplements or anything else. The routine of the months since the purchase of the Bronco was disrupted and radical changes required in the patterns of our days. My mother retired from work as quickly as she could — a heartbreaking event for a woman who had so loved her career — so she could be at home with my father. Together they did the things my father had previously been able to do alone — pick their grandson up from school, spend at least parts of the weekend with me.

Looking back, it's easy to see that my father was much more aware of his memory problems at this stage than we were, as he was able to hide a great deal from us. It's also easy to see that the problems were taking a terrible toll, that his anxiety levels must have been almost unbearable during the periods of his days and nights when he was completely lucid — he alone knew how much he could no longer remember. Yet despite his efforts to remain in control, the man who had been our leader and guide in many things, grew more dependent and was increasingly becoming a follower and in need of our guidance; the man who had been our strength, was desperately in need of ours. We increasingly made the plans, set the agendas and he followed our lead.

I know my father wouldn't want me to feel any anguish over my inability to understand or recognize what was happening in the sixth year before his death, but there is within me an element of guilt I may never completely dispel. I ask myself whether or not my father was being expected or allowed to do too much, if we were putting him and others in danger. I ask myself if there was more he needed from me that I did not give. I ask myself if there is any way I could have eased the pain being caused by his own awareness of his disintegrating memory and confidence.

Would it have been somehow better if we'd been able to see the subtle changes more clearly while they were happening? I don't know. Would it have been better to know what the ultimate outcome would be, that my father was suffering from Alzheimer's and would experience immeasurable anguish before his death? A large part of me says no, because the elimination of hope would have been devastating; a small part says yes, though for what reason I'm not sure. Ultimately, it doesn't matter. I admitted to myself, long before my mother did, that my father had Alzheimer's (or at least something so like Alzheimer's that it really didn't matter what the label was), but that realization was still many months away. In the meantime, we simply got out of bed each morning and went to our beds each night, sometimes completely aware of the painfully changing patterns of the days, other times unable even to acknowledge them.

When life asks

that you become leader instead of follower,

remember the times

when the hand you now hold

gently held yours,

and guide as well as you possibly can.

8
A Bed of Roses

Early in the morning on a cold, dismally gray and foggy day in late November, when I was just fourteen years old, I sat on a bed in a hospital outpatient clinic and learned I would be going into surgery within days. The diagnosis: bone cancer. *Possibly* another extremely serious and very rare condition of the bone, but that possibility was so unlikely it was entirely discounted. In either case, the best case scenario was that I would walk forever with a straight leg. The worst case scenario was obvious — loss of leg or even life.

The terror that filled me at that instant etched those moments on my mind and in my heart as if they were scenes from a slow motion horror movie I would replay over and over again in my mind for years to come. I developed an intense and immediate hatred of and fear for everything about the hospital, any hospital, and the doctor that stood before me, despite the fact that his face was unable to hide the compassion in his heart.

After a few moments, my mother stepped outside the room to protect me from the intensity of her own fear and from the answers to questions she didn't want to ask in my presence. My father stayed in the examining room, but almost fainted after the others left, and it was the severe whitening of his face as he swayed beside the bed that must have finally penetrated my shock. He lay down; I sat beside him and cried. And cried and cried and cried.

We spent the rest of that day shopping for the clothes you take into a hospital — nighties, dressing gown, slippers. The day's defining feature was the fog. It was thick, oppressive, damp and heavy, seeming to add to a weight heavier than any I had ever carried. It seemed to me that we met more friends and acquaintances than usual that day, and I would stand silently as my mother explained she was not at work because I was going into the hospital — *a problem with my knee... a rare condition and, yes, a serious one... thank you for your kind wishes and please, if you don't mind, could you please say a prayer.*

The next morning, when I was admitted to the hospital, I was 5'8 1/2" and weighed ninety-six pounds. During the months that had passed since we'd discovered the section of iceberg on Bellevue Beach and placed it for safekeeping in our freezer, my knee had continued to deteriorate, my walk slowing as I dragged a heavy and weakening leg. I concentrated on being a Grade 9 student — dreams of still making the volleyball and basketball teams, of boyfriends not yet met and dances not yet danced. I also carried inside me a profound fear that was sometimes just beneath the surface and other times buried so deeply I was almost able to ignore it, until the morning I awoke to find my knee swollen to illogical and unreasonable proportions and realized it contained lumps that, when pushed, would dart suddenly from one part of the joint to another.

What my parents must have felt when I walked into their bedroom that morning to show them my knee, I can only imagine. My mother says she began to pray immediately — we were a Catholic family and had always attended church on the weekends (even when the service was at 7:30 a.m. on Sunday morning). We prayed most regularly to St. Anthony and it was widely known by friends and relatives that if you'd lost something important, all you had to do was call my mom, tell her your dilemma, she would say a prayer to St. Anthony and the item would be found. It's true — a custom-made shoe for a child was recovered after it had been buried on Bellevue Beach by the small child who owned it, wedding rings were retrieved, valuables of all sorts were located. My mother always seemed to know when St. Anthony would be able to find something, and she'd explain this to whoever was seeking her help. She didn't mention it to me at the time, but she felt, on this particular occasion, that St. Anthony was telling her he was dreadfully sorry, but this was too much for him. He couldn't help her this time.

Sometime over the next two days, in the midst of x-rays and doctors, tests and examinations, appointments and buying nighties, Esther, one of my mother's colleagues at the School of Nursing in the hospital where I would be having surgery, showed her a photo she'd brought to the office for another instructor. It was a 3" x 5" black and white photo of a young nun. *This is a photograph of St. Therese,* she said as she explained how she'd had a copy made for one of the other nursing instructors. My mother looked across at her, told her quietly that I was very very sick and she really didn't know who to pray to this time or how we could cope. *Could she please have this photo,* she asked. *Would the other person mind waiting a little longer for another copy?* Esther gave my mother the photo with the explanation that St. Therese, who was known as the Little Flower, had died when she was in her twenties. If you prayed to her and she was able to grant your request, she would send a sign — roses. We prayed.

They leave you with so little to grasp when they say you must prepare yourself for bone cancer. Years are added to the day you spend waiting for surgery. You are paralyzed and eventually become numb. They come to your bedside and blankly you stare at the nurses who try to be kind; you stare at the doctors and build walls against their expressions of barely hidden concern and pity; you watch the ceiling; you watch the sun rise and set; you count the footsteps in the corridor; and you're so afraid, but you laugh at the silly jokes that are made just to cheer you. At night I didn't sleep. The sheets were on fire and I'd lie awake watching the nurses as they checked my room, clinging desperately to the doll I hid under the covers. Susie, the doll I'd had forever.

They scheduled my surgery for 12:30. My dad waited with me through the morning, and I know that I took as much of his strength with me to the operating room as my own. They poked me with needles; they pumped me so full of drugs that everything grew hazy and so, so dry. I couldn't swallow, but I fought to hold onto my consciousness and my mother's and father's hands. Until I had to let them go. We had prayed, we had looked for a sign, but we had seen no roses.

My parents waited back in my hospital room while I was in surgery. *Save her life,* they asked. *If at all possible, save her leg, but please save her life.* My mother walked from the room periodically, too restless and worried to stay in one place for long. She knew everyone at the nurse's station — they'd been her students or her friends or both; they knew nothing of wishes for roses, but they were kind and caring.

The surgeon made a large incision on the front of my knee, a curved cut that would allow him to fold the skin back and work on the bone. He cleared away the remnants of the front of a joint lining that had become calcified and was breaking into lumps of various sizes. Beneath, the bone was healthy. We're told that the doctor smiled — a huge smile of surprise, relief and joy. It wasn't bone cancer; it wasn't even the serious but discounted condition; it was another rare disorder that didn't match the symptoms or the history. My mother also smiled; she'd seen a greeting card that had, at some point in the afternoon, been placed on a shelf by the nurse's station. On the card there was a rose.

When I was wheeled back from the recovery room later that evening, three pink roses followed immediately behind me, a gift from friends of the family who knew nothing of our prayers but somehow became part of our answer. I'd entered the operating room awaiting a death sentence and left with my leg and my life.

Much of the pain, the unhappiness, ended that day, in an operating room full of people pulling for me. But the only thing I really remember of that night and much of the next twenty-four hours was that through the haze of heavy medication, I was supposed to move my toes as frequently as I could; otherwise there could be serious complications. For the first time in my life, movement was severely restricted, my leg immobilized by a full-length bandage designed to provide the kind of protection necessary after such invasive surgery. Aware that I still had my leg, experiencing a pain unlike any I had ever known, I moved my toes constantly through sleep and brief moments of semi-awareness.

Life, I sometimes think, is a series of intertwined endings and beginnings. For us, this day in late November was the end of one part of our journey and the beginning of another. Smiles came much more easily than they had in earlier months as we shared the incredible story, but the tears continued to flow.

I spent five painful months undergoing physiotherapy. For the first two months, the treatments started at six in the morning when my father would awaken me despite the winter darkness to apply warmth to the muscles in my leg in an effort to ease the stiffness before the trip to the hospital; it ended with him gently manipulating the knee before tucking me into bed at night. There was electric shock to stimulate the muscle, pain until I could no longer hold in the screams.

I was incredibly weak and still terribly afraid through this entire period. I was also coping with the news that I would be facing another round of surgery to remove the lining from the back of the knee joint, the area that couldn't be reached with the first incision but which was affected by the same condition. January was set as the first possible date, but as Christmas came and went, I was still too weak for another operation. When advanced physiotherapy finally resulted in a breakthrough in the movement range of my knee, something that was becoming an increasing concern, we decided it would be better to let me return to some sort of normal life for a short time and build my strength before the next bout of surgery, so we moved it to Easter. As spring approached, I began to feel strength returning for the first time in months and begged the doctors to delay the surgery again. *Please. Let me wait until summer. I can't do this again. Not yet. Please.*

They agreed and we waited, and the day before school ended for the summer, I returned once more to the hospital for my x-ray. The day after school closed, we returned to the clinic where my life had been changed forever the previous fall. Steve, who had looked at my mother after the initial diagnosis and asked why it had to be me, why it couldn't be him, drove me there in dad's green Land Rover. We entered the examining room and watched my doctor walk back and forth in front of a long series of x-rays which were mounted against some sort of fluorescent-like viewing screen. The look on his face was a mixture of bemusement and happiness as he turned to me.

It's gone. There's absolutely nothing there. Nothing at all. It's impossible of course, but it's actually gone. Just look at these x-rays. You see, it was here three weeks after the surgery; it was here at Easter; and now it's gone.

And you know why that is, don't you, my mother said.

Yes I do. And he pointed towards the sky. Another ending. Another beginning. Another believer. Roses.

How is this story relevant to the larger story of my father? First of all, there is no doubt in my mind that the prayers of my parents, their intense faith, their kindness, gentleness and strength, were the channels through which the spiritual energy of this experience could flow. I also know that even without the cancer, I had virtually no strength left to suffer through the physical agonies of the recovery. They gave me theirs.

My dad would get up between 5:00 and 5:30 a.m. every morning, boil the water for hot water bottles, and turn up the heat in the house so things would be as comfortable as he could make them before he had to wake me. He would bring me those hot water bottles, pack them around my leg, and help me loosen the knee enough so that the morning's physiotherapy session would be more bearable. And he would work with me just before bed at night, gently moving the knee and willing it to stiffen a little less throughout the dark hours to come. He made sand bags, each carefully sewn and weighed, to increase the number of exercises I could do at home and decrease the number of hours I had to spend at the hospital. And when I couldn't eat anything, when I physically shook with weakness and fear, when I cried in frustration, anguish and pain, he would stay with me, sit by me and offer nothing but silence, his hand or his shoulder, some quiet words, whatever I most needed at the time.

We had approximately four months to celebrate and recover after the last trip to the doctor, and then the unthinkable happened. I came home from school one evening to learn my father had fallen from a ladder at work and because of the injury (about which neither my mother or father would provide details), he would require some sort of chest surgery. We were never able to determine what he was doing on the ladder; he wasn't supposed to be there. Nor were we able to determine how or why he fell; he couldn't remember. But my mother had received a call at work and they'd spent most of the day in the emergency room.

Two days later I walked into the kitchen, told them I knew that there was a great deal more going on than dad having a few sore ribs and requiring minor surgery, and demanded to know what was really happening.

You know you can't hide things from me, so you might as well tell me what it is.

The x-rays taken after my father's fall had revealed a cancerous lesion on the middle lobe of his right lung, and there was no doubt at all about the diagnosis. He was to enter the hospital for surgery in a few days to have the lung removed; the prognosis wasn't good. However, I was not to tell Steve who was leaving the next morning for meetings in Ottawa, to represent the medical school at which he was studying; he would refuse to go if he knew the truth and this was not an opportunity my parents would allow him to miss. I remember my father standing with his back to me as my mother explained this, though I have absolutely no memory of what I said or when he turned to face me. I have no memory of how long I sat there or where I went when I moved. I know only that I was devastated, and trying desperately not to show it.

On the Saturday before my father was to go into the hospital, my mother called to me from the living room of our house and pointed to a florist's van parked in the driveway of the house across the street. We'd been frantically cleaning the house — dusting and vacuuming with an intensity reserved for days when growing desperation cannot tolerate even an instant of inactivity.

See that van across the street? Don't ask me why I'm telling you this, but that van is not going to Mrs. Boone's (the neighbor who lived in that house); *he's coming here and he's going to bring me one red rose.*

I watched the driver get out of his van, look up at the number on the house, shake his head, get back in, reverse out of that driveway and pull into ours. Removing a small package from the back of the van, he turned and walked up the steps to the front door of our home where my mother met him. When she turned to me she held a single red rose floating in a bowl and had tears flowing from her eyes.

Your father is going to be fine. I asked St. Therese for one red rose if he was going to be fine and she's sent it right to our front door.

My mother's friends and co-workers spent the time remaining

before the surgery trying to convince her she had to accept the inevitable, telling her she was denying reality but had to accept her husband had lung cancer — for her sake, for his sake, for the sake of the children. She did not; we did not; and my father, like his daughter before him, entered the operating room with a death sentence, and left with his life. The lesion that was found on the lung was inconsistent with what had been seen on the x-ray; a lobe of the lung was removed so that there would be no chance the lesion would ever become cancerous; and my father began the process of his recovery.

I spent many quiet hours beside my father's bed, late into the evening after school. Happy just to sit, to fix his sheets, to place the blankets gently over his shoulders as he settled in for sleep, to watch him in the semi-darkness, to be there if he needed something. When he began to stand and walk again, I would help keep the intravenous trolley from falling as he dragged it behind him. He'd been told his shoulder would sag because of the ribs that had been removed during the surgery and he refused to let this happen. So he would practice standing straight and tall, walking back and forth in his room, stopping only to ask whether or not any droop could be detected. The days and nights that followed were not without pain, just as mine had not been. But my father stood just as straight after the surgery as he did before, and the smiles came more easily and more frequently.

I wondered then and will always wonder whether or not my father asked for the opportunity to trade his life for my own the year before. If he was somehow granted that opportunity, but then given an extension because he had more to do during his time in this world. Did his faith heal me? Did ours heal him? Are these questions that can ever be answered?

Single red roses became particularly important to my father from that time forward, just as three pink roses held special significance for me. St. Therese became our constant spiritual companion as we continued to face different, but numerous struggles. The photo that was given to my mother just before my surgery has a permanent place beside my bed. And we accepted, without question, that messages could indeed be sent in ways many people would ignore. Just as my father and I had set out in search of a piece of iceberg with little to sustain us but belief, we traveled the journey of these two years with faith as the main source of our strength. And just as St. Therese sent roses, my father sent stargazer lilies. Would I have recognized his flowers had it not been for my belief in hers?

On my father's last birthday the August before he died, I went to the florist shop and selected a single red rose. I brought it to his home and placed it in a vase. And I kissed his forehead as he lay on his bed and quietly sent him my love as I placed the rose where he could see it. He didn't know it was his birthday. He didn't know me. But I could think of nothing more appropriate to give him. A daughter's gift. A daughter's belief. A daughter's faith.

Early one morning during that same summer, my mother found my father lying in bed with tears in his eyes and a peculiar expression on his face. Although she didn't expect an answer... the time for words having essentially passed... she took his hand gently in hers and asked him what it was, what had happened.

It's St. Therese, he told her. *She was here, standing beside the bed. And she told me not to worry, that she will take care of me.*

At a time when he could not remember anything that happened even a second before, when he could rarely use words, this image stayed with my father throughout that day and into the next.

It stayed with us far longer.

If you cannot believe in miracles

remember a fourteen-year-old girl

and her three pink roses.

Remember a father

and his one red rose.

And know that there is always hope.

9

Forget Me Not

A few months after my father's death, I sat thousands of feet above the ground on an airplane taking me to an early morning out-of-province meeting and read the account of another daughter who was coping with her father's recent death from Alzheimer's. She spoke from her heart, in an article published in a national newspaper, and told of some of the anguish she felt as she had watched her father suffer. However, she had always been able to gain comfort from the fact that no matter what else her father forgot, he always remembered her. As I finished the article, I bent my head forward and raised my hand to cover my eyes and my silent tears. The sorrow of knowing my father had lost every memory we'd made together was as raw as it had ever been, the devastation of having lost him long before he died like a knife twisting in my heart.

Fortunately, the plane wasn't particularly full that morning and no one noticed my behavior. By the time the flight attendant passed my seat, I'd removed my hand from my eyes, raised my head and calmly wore the mask behind which I'd hidden the anguish of loss for more than five years. I'd also put the refolded newspaper aside and brought out the laptop computer to begin some work. What else was I to do? This was my pain, not theirs.

I began grieving for my father many years before he physically died. And I remember exactly when the process began. In the spring after my mother's early retirement, my parents took a trip to visit Steve and Glenna in Vancouver. They had planned a two-week vacation but ended up staying almost eight because when they arrived, my father lost all sense of time and place. Sometimes he thought he was back in Korea; other times he was simply unable to name any possible location. And he'd completely lost the ability to judge the passage of days and nights. It seems that at this stage he still knew the people around him — his wife, son and daughter-in-law — though I wonder if it ever occurred to him, during the hours he believed himself to be in Korea, that their presence was an impossibility. I suspect not.

I spent those eight weeks feeling helpless, waiting for the next phone call to find out if my dad *was coming out of it yet*. Steve, now a doctor, spoke in his best clinical voice, of the dementia our father was exhibiting, and refused to let him travel again until his condition had stabilized somewhat. It must have been tremendously difficult for him. One of the reasons for my parent's visit at that particular time was that my brother's wife was ill — suffering from environmental allergies so severe that she was confined to the small guest house of their home since it had been reconstructed using only 'safe' materials which didn't adversely affect her. My parents were going to provide support, to help, to be with their son and daughter-and-law.

But the drastic change in location caused a drastic change in my father's condition. Additional tests were run; intensive vitamin supplements were started; and my father did eventually begin to understand where he was and why. I remember an intense relief flooding through me the day after they came home. It was obvious my father was intensely happy to be on familiar ground, and his house and mine were still familiar. He was actually able to joke about the fact that half the time he was in Vancouver, he'd thought he was in Korea — must have been because they were staying in a room in the basement and the only things he could see through the small window were the bushes outside. He was able to recognize us upon his return; he was able to recognize his home; and that was reason for joy. My mother, however, vowed she would never again take him somewhere so unfamiliar, never again subject him to the anguish she'd witnessed as his present blended with his past and the weeks slipped by unnoticed. For her part, even though she'd coped with the trip in the same professional and competent manner she'd always dealt with the tragedies at the hospitals of her career, beneath her calm veneer lived a heart and soul that had been ravaged.

Did life ever return to normal after that? A new normal, I suppose, but certainly one with a growing list of things that were not longer possible.

Spring edged into summer and we began to prepare for my second brother's wedding to be held in Vermont in September. Before the trip to Vancouver, we'd expected everyone to be going. The entire family realized, however, that if my father was subject again to completely unfamiliar surroundings and many unfamiliar faces, the impact on him would likely be catastrophic. I wanted to stay at home with him, let my mother go, but in keeping with the pattern she would continue to follow until the morning of his death years later, she refused to leave his primary care to anyone else.

Thinking back, I realize I wasn't capable at that point, of really paying much attention to how my brother, Rik, must have felt about this, particularly since Steve wouldn't be attending either because of his wife's condition. Rik had been closer to both my father and brother than he had been to me, and it must have been a deep disappointment that his sister, brother-in-law and nephew would be the only family representatives. I was dealing with complex emotions that ranged from anger and bitterness to devastation and despair to hope and occasional happiness, and I prepared for that wedding with dread.

By the time we arrived in Vermont, I was completely exhausted

— physically and emotionally — something I was forced to admit when I was hit with intense vertigo the morning after our arrival. I ended up at a hospital where I was given medication that would control the dizziness and other symptoms and see me through the week that followed until the flight home. We left the city where we were staying for the first couple of days and drove to the small community where the wedding would be held, and I managed, by leaning (psychologically and physically) on my husband and small son, to survive the thirty-six hours during which my presence was absolutely required. Then I fell into the passenger seat of the rented car and slept all the way back to the city.

Despite the walls I'd erected around my emotions as I met the people who were welcoming my brother into their family, the reason for the absence of my parents was an almost unbearable anguish. I stayed as long as I could bear after the ceremony and reception, then all but ran away, escaping from the beauty of the community, from the joy, the laughter, and the celebrations. Feeling, all the time, that I'd let my family down and been a most ungracious representative, but absolutely incapable of doing any better. I hope they can forgive me.

It was shortly after we arrived home that I realized I was actually grieving the 'loss' of my father. I'm not sure this makes any sense, but I really did grieve — silently and privately so that the only person who knew my feelings was my husband. I carried around an intense unhappiness and an intense loneliness. But I wasn't just grieving for my father; I was also grieving the loss of my mother. I never told them this. How do you walk up to two people who are living and say: *Don't worry if I seem sad... I'm just grieving for you. No... No... I know you're not dead. But well dad, you see, you're going to forget me and as time goes on be able to do less and less, and then you'll die. And Mom, well, you're growing so angry and so bitter, and I'm losing you right along with dad. Just in a different way. So I'm grieving, but I'll be OK. Don't worry.*

The decision not to attend the wedding had been a relief for my father — a disappointment, but also a relief. The situation was, however, particularly hard for my mother, much harder, in fact, than I suspect she admitted at the time. Despite her intense commitment to my father and her own decision to take care of him as long as she possibly could, she was filled with a growing anger and bitterness. The unfairness of the situation was beyond comprehension. They'd worked incredibly hard to provide for three children and help many relatives. They'd never been able to travel together or do so many of the other things many couples accept as commonplace. And just when they were reaching the point in their lives when she and my father should have been able to enjoy retirement, life began to fall apart. She felt thoroughly cheated and deeply devastated. She was also intensely lonely as she began an excruciating process of watching her husband die slowly before her eyes.

For a number of years from that time, I never knew, when I visited or called her, whether she would be calm and pleasant or frantic and deeply distressed. I never knew if she would be accepting or intensely critical of some perceived or real failure on my part. I never knew whether I would walk away from the encounter in one piece, or feeling as if I'd been shredded. I say this with no malice — she didn't mean to be cruel; she would never have knowingly hurt me; and her suffering was all but unbearable. So I grieved for my father, for what he had lost and what he would lose. I grieved for my mother, for the changes in her life and her loss of happiness. I grieved for our closeness and friendship. And in my grief, I shaped the role I would continue to play and built the walls required to hide from almost everyone, my own pain. I wrote less than I should have, mainly because I couldn't bear to release my emotions. I was unable to admit to myself that the situation and my reaction to it was placing enormous stresses on my own home, even as part of me recognized them. And I continued to grieve even though I stopped admitting it. I'm not sure I've ever really stopped.

My father's deterioration and my mother's anguish ravaged me. Learning to accept unwanted changes in relationships and roles aged me. And trying to keep everything together changed me, making me stronger in some ways, weaker in others.

Shortly after we returned from Vermont, my father added a new habit to the routine of his visits to my home. He would arise from his favorite chair or leave the game he was playing with his grandson and restlessly walk from room to room. I'd use the sound of his footsteps to track his movement through the house, and when they'd grow silent, I'd quietly go to him. Most times, I'd find him standing in front of the corner window in our living room, his hands thrust deeply into the pockets of his khaki pants, his eyes staring out the window with an intensity that pierced my soul. It was as if he was searching for an answer to a question, as if he was willing himself to find something familiar in what had become unfamiliar. I'd usually go to stand beside him, look out with him and make some comment about the weather, or the grass, or the fence. Something. Anything. In the early months after Vermont, he'd usually smile at me and answer. As time went on, he simply remained silent. Eventually, I stopped walking to the window.

To watch a loved one suffer

and be unable to ease the pain

is to suffer also.

You may hide it from others.

You may even hide it from yourself.

But there is pain.

10

Dick and Mrs. Barron

Children always called my father by his first name. In an era when only the title 'Mr.' would have been seen as appropriate by most adults, he wasn't Mr. Barron, he was Dick. My mother says my brothers called our dad by his first name for many years, though I always called him daddy or dad. She also says neighborhood kids were forever coming over to the little house they lived in when I was born, knocking on the door, and saying: *Hello, Mrs. Barron. Can Dick please come out to play?* Or they'd see my parents somewhere and happily shout: *Hello Dick and Mrs. Barron.* My mother was always Mrs. Barron (or Mom, to the hundreds of nursing students she worked with through her career). My father was always Dick. Neither took any offense to their respective identifications; they accepted them graciously and with twinkles in their eyes.

Kids would come to see if Dick could come out to play. To see if they could help Dick work on something in the garage. To see if Dick could fix their broken bikes or flat tires. Just to see if Dick was around, so they could follow him as he worked outside the house and chatter on about whatever was on their minds.

Children and young people of all ages found that my father was the sort of man who was easy to talk to and be with. He would always find time for them — to repair the bike tires, pitch tents in back yards, repair fishing rods, rebuild Land Rovers, offer advice when asked, share his own experiences when necessary. He was a talented storyteller with a mischievous twinkle in his eyes, and he had a wonderfully contagious laugh that would fill the house or yard. And, perhaps most importantly, he would always find time to listen, really listen. His seemingly simple habit of paying attention to our words and his genuine interest in what we had to say was an extremely special trait, and a precious gift to all of us who shared his company.

It wasn't until I reached my teens, however, that I really began to realize that having a father who really listened wasn't as common as I thought. Most of my classmates, even my friends, didn't talk to their parents much — I talked to both my mother and father about everything and anything. Many of my contemporaries were feeling misunderstood, unappreciated, even unloved; I wasn't. Many were seeking ways to rebel; I didn't feel I had anything to rebel against. My father was one of my very best friends, and in many ways I felt much more comfortable and much happier in his company than I did with all but a few of my contemporaries.

With him I didn't have to pretend; because of him, I found the strength to set my own limits and do only those things I believed were right for me — when most people were living life by the rules of peer pressure. If something felt wrong, I didn't do it. I suppose I lost some 'friends' because of this, but if I did, I no longer remember who they were. Their acceptance wasn't as important to me as being true to myself.

In the years since my teens I've often chuckled that my father was an amazing psychologist because when I was seventeen years old he gave me a car for my birthday. This was not insignificant — my family was not rich by any estimation — but I was the only person in my group of friends who had his or her own vehicle. I'd spent two or three weeks checking out all the car dealerships with my father. As far as I knew I was helping him pick out the car my mother, my brother and I would drive (after I got my license). We finally decided on a small, red four-door Dodge Colt — affordable, yet sporty enough to satisfy my seventeen-year-old tastes. I didn't find it strange that I was the only one involved in the choice; my father and I had picked out vehicles together before.

We brought the car home on a Saturday morning. I spent part of that afternoon sitting on the floor in our living room, surrounded by the fabric and pattern pieces needed for whatever sewing project I was embarking on. When my dad walked by, I heard something drop to the floor next to me and looked over to see a set of car keys. I reached for them to pass them back up to my father when he smiled down at me and winked. *Happy Birthday*, he grinned. I remember asking him, rather stupidly, what he said. I also remember his eyes twinkling as he told me this was my birthday present, a little late, but my birthday present nonetheless, and that he knew I'd like it because I'd helped pick it out. I was still speechless when I jumped up and hugged him.

You can look at this any number of ways — that my father was spoiling me rotten was perhaps the most common perspective. But when I took those keys in my hand and accepted his gift, I also accepted the responsibility to care for my vehicle as my father would care for his own. When drinking and driving was much more common than it should have been, I became the self-designated driver, because I couldn't imagine my father hearing one night that I'd crashed the car he'd given me because I'd been drinking. I knew how much the car cost; I knew what his monthly payments were; I knew he would do without other things so I could have something both dependable and fun to drive. I also knew that he trusted me with this gift and it was inconceivable to me that I would do anything to betray his trust or his faith.

I don't think I actually told him of the impact of his gift until approximately three years later — instead I tried to show him how much his gift meant, by bringing the car home safely day after day and night after night. When we did talk about it, we did so after the death of a younger cousin in a car accident, a cousin who'd been drinking with his friends before getting behind the wheel on this particular night to drive home.

It was a tragedy that affected everyone deeply and as my father and I were driving home the night after he died, having brought my mother to the community where she'd stay with her sister (my cousin's mother) until after the funeral, we began to talk. One of those long, heartfelt, deeply serious talks about life, the reasons we travel the paths we do, and whether or not parents can really make any sort of difference. When we arrived home, he backed his Chevy Blazer into the garage, and we kept on talking, well into the early morning.

Most of the details of the conversation are gone from my memory, but there was one segment that explained a great deal about my father, why he was such a powerful influence in my life, and why people, particularly young people, sought his company and counsel. The topics varied widely. From discussing the cousin who'd just been killed, we started talking about the kinds of things most of the people my age were doing. We talked about other people — two teenagers who'd become pregnant and were sent away from home by their father to have their babies alone. *Would you do that,* I asked. *Would you have sent me away if I'd gotten pregnant? No,* he answered, *I would never do that to you. I wouldn't exactly be happy about the situation but I couldn't send you away. You'd need our help more than ever. Everyone makes mistakes.*

Then I asked another question.

Dad, what's your philosophy? What did you do to make me believe that I should always be the best person I can be; why is it that I haven't and won't do a lot of the things most of the people I know do because it would break my heart to hurt you? Why is it I can sit here and talk to you about anything? What did you do that was so different from most of the other parents I've met?

At first he just looked at me, without saying anything. Then he shrugged a little and answered quietly.

I don't really know. It's just that from the moment each of you was born I respected you as people, as individuals. And I always tried to treat you with respect.

I remember sitting there thinking, yes, that's exactly what you did. So simple. You didn't just love us, you respected us. And that was unconditional — because you didn't expect us to be perfect; you expected us to be who we were and whoever we were was perfectly fine with you. You shared our failures and our mistakes; our successes and our joys; our first loves and our broken hearts; the big screw-ups and littler ones and everything that goes along with growing up; and you never made us feel small or insignificant or stupid. You gave us the room we needed to fall flat on our faces or to soar with the birds, and you were there beside us to ensure we learned from the experience. You always listened, you always gave, and when we tried to give you something, no matter how small, you accepted our gifts as if they were precious gems.

Of course my father wasn't perfect. No human is. He got angry when vandals would throw rocks through the fence he built around our yard; he hated being taken advantage of; he always got irritated when he was putting the Christmas lights in the window — I don't know why, but he did; he didn't like having to remind us to do the things he thought we should do without his direction — like shovel the snow left in the driveway by the latest storm. And he worried and hurt and feared just like any man; more, I suspect, than many.

But the foundations of his life were respect and non-judgment. These were the principles that touched not just his own children, but the children who wandered in from the neighborhood and the friends who were lucky enough to share some of our time with him.

Children called my father Dick because they knew, instinctively as children know these things, that he would not ridicule their ideas and feelings, their projects and their dreams. Children called my father Dick because they knew that in his eyes, they were real people who really mattered. Because they knew he respected them.

What thanks can I give you

for your respect and your acceptance,

for your support and your faith,

for your unconditional and unwavering love,

except to live my life

so that you would be proud

to call me daughter.

11

Happy Birthday to You

My father didn't live in the past until Alzheimer's gave him no choice, and I decided by watching him throughout my childhood that I shouldn't live there either. While our personal histories help determine who we are at any given point, spending today emotionally or psychologically trapped in yesterday can hamper our ability to experience what is happening around us, impede our ability to grow, stifle the happiness that could otherwise be ours. It's a principle I've not mastered as completely as I'd like, however, despite my conviction that I must do so. As a result, many of my experiences throughout my father's illness return to overwhelm my senses at seemingly innocent times or in seemingly harmless places. Simple questions, like what day is it. Simple tasks, like buying birthday cards. These are different for me now. Reminders, windows backwards, drawing me into our past.

In that past, no one is exactly sure when my father no longer knew what day, month or even year it was, though we suspect he kept this particular agony from us for quite some time. Later, when asked if he knew what season it was by health care professionals assessing the deterioration in his condition, he'd answer almost impatiently: *Of course I do — it's summer,* even though the ground was covered in snow. *Or it's winter,* even though the sun was warm and the grass was green. Eventually, he wasn't able to answer.

The evidence was there, of course. But since his life was no longer structured around the need to be at work at certain times on certain days, it wasn't as obvious as it would otherwise have been. The one thing I can say I noticed initially — really noticed and admitted — was a need to remind him of days and dates he'd never been in the habit of forgetting — in his case birthdays and anniversaries.

Now, when I stand in front of a greeting card display, it's as if a memory steals in to stand beside me – the memory of the barely concealed pain I would see in his eyes when I asked him if he'd like to come with me to buy Mom's birthday or anniversary card; the memory of that barely concealed pain combined with his enormous and unwarranted gratitude.

My heart would cry out as I stood beside him in the store while he looked through the display of cards — his hands shaking until he made his selection; his grip on the card he would eventually choose so strong it seemed he was afraid to put it down, terrified if he did it would slip forever from his thoughts; his barely control anguish enveloping father and daughter as he suffered the knowledge of yet another gap in his memory, something else of importance erased.

He would have been devastated had we shown up with a gift for my mother on a special occasion that he'd forgotten, and so we brought him to buy cards and presents. We helped him hide them when he brought them home until eventually we kept them with us. In doing so, we helped him retain some semblance of normality as long as we could, always aware, however, that there was a price because each reminder of a special date created new anguish. We were easing his pain in one regard and increasing it in another. As for my mother, by this time she'd ceased to feel joy in such occasions, her pain tinged with a bitterness so acute that at times I wondered if we shouldn't have just let birthdays and anniversaries pass unnoticed. For her sake and for his. It was difficult and terribly sad.

My father had suffered his initial memory lapses in isolation. But the numerous incidents leading to my mother's retirement meant the increasing dementia couldn't be ignored (even if we didn't know the cause and didn't have a diagnosis) and there was so little we could do to ease the pain of the situation. So we did what we felt we could do, what we felt we had to do, what we felt he would have wanted us to do.

My father was still able to remember a great deal and do most things when he first started forgetting the important dates in our lives; he still knew what birthdays and anniversaries were and I believed he would not have wanted to forget them. He was trying hard to be who he had always been, to live as normal and complete a life as possible. We simply tried to help him do that, and so, for as long as it seemed right, we helped him remember.

Once he could no longer choose the cards himself, we'd select them for him and bring them for him to sign, though we stopped doing that on his second last Christmas. We'd arrived at my parent's house on a cold, snowy Christmas afternoon, our arms filled with brightly wrapped packages, our hearts filled with a mixture of hope and dread. Mother, daughter and grandson went to the Christmas tree to lay out the gifts. Peter went immediately to my parent's bedroom so he could show my father the card we'd chosen and have him sign it.

I had no problem imagining the scene when he described it later — he led my father to his desk, showed him the card for my mother, passed him a pen and asked him to sign it. My father took the pen with an unsteady hand, looked at Peter with an expression that was part blank, part confused, then proceeded to sign 'Richard J. Barr...' Peter tried to stop him, saying: *No, this is a card for Mary and all you need to do is put 'Love Dick'*. He couldn't — my father could still sign his full name, but that was the only name he could sign. We hadn't known that; I'm not even sure my mother knew until she saw the card and heard the explanation. What we had thought was a kindness became a cruelty; my father forgot the incident almost immediately, if it registered at all. My mother has never forgotten.

At about the same time we started reminding my father about other people's birthdays, we also started reminding him about his own. He had never been difficult to buy for. Over the years, he'd chuckled happily at remote control Jeeps and robots as he'd send them to sneak up on people in other parts of the house; beamed when we bought him another tool for the collection in his garage; taken books we gave him to his bedroom so he could read them as soon as he finished whatever volume he was currently immersed in. He wore the leather flight jacket my brother sent him with a wonderful air of pride, and the pants I'd sewn him, saying how he'd never had a jacket or pants that fit as well as these did, and how perfect the side patch pockets on the pant legs were. If he ever disliked anything we gave him, he certainly never gave any indication. And we were always delighted by his graciousness; he had a way of making us feel our gifts were deeply appreciated.

At first Alzheimer's made him forget his birthday, but only until we showed up with gifts and cards, to gather around the table and share a special meal and cake. I remember the birthdays when my son would run to the couch with Dick after supper, jump up beside him, and pass him the cards and presents one by one. His animated voice would mix with my father's exclamations of pleasure, their laughs and chuckles filling the room.

Later, his battle with Alzheimer's meant that sometime during the meal, he'd forget what the occasion was, and have to be reminded about the presents waiting for him. The scene would then play itself out almost exactly as before, except there'd be an edge to our smiles as we watched a small boy trying to help his grandfather, not quite certain why or how anyone could forget about presents, and their laughter and conversation wasn't quite as easy as it had been the year before.

I think it was on my father's second last birthday that Rik, who was still living in the city at the time with his wife Sarah and daughter Mae, planned a party at his home. His wife's parents were visiting from Washington and he saw it as a great opportunity to get everyone together. Taken out of his own environment for the afternoon, my father had no idea the occasion was a celebration for him. He sat in a chair while we brought him food, my mother making every effort to deal with the lapses in conversation caused by his uncomfortable silence. When a cake glowing with candles was brought to where he was sitting, he looked at it in confusion. *Nice cake dad? Yep. It's yours. Oh. You have to blow out the candles. Hhm?* He laughed when Kenneth and Mae ran to show him what to do, the uncomfortable, inappropriate laugh I'd come to hate. His gifts were opened for him and one of his cards was taken from his hand and turned right-side up; he'd been holding it upside down, only pretending to read.

By this time, buying presents was no longer easy; it hadn't been for a few years. We tried desperately to find things we thought would give him some continued pleasure. But things would go unused; books would go unread. I suppose he was like a young child who excitedly unwraps a package then tosses it aside, since the unwrapping is itself the focus.

The one thing that seemed to give the most pleasure for the longest time were framed photographs. He'd hold them in his hand, smiling. Then we resorted to articles of clothing he needed — new belts, new gloves, new shirts, new shoes. And finally, on his last birthday, when my mother could no longer bear the idea of any sort of celebration and he would have been physically unable to endure it, I gave him a single red rose and a simple card that told him I loved him and wished him god's blessings.

Whatever a person's traditions when it comes to things like

birthdays or anniversaries or Christmas, Alzheimer's changes them. For my father, every year after my mother's retirement brought steady deterioration, and so we changed traditions and patterns of behavior in an effort to make things as easy and 'happy' and normal as they could be. We did stop celebrating my parent's anniversary, at my mother's request. At that stage she could feel no joy in being reminded of the day they were married or the years they'd spent together. We didn't stop celebrating the others, though I can't help but think we never quite got them right. Actually, I can't help but think that when it comes to Alzheimer's, maybe there's no such thing as getting them right, no matter how hard you try.

Which brings me back to the greeting card displays. As the memory of my father's pained choices steals in today to stand on one side of me, the memory of trying to find a card that was appropriate for him in the situation steals in to stand on my other side. I couldn't bear to give my dad birthday or Christmas cards that talked of a future that was bright; I couldn't bear to give him cards that spoke of happy days gone by since he couldn't recall those memories; so I would search for a card that told him, simply, how much he meant to us, had always meant to us, would always mean to us. Even though I knew, in the last couple of years, the words held no meaning for him. The right cards, in those years, were very hard to find.

Days of celebration

may become sorrowful reminders.

Words once taken for granted

may be silenced by circumstance.

And yet the most important message remains.

12

For the Love of Land Rovers

My father's favorite place in our house was the garage. That's where he spent most of his free time — working on vehicles, organizing projects around the house and yard, fixing things, making things. I spent my childhood as a skinny, wispy-haired blonde little girl who hung out there with him whenever I could. He'd wear coveralls — usually dark green but sometimes navy blue; I'd wear worn-out jeans or shorts and my oldest t-shirts and sweatshirts. Sometimes we'd have to stop in the middle of whatever project occupied our time and clean up enough to drive to a building supply or auto parts store. We'd smear a gel-like cleaner over our hands — I loved the feel and smell of the cleaner, and the way it made the dirt disappear as if by magic — and trade our greasy or paint-smeared clothing for something that wouldn't leave marks when we jumped into one of our vehicles.

My father's garage was probably as clean and organized as a garage can be. You could enter it through the main garage door, through a door from the back yard, or from one of two inside entrances off the main porch going into the house. We didn't have an electric garage door — the kind I have today that allows me to sit comfortably in my car, push a button and wait for the door to smoothly roll to the ceiling. Every time we took a vehicle in or out of the garage, someone would have to lift a ten foot bar that held the two doors in place, fold the two sides back against the walls and anchor them with wooden door wedges my father had made. Closing the doors meant reversing the process.

Inside the garage, the floor was concrete. There were three windows near the top of one of the side walls — too high up for me to see anything besides a small patch of sky but large enough to let the outside light brighten the room during the day. There was space for two cars, parked end to end; there was also space for shelves, work benches, desks, and a small storage closet. A ladder attached to one wall led to an attic.

Over the years the exact configuration of the benches and shelving, even the storage areas changed, as my father made adjustments to suit his particular needs at the time. His collection of tools grew steadily over the years. There was every kind of nail and screw, every size of drill bit. There were paint tins, cleaners, brushes and rollers. There were shovels and rakes and lawn mowers, axes, saws and hammers, and various auto parts. There was an assortment of rags, work gloves and clothing, even shoes and boots just for the garage. Everything had its place and everything had its own unique smell.

When people came to borrow things, as they frequently did, or when someone needed a particular size screw or nail, my father could instantly locate it. Or give directions to others so they would be able to find it without delay. Same thing when I was working there with him. He'd be lying under a vehicle that had been jacked up, the bottom three inches of his coveralls and his boots the only parts of him that were visible. *Duck,* he'd say, *I need my 3/8 inch wrench; it's on the second shelf, third row, over the desk.* Which is exactly where I'd find it.

The garage was painted at least once a year — floor to ceiling. There was no particular season or schedule for this activity; it occurred whenever my father decided the constant traffic or activity meant it needed doing. The floor was generally a deep shade of grey; the walls were sometimes the same colour; at other times the upper or lower half was grey, with the remainder being a contrasting colour — rust, deep green, a darker or lighter shade of grey.

I don't always remember there being a radio in the garage, though there certainly was in later years, after I'd grown and moved away and was no longer there to chatter on. Eventually, there was a tiny TV — one we'd given my dad for his vehicle so he could watch while he waited when he was picking my mother up from work, but he kept it on a shelf above the desk instead.

My mother says the main reason they initially bought the house where I grew up was that it had a garage, because she had worried about my father when he was lying on the cold driveway in all sorts of weather, working on one vehicle or another. The house wasn't her dream house. It was also just outside the city limits when they'd planned to live inside the city. But it had a garage, a place where my dad could stay warm and dry, and so this particular house won out over the others they looked at.

There's no doubt that purchase gave my father countless hours of pleasure; I just hope he always knew how much I treasured the hours I spent with him in his garage. Why was I so happy in the garage with my father? I think the answer is simple — I was happy because I knew I was welcome there. Because my father always found some way for me to help and never made me feel that I was in his way or slowing him down. Because he welcomed and accepted whatever help I was able to give and made me feel that I had somehow made his task easier. Because we could talk if we felt like it or be perfectly quiet. Because I shared in his sense of accomplishment at a job well done. Because I could get my clothes dirty and my hands greasy and he loved me anyway.

We spent a lot of our time in the garage working on one vehicle or another — that's what he most loved to do. And the vehicles he loved most were his Land Rovers, his green Land Rovers. Even now old friends and acquaintances still refer to his Land Rovers when they talk about how they remember my dad, how his Land Rovers seemed to suit his tall, straight bearing, how his preference for wearing khaki clothes made them think of safari, of my dad being the explorer of far-off lands.

When my brothers were small, my parents had only one car, but from the time I was fairly young (after my grandmother had moved in with us and my mother had gone back to work) there were usually two. That number steadily increased as my brothers and I began to drive and I remember Land Rovers as being a constant part of my childhood. My father took great pride in keeping every one of our vehicles in mint condition. He seemed to know instinctively what needed to be done and when he should do it. In fact, all he had to do was hear a car running or drive it himself for a few moments to figure out what the problem was. Even when there was no particular repair to make or no maintenance that was required, he'd tweak and adjust and fine-tune. He was always working on something, always fixing something.

I didn't inherit my dad's seemingly instinctive understanding of the automobile, and despite the fact that I spent hour upon hour working with him in the garage, I never picked up his ability to fix them. But I realized a long time ago that the point of all those hours had little to do with learning to realign the steering or change the spark plugs and everything to do with simply spending time with my father, seeing things through his eyes, showing things to him through mine, learning from his example and his patience, sharing a special friendship.

Sometimes the projects we worked on took just an evening or two; sometimes they lasted for days or weeks. One summer, for instance, we spent all our free time refurbishing a camper that fit on the back of a truck. When we'd bought the truck-camper, we envisioned a whole

new level of camping comfort. The only thing was, the camper was
home made, and not quite complete. But it was what we could afford
at the time so my dad and I were more than confident we could finish
it. We did — we hammered and screwed and sanded and built and
made more trips to the hardware store than either of us could count.
We used that camper for just one season, then sold it the next year and
upgraded to a factory built truck-camper. But at the age of thirteen,
I'd learned something of the commitment, patience and determination
needed to see an extensive project through to its conclusion; my dad
had shared his with me.

I wasn't the only person who got to spend time with my father
in Dick's place, as our garage came to be known, to learn from his
examples. I remember one winter — a year or two after our truck-
camper summer — when we had two Land Rovers parked face-to-face
in the garage. One was ours; the other belonged to my oldest brother's
friend, Joe. Ours was in good working condition; Joe's, on the other
hand, needed some work. I think they were doing a realignment of the
wheels on Joe's vehicle (though I can't remember for sure) using ours
as a guide.

I spent New Year's Eve that year hopping in and out of the driver's
seat of our Land Rover, following my father's instructions to turn the
steering wheel this way or that. Fetching tools, holding lights, offering
opinions on how the exposed front of Joe's vehicle compared with the
exposed front of ours. An odd way to spend the evening perhaps, when
most of my school mates were experiencing their first real New Year's
Eve parties, but my father was my truest friend, and I was happy to be
with him. I was also proud, because I knew he was happy to have me
there.

I miss those hours with my dad in the garage — they were peaceful,
fun and exciting, and they taught me many things. There was never
a possibility, when my father and I started a project, that it would

go unfinished. There was never a possibility that the problem being addressed would go unsolved. In my father's garage, there was no such word as can't — we simply worked until we figured out how, he accepting my opinions and input, me learning from his experience.

Our Land Rovers weren't always in the garage, as you've probably guessed. Most of the time, in fact, they were on the road filled with everything from groceries to fishing rods to sports equipment; filled with the laughter and conversations of my family and our friends as we traveled to work and school, to cadets and piano lessons, to ponds and beaches and the homes of relatives.

I loved driving around in them just as much as I loved working on them. Especially in the winter when my dad would let me operate the controls for the snow plough he'd installed so he could clear the nearby driveways and even the road where we lived — not for payment but because that's what good neighbors did. Especially through stormy streets as we made our way home in the middle of a huge snowstorm — taking hours while we picked up and dropped off others who would otherwise have been stranded. Whenever we sat in the Land Rover, it was an adventure and my father was the adventure guide.

I eventually got to drive our Land Rover. After I'd gotten my license, he offered one day, to teach me to drive a standard transmission — to drive his Land Rover. It was and still is the most stubborn and most wonderful vehicle I've ever driven — the gears were hard to move, the steering was cantankerous beyond reason, and it actually seemed to jump over even the tiniest bumps in the road. Not to mention being totally unforgiving if I didn't release the clutch at the exact second it wanted to be released. My dad lurched and chuckled his way through most of the early lessons, gently coaching me with a twinkle in his eye; I laughed too, even though I couldn't help but feel utterly mortified as we hopped our way across vacant parking lots. It would be incorrect to say I eventually mastered the vehicle, but we did come to a happy understanding.

Possessions didn't mean a great deal to my father, but he loved his Land Rovers. What did he do for me when he trusted me to drive the last one he would own? He showed me he trusted me to care for it as he would. He showed me I could do anything my brothers could do (they'd also learned to drive the Land Rovers and had been driving them long before I could even get my license). I think he even helped me land my second, or perhaps it was my third boyfriend, a Land Rover fan who said I was the only other person (not girl, but person) he'd ever let drive his Land Rover. In trusting me to drive his Land Rover, my dad did what he'd always done; he showed his respect for me, his belief in me; he let me try something new without fear of his displeasure at my failure; and he treated me as an equal. For those gifts, I can never thank him enough.

After my mother and I visited the funeral home on the afternoon of my father's death, I called Steve in Vancouver, who was making his flight arrangements to come for the funeral, to tell him everything had been taken care of and I'd picked out the best casket I could find. He chuckled and said a casket wouldn't do — we needed a Land Rover because that was about the only thing dad would be comfortable in. I chuckled right back, saying no, I hadn't been quite able to manage that but had picked a rather classy green casket — their best copper one. Not many people would understand I picked green because of my father's love for his green Land Rovers, but my brother and I did.

Recently, Steve got a Land Rover of his own. It isn't green, it's silver, and it rides a lot more smoothly than the kind we both learned to drive, the models they stopped bringing into the country in the early 70s (which is why, by the way, my father stopped buying them). But somehow it feels the same. My father would have loved Steve's Land Rover, and my only sadness when we rode together from the airport to Steve's house outside Vancouver, was that my father wasn't sitting there with us. Then again, I have a feeling he was. Just as I have a feeling he was standing next to us in the carport when Steve was explaining exactly where he was going to build his own garage. And he was chuckling, the rich, deep chuckle of our childhood.

Welcome a child into your world

to try without fear of failure,

to experience without fear of judgment,

and teach, through your belief

in his ideas and abilities,

that he can do anything.

13

Sinking Deeper and Deeper

During the last four to five years of my father's illness, he never looked at me and asked the question many Alzheimer's patients do — *Do I know you?* I'd like to say that's because he knew exactly who I was until and beyond the moment of his death, but that isn't the reason. He'd become quite adept at making people think he knew who they were when all he instinctively knew was that he should remember these people. Because he'd always been a relatively quiet man, people who would only meet him intermittently would see his smiles and nods, return his still firm handshake and walk away unaware of the confusion they'd caused him. Because he continued to behave in the gentlemanly manner they'd come to expect, because his hair was combed carefully back in his regular style, because the style of his clothing exhibited no change, people didn't readily recognize the hidden turmoil and irreversible changes that were taking place. How could they?

While Alzheimer's is known to cause massive and quite obvious personality shifts in many patients, it did not appear to do so in my father, at least not until the last months. Always a quiet man, always a patient man, he essentially remained so. But for about three years following my brother's wedding in Vermont, there was an increasingly evident pattern. My father would experience a bad day — he'd be physically ill and mentally more confused than before. Even after he recovered physically, it would be evident (sometimes more evident than others) that he'd lost more of his mental abilities. At first, he was still able to participate in much of our lives, but over time he needed more and more help. And the relationships changed, often without us recognizing just how much they were changing, as we took over more and more of the tasks he would normally have done himself.

When my mother realized he had no idea what the day or date was, she tried to help him keep track by having him mark the days off on a calendar. When she noticed he'd failed to put clothes that needed to be washed in the laundry but worn them instead, she began laying out his clothes. When it seemed he should no longer be driving, she suggested to him that she should learn to drive in the winter and took over that task. When he could no longer write the cheques to pay bills, she took over his share of those tasks. And when he was with us, we questioned and directed and guided as much or as little as we needed to, even in situations where he would normally have led. Through this period, we didn't notice a daily deterioration — we dealt with the bad days then adjusted to his changed abilities. In fact, when I think back and try to piece together the path of his disease, it's impossible for me to even remember the sequence of events.

Did my mother start selecting his clothes before she started driving all the time? Was she selecting his clothes when he was still more than capable of sitting and playing happily with his grandson? Was he still capable of making decisions about the food he wanted to eat when he was no longer aware of the season? When did he stop repeating a single comment or a single question and instead grow more and more silent? When did he begin to take his shoes off, then put them back on, then take them off again, then put them on again, then take them off again, completely unaware of whether he needed them on or not? When did he no longer know his way around my house, so that he couldn't find the bathroom, the kitchen or the porch? When did he stop knowing his way around his own house? When did he stop doing anything meaningful in his garage? When did he stop reading bedtime stories to his grandson? How long was he pretending to read books and magazines when all he was doing was holding them and turning the pages? When did he stop being able to taste things? When did his hugs take on an element of desperation? When did he no longer worry about being sick, because he no longer remembered that he was forgetting?

I don't have answers to these questions and I don't have answers to hundreds of others. I don't remember the exact path of his deterioration; but if I sit quietly in the rocking chair that stays empty now, the one he usually occupied when he visited our house, I can feel the insidious stealth of the disease as it swept over him and I can see certain aspects as clearly as if they were playing themselves out before me in holographic form. But it's all a terrible jumble — in terms of what came first or second or third or fourth. Maybe that's because the process wasn't really like something that moved from beginning to end in a series of steps. It was more like watching the surface of the ocean after you toss a beach rock into the water and see the series of rings it creates. They completely encircle the point where the rock hits the water, reaching out farther and farther as the rock sinks deeper and deeper until finally, there is nothing. Absolutely nothing. No rock; no rings. And the beautiful rock you picked up on the beach is lost forever.

My memories aren't of a series of days, or months. Rather, they're of moments, series of moments in time that anchor me to the reality of those days.

Moments...

I remember, after I changed jobs some four years before my father died, that one of my greatest sadnesses was he couldn't retain the new information about where I worked. I was doing some of the most significant and rewarding work of my career to that point, and I desperately wanted to share it with him, so I'd 'natter on' whenever I was in his company — telling him about the new magazine, that day's news conference, how we feared a strike would be inevitable, the reaction I'd gotten to an article I'd written — knowing he'd remember none of it. I'd show him the things I was most proud of because I knew how proud it would have made him, even though I realized he couldn't comprehend what it was or how it related to me or him. I did believe he was able to read people's moods much as a young child instinctively does and I believed he could feel that I really wanted him to know these things, that I was talking to him because he was important to me. And so I struggled to avoid what would have been an all too easy slide into a habit of silence. Only on one instance did he seem to connect me to the work I so frequently told him about. We'd just released the second issue of the professional magazine I edited. Its theme was on Global Education and the editorial I'd written introduced the topic by paying tribute to my father for the lessons he'd taught me:

I think I was very lucky as a child. My father had traveled the globe before I was born and whenever I asked a question... and often when I didn't ask... he would fill my heart and soul with stories.

He told me about Australia, the Soviet Union, Japan. He told me about Korea and the West Indies, North and South America. He talked about oceans and lands. He talked about destruction and life. He talked about people and customs, differences and similarities, and the importance of respect and acceptance. Whatever his personal tragedies from World War II and Korea, he never said, or even hinted, that one people was better than another. That one people deserved more or less respect than another. And in the way of gifted storytellers, he filled his words with significance, so that even when the details of the stories passed... as did the time for telling them... the basic message remained clear. This really is a very small world. And we really are one people. (Reprinted from *PRISM, The Professional Magazine of the Newfoundland & Labrador Teachers' Association,* Fall 1992)

The article went on to talk about the other influences in my life, of teachers and professors, as it set the stage for the rest of the articles in the publication. My mother gave my father the article to read, knowing the chances of him remembering it were slim, knowing that at this stage, if I wasn't in his company I was essentially erased from his world. But she gave it to him anyway and later told me he did indeed appear to read the article... slowly and completely... then looked at her from where he sat holding the magazine. *She's a good girl, isn't she?* he asked with a smile. *Yes,* my mother answered. *She is.*

Sometime in the year leading up to his death, I looked up one day to see my father standing in the door of my office. He was wearing his khaki pants and shirt and he was smiling at me. I stood up and walked around my desk towards him as he stepped slowly inside. We hugged.

How are you? I asked.

I'm OK. How are you? he grinned. *I have to go, but you be good now OK?*

I will. I answered. *You be good too.*

I smiled at him, we hugged and then he left. It was a dream of course — my father never did physically visit my office. But when I awoke in the middle of the night with tears streaming down my face I was certain that this was a goodbye — one he chose to say while he could still say it. And it was many days before I could hear the phone in my office ring without thinking this would be 'the' call from my mother asking me to come to the house.

Perhaps the reason for that dream was nothing more than my intense wish to find the connection that had been lost with my father, to share with him a part of my life he could no longer share. Perhaps he really did come to say hello and goodbye, an astral self coming to meet me when there was no longer any other way to bridge the gap. I'm not sure it matters. I do know, however, that while on the surface I calmly acknowledged I was no longer known by the person who had always loved me — simply for who I was — in my heart and in my soul, in waking and in sleeping, I silently longed to be recognized.

Moments...

It was summer and as always during the summer, there was a steady stream of visitors to my parent's house. Kenneth was spending parts of each day there waiting until I began my vacation, spending his time with my father in the garage and in the yard or in one room or another with whatever toys were of most interest at the time. Enjoying the hash browns and bacon my mother would prepare for his lunch. I went to pick him up one afternoon and walked through a house filled with the animated voices of visitors excited to be in one another's company. However, the house was also burdened by the weariness and frustration of my mother, who was finding it harder and harder to deal with my father's illness, particularly when combined with the responsibilities associated with a house full of guests.

I found my son and his grandfather sitting on the royal blue carpet in my brother's bedroom, surrounded by a sea of red, yellow, white, blue, black and brown Lego building blocks. Launching into a report of the day's activities, Kenneth proudly displayed the ship they'd made together. I hurried him out of the room to find the containers and bags he needed to pack everything away — partly because we had to pick Peter up from work and partly because some days I simply couldn't bear to be in the house. I must have been unsuccessfully trying to explain to my dad why we needed to leave quickly, because he looked at me, with an expression that was a mixture of desperation, bitterness and self-loathing. *I wish I could leave,* he said, as he picked the ship up from the place on the floor Kenneth had placed it. *I wish I had a ship like this one because I'd sail away and never come back. I'd sail away now. While I still can.*

It was the only time I had ever or would ever hear my father express a desire to leave everything and everyone he loved, and the depth of the anguish that led him to make those comments was almost immeasurable. These were the hardest moments — when he knew how ill he was; when he knew there was no going back to the way he had been; when he didn't know what loss tomorrow would bring. I didn't say anything for a moment — didn't know what to say — and when I was able to comment, my words were simple and full of my own anguish. *If you did that, I'd really miss you.* But the truth was I already did. And the other truth was I could understand exactly why he said what he did. Because as much as he wanted to be free upon the ocean — reliving a youth where the salt air of the sea filled his lungs and the stars guided his path instead of being bound by a prison that became more and more secure everyday — I wished, for him, that same freedom.

We tried, we really tried, to help Kenneth understand what was happening to his grandfather, why things like requests for bedtime stories and certain play activities were no longer possible. We also tried to help him understand how the pressures of his grandfather's illness were affecting his grandmother. And in some regards, I think we were reasonably successful, not because of our own wisdom or any particular insight, but because we are blessed with an intelligent and observant son whose natural curiosity drives him to seek explanations. To ask every question he can until he's gathered enough information to formulate the answers he needs. But it was so acutely painful to watch his relationship with his grandfather change. And the experience was deeply painful for him.

Moments...

It was nearing Christmas and Peter and I had been trying to find an evening when we could shop for Kenneth, without him being present. We no longer left him alone with my parents for long periods of time. His sensitivity to the illness was making his visits there increasingly difficult for him, partly because of my father's forgetfulness and partly because it was impossible to ignore my mother's frustration and intermittent depression. We worried about Kenneth — the impact of being in an increasingly negative atmosphere. We worried about my parents — the impact of lessening the frequent contact they'd enjoyed with their grandson. So usually we compromised and instead of leaving him there on his own, one of us would stay with him, our presence acting as a safety net should one be needed.

But on this particular cold December evening, we set aside our concern long enough to spend three hours mingling with the other Christmas shoppers, searching through toy stores and sharing the task of carrying the packages. With no trunk to hide the gifts in — we drove a station wagon — we decided I should drop Peter at home then pick up Kenneth, giving Peter just enough time to hide everything.

When I arrived at my parents' house, Kenneth's bag of toys was packed and he was sitting in the family room waiting for me. My mother or father or both must have been with him, though I don't remember for certain. I only know that while his face was calm, his eyes were tortured and his small body rigid with self-control. We hurried out of the house and I opened the door for him so he could climb into the passenger seat.

What's wrong? I asked. *What happened?*

He didn't answer for what seemed like a long time. Instead, he sat there with his shoulders lurching as he sobbed uncontrollably, tears flowing down his reddening cheeks, his chin dropping to his chest. I sat there quietly, letting him cry, waiting for him to talk. I hope I held his hand and said whatever he needed to hear. I don't remember. I only remember his tears, and when they began to ease, his words. *I just don't understand. I just don't understand what's happening to Dick. And I don't understand why Mary is like she is, why she seems so mad all the time. I just don't understand.*

As it turned out, nothing extremely unusual had happened that night, nothing that would be labeled as horrifying by most observers. My father and his grandson had simply played together. But the play was changing, my father's ability to be a partner and friend was disappearing, and it was breaking the heart of the small boy who loved him dearly.

Change is sometimes so gradual

we do not recognize either

its severity or its impact.

Until we take a moment

to see through a child's tears.

14

The Simple Act of Being There

I started sewing my own clothes when I was twelve. My mother had sewn frequently throughout the years and had a wonderful early model Singer sewing machine with foot pedal action that I used at first, though I worked primarily on a more modern Kenmore model. The first item I made with the help of the volunteer instructors at school and my mother at home was a pink, floral dress. It was short, had cape sleeves and a pink wool drawstring through the neckline. I was so incredibly proud of that first creation, though never wore it much. Certainly, I kept it for years until I decided that perhaps I was too old for a sentimental attachment to a piece of fabric that no longer had any practical use.

My next undertaking, this one much more ambitious, was a pantsuit. I chose a stiff, natural-colored cotton that was covered with the signs and names of the zodiac in deep red. The pants had a flat front, back zipper and were flared slightly at the bottom. The jacket was waist length and bomber style. It was a much more complicated undertaking than I would now advise someone of my experience to tackle, but I was determined. And so I cut and pinned and sewed. I do remember thinking, when I was finally finished, that it wasn't exactly perfect. But I didn't really care and wore it nonetheless. What would have happened if either of my parents had looked at those first attempts and pointed out the flaws instead of admiring what had to be quite primitive work? I guess I can't know for sure, but I suspect that at some point I would have decided to stop.

From the time I started sewing, my mother and I would often choose fabrics and patterns together, so I essentially had her buy-in before I even started, her stamp of approval. My father would watch, generally without comment but often with a chuckle or a grin, as we walked into the house with yet another bag from a favorite fabric store. Sometimes I'd pull everything out of the bag right at that point and tell him what I was going to make; sometimes I'd show him when I was cutting it out; sometimes when it was at the first fitting stage; sometimes not until the outfit was complete. Sometimes I'd asked him to tell me if the pant legs were even, if the skirt was too short or too long, if the lining was pulling. It didn't matter what I made or how inexperienced the construction, my father always made me feel proud of what I'd accomplished. There may have been an extra bright sparkle in his eye when I 'modeled' something he particularly liked, but there was always a twinkle and a smile.

I started sewing because I liked it. I continued because it was the best way (often the only way) to find the kind of clothes I wanted — partly because of the fit (I was tall and embarrassingly waif-like) and partly because we lived in a small city. But I also enjoyed shaping and moulding the fabric — creating things. I still do.

When I look back, I realize that my father's support of this interest was really quite a simple and quiet thing. A few encouraging words, light-hearted teasing, sincere compliments, smiles, a twinkle in his eye. He wasn't prone to long, flowery compliments — *Oh dear, what a beautiful job. You are so talented and that outfit makes you look like a princess. How absolutely precious you are.* These were not the kinds of things my father would say, but his support and acceptance were evident in other ways. He never asked why we were buying more fabric (just because it was on sale) when we already had more than a few pieces we hadn't gotten around to sewing yet. He never asked why I was making another skirt or pair of pants or top, even though these would have been quite legitimate questions. Instead he watched, smiled, accepted, and I believe instinctively knew, that just as he loved his vehicles and what he could do with them, I loved my fabrics and what I could make with them. If he'd acted differently, he could have taken something incredibly important from me — at a simple level, the belief that I could be a competent seamstress; at a much deeper level, the self-confidence that was enhanced with the completion of every sewing project. I didn't recognize this at the time, of course. I just accepted his smiles and smiled back, my head a little higher as I walked out the door to the car on my way to a Grade 8 dance. A portion of my self-confidence and sense of self-worth still intact when I'd return home a few hours later without having been asked to dance even once.

Being a teenager can be incredibly difficult, particularly the thirteen to seventeen period. I was much taller than most of the boys; my marks were high; I wore clothes I'd sewn myself as opposed to buying what most of my contemporaries were wearing; I was tall and thin; I spent much of my Grade 9 year in hospital and at physiotherapy; I wasn't popular with the 'in crowd'; my hopes of being athletic like my brothers were derailed by knee surgery; I didn't want to smoke or drink; I didn't fit easily into any group. And I strongly believe that if it hadn't been for my home environment, I would have had a much more difficult time finding the courage to be who I was, to find my own ways to grow and explore. Sewing was one example, but there were many others.

In Grade 7 my class was taking a trip to the small French island of St. Pierre, which was located a short ferry ride from the tip of Newfoundland's Burin Peninsula, but number restrictions meant that only two-thirds of the class would actually be able to go. Get your parents' permission first, we were told, then if you're allowed to go and want to, you can put your name in with all the others and we'll draw from those. I'd never been away from home without my parents before and I was nervous — in many ways I was a young thirteen year old. My mother was hesitant — imagining, as was her habit, everything that could go wrong — from the boat sinking to something happening on the island. So we went to my father and asked him what he thought. I can see him to this day, sitting on the edge of his bed. *Well duck, this sounds like a good opportunity, but it's up to you. If you'd like to go, then that's fine with me. If you don't that's fine with me too. I know you have to start going sometime.*

There was something about the way he said *you have to start going sometime* that has stayed with me in the many years since then, one of the defining moments on my path to adulthood. Because while, on the surface, we were talking about a three-day trip to St. Pierre, I knew we were talking about a great deal more. We were talking about his trust in me. We were talking about the fact that I was growing up and that meant changes — a lot of them — changes that would separate us. I sensed some mixed emotion in his voice; but I sensed no hesitation, no wish on his part to hold me back in childhood. And I knew, as I had always known, that his belief in me was complete.

I did decide to include my name on the list of people who wanted to attend and had parental approval, but I wasn't one of the students selected when the draw was made. I was disappointed, but also a little relieved, because while my dad was ready to let me go, I'm not sure I was ready to leave.

I had fewer boyfriends throughout my teens than most of my classmates. At first, that was because fewer people were interested in a tall, skinny, brainy girl, and later, because I saw no point in having a boyfriend simply for the sake of having one. I had what might be considered a rather odd thought process about the whole thing: if I was dating someone simply for the sake of having a boyfriend, then happened to meet someone I really liked, then the person I really liked wouldn't call me because I already had a boyfriend and so the relationship was doomed before it even started. When at age sixteen I finally met someone where everything (well most things anyway) clicked, I was understandably excited. He was 6'2", blonde and wore a white silk scarf with a long navy blue winter coat. I can still picture him standing in the gymnasium at the school dance when he first approached me. I can still remember thinking how staggeringly handsome he was.

The relationship lasted three months before he dumped me — on Thursday night before the Easter weekend and less than one month before the senior prom. To make matters worse, he dumped me for one of the most popular females in my class. The boyfriend experience was new; the break-up experience was new; and I'd definitely liked the first part better than the second. So what did my father do to help me through the adjustment? He took me for an unusually long driving lesson.

Actually, he didn't say a word about the break-up. I'd told my mother when I came home early on that Thursday night, just before escaping to my room. She had to work the next day, but my father was home. Somewhere around mid-day, after we'd made the annual Good Friday trip to church, he suggested today would be a good day to learn how to park. We drove to the empty parking lot of the local Arts Centre; I got behind the wheel and, over the course of the next few hours, improved my angle and parallel parking skills significantly. The only reference made to my crisis — *You know Steve broke up with me last night, do you dad? Yes,* he answered, *I know.*

An afternoon of parking did not, I am the first to admit, cure that particular crack in my heart. Being dumped hurt a great deal and for a great deal longer. But I needed support that day, particularly that day — quiet understanding and unquestioning support — and my father, in his own way, gave me exactly that. I don't know how he could have known what I needed. I don't know how he always seemed to know. But he was amazingly perceptive and skilled in the simple act of being there, when and where I needed him most.

There's a little more to this break-up story. My ex-boyfriend did indeed offer to take me to the prom despite the new status of our relationship; he said he felt badly that I was now without a date and it was likely too late to find someone else. He seemed sincere, but to me it was inconceivable that I would attend the dance with someone I knew wanted to be there with someone else — to me that would have been even more humiliating than the breakup. I didn't go to the prom and I can honestly say that to this day I have never regretted the decision; in fact, I really did gain satisfaction from the fact that I didn't let anyone pressure me into doing what they thought I should do when I knew it wasn't right for me. What did I do when all my school friends were dancing the night away? I spent the early part of the evening out and about with my father and the latter part in the garage.

Sometime after high school and that first breakup, and before university and the next boyfriend, I got my hair cut. I'd agonized over that particular decision for more months than anyone might ever believe possible, but unlike the clothes that could be changed quickly if they didn't *feel* right, hair didn't grow back quickly, and I was (still am, actually) extremely cautious. Having finally made an appointment, I found myself in Donna's chair — the person who would guide me through the evolution of the next decade. She took about six inches off the back of my long straight style and gave me bangs. I watched the transformation with a mixture of excitement and terror and left the salon pleased but more than a little apprehensive.

As we pulled into the driveway, my father came out of the garage where he'd been working with the doors open. I asked him what he thought as soon as I stepped out of the car. *Well, I think you look like Purdy from the* The New Avengers *and she looks pretty good.* He grinned at me. *Really?* I beamed back. *Really.*

That particular day was, for me, very much like the day in Grade 7 when he'd been ready to let me go on the school field trip to St. Pierre. His words were one thing; the look on his face and the expression in his eyes another. Another mark of more time passing. Another defining moment. I'd been transformed from new high school graduate to sophisticated young woman in just a few hours. And he accepted and approved.

If my relationship with my father changed at all when I was a teenager, it only strengthened. He didn't lecture. I didn't shout and scream or believe his purpose in life was now to limit and frustrate me. I didn't fear that he no longer understood me; in fact, I sometimes think he understood me more completely than I understood myself. He occasionally told me to turn down the music or to stay home from a particular party or dance because the roads were too slippery and snow-covered. But he didn't look at me and complain that he'd lost his helper in the garage. He didn't keep me from taking my first trip out of the province and country — to England when I was just sixteen to stay with the daughter of our neighbors. He didn't criticize my clothes or shoes or the dates who came to the door.

He watched, he led, he gave advice when he thought it was warranted (or when it was asked for). And I knew that if he expressed an opinion that was opposite of what I was intending to do, it would be in my best interest to listen because it was quite likely my own analysis of the situation had failed to include a particularly important point or two.

I've already spoken of the power of my father's trust. I've already spoken about his philosophy of respect and his unconditional love. And whenever I hear the Celine Dion song, "Because You Loved Me", my father is the person who comes to mind. Because I know, with as much certainty as I know the sun is shining outside the window as I sit at my computer and write this, that I am who I am today, that I see myself, my husband, my son, my dog, my mother, indeed, I see the world the way I do in large part because of my father, because my father loved me. I've read a lot of books and heard or watched a lot of stories about people who were not blessed with the kind of relationship I had with my father. I read and hear about emotional cruelty, physical abuse and abandonment, and so many negative factors. I hear the personal accounts of friends and acquaintances who suffer immensely because of cruelty. I even recognize those parts of my own heart and soul that have been marred by people who make it their business to judge and hurt others.

But I know from experience that not all people are like that. I know from experience that we don't just learn from hardship or pain or cruelty, that we can learn valuable and remarkable things from the people in our lives who provide a constant source of light. And I believe their stories must also be told, because their light and their example can help and guide others.

Throughout his life, except for the period during his Alzheimer's struggle when mind, soul and heart were locked inside windowless walls that grew thicker and thicker everyday, my father was there for me, for all of us. It was incredibly important, this simple act of being there, of knowing what was needed and giving it. It was one of my father's greatest talents, my father's greatest gifts, and he was our brightest light.

When you are tempted to spend

even more time away from

your son or your daughter

your husband or your wife.

Remember my father.

Remember a prom night

spent in a garage.

And know how precious

the gift of your company.

15

Living with Dying

As I grow older I believe less and less in coincidences. It was a Saturday morning, and I had found my seat on the tiny city-link airplane that would decrease what would have been a two and a half hour drive to a large airport to a thirty-minute trip through the clouds. I didn't stare at the older gentleman who had arrived before me to take his window seat, though I wanted to. He was wearing straight leg blue jeans, a khaki jacket. He wore glasses and his thinning white hair was combed back, held in place by a shiny, but not too shiny substance. His hands were dark. Tanned. Strong. Weathered. Hands that told their own story of the great deal of work they'd seen. But also hands that seemed disproportionately large for the thin wrists and arms. Like my dad's had been in his later years.

I asked if you'd keep me company on this trip, dad, I thought. But did you have to seat me next to someone who could have taken his clothes from your closet and who wears his hair in the same style you always did? The man fiddled with his seat belt, opening and closing it repeatedly with a kind of nervous energy. Even though I could see the movement only through the corner of my eye, I began to wonder if he suffered from dementia. I guess I am unusually sensitive to those sorts of things.

As the plane began to taxi along the runway, I heard a voice in my ear. *You see that dark green land over there,* the voice said. *That's where I grew up.* The man was smiling as he looked at me, one hand pointing at the horizon.

William had grown up in Lethbridge, Alberta, the city where I now lived and the place we were leaving. He earned $5 a month when he joined the navy at the age of seventeen. He was married for fifty years to a woman he had known for fifty-three. She'd died just over a year earlier — a victim of Alzheimer's. *They didn't put her in a home, though,* he said. *The hospital had everything arranged, organized, settled — she would go into a home the next day. Like hell,* he said. *When you love someone like I loved her, you don't let that happen.* Now he travels, chasing memories. British Columbia. Alberta. Home to Ontario three weeks early because he misses his children and grandchildren. *A good reason to go home,* I smile. *I think so,* he answers.

The noise of the plane prevented me from hearing everything he said and I hoped his repeated questions to me were because he was also having trouble hearing. Or perhaps it wasn't the outside noise that caused him problems; perhaps it was the noise of joyous and painful memories as they replayed themselves over and over again within his heart and mind. The one thing I'm certain he heard and understood was my explanation that my father had also died of Alzheimer's. And so he talked about his wife, his family, his days in the navy while I told him a little about my dad.

Before the flight ended, I opened my purse and removed a small wallet — the one in which I've placed two of my favorite photos of my father. *This is my dad,* I told him, *on his way to Korea.* It was a tiny black and white photo, no more than an inch and a half square. My dad was sitting on top of a vehicle when it was taken, wearing his uniform, grinning. Three friends, also in uniform, were standing in front of him. A sign behind my father's head said Jasper — William noticed that. It's a favorite photo of mine and has been since I found it as a small child in the large white boot box under my parent's bed

— the one that served as their photo album before there was time to sort and arrange. William reached into his pocket after he'd handed my wallet back to me and pulled out his own thick, dark brown, worn leather billfold. Opening it, he turned to a black and white photo of a young, beautiful brunette. A photo of his wife taken in 1944. He also carried her obituary from the newspaper. His tired eyes were moist. *She's beautiful,* I said. She was.

The plane landed and taxied to a stop. William patted my hand, squeezed my fingers. *I've enjoyed talking with you my dear,* he said. *I've enjoyed talking with you too,* I answered.

William continued his journey and I continued mine. I walked through the second airport of the day, thinking about the way he'd held his hands, folded and unfolded his arms, tugged at his jacket — all mannerisms I'd witnessed so many times before. I thought about his pain, still so near the surface and his love, still so intense. I thought about his loneliness and the haunted look in his eyes.

When I'd arrived at the airport that morning, my seat-sale flights and their pre-selected seats had been mysteriously cancelled. The airline agent could have refused to honour the tickets; she could have insisted that I pay full fare, but she didn't. Instead she smiled at me, reissued the tickets and gave me new seat assignments. I later learned my travel agent's records showed she'd cancelled my booking, although she can't explain why — in fact she was appalled and extremely apologetic because she knew I hadn't asked her to make any changes. I told her simply that it was OK — things had worked out and I knew she hadn't intentionally tried to disrupt my travel. I didn't tell her that part of me looked on the whole incident as a tiny piece of destiny, a coincidence that wasn't really a coincidence at all. I didn't tell her I believed the tickets were cancelled so I would sit next to William that day. So that I would remember the past, share a moment of pain, and find the inspiration and strength to continue this story.

The story of my father's illness, the way his hands and eyes revealed the reality of his terror even when he could not or would not admit it. The story of my hopelessness when sitting beside him in the back seat of the car, on a day trip we had made hundreds of times when I was a child, explaining where we were going, what road we were on, and what we could expect to see next. The story of my father looking at me and saying it was odd, but he didn't remember ever being on this road before. The story of his body growing more and more rigid on a day we'd hoped would give him some pleasure, because he knew we were going to his hometown and yet he knew he was totally and utterly lost.

William reminded me of that, but he also reminded me of another part of the story — the story of what my father's illness did to my mother. The story of a woman who began to twiddle her thumbs as my father did when she was sitting somewhere quietly or riding in the passenger seat of a vehicle. Whose eyes began to dart nervously about her as she moved from one place to the next. Who began to worry if she thought she forgot something. Who isolated herself as much as she possibly could. Who stopped laughing.

The story of a woman who had pursued a career with the full support of her husband in an era when that sort of commitment was still widely unaccepted. The woman who always knew that no matter what, her husband loved her and was her greatest supporter. The woman who turned from her career to stay at home with my father because she could conceive of doing nothing else. The woman who lost the opportunity to travel with her husband, enjoy her grandchildren with her husband, spend some time, alone and in love, with her husband. And who grieved deeply and bitterly at the unfairness of life.

The pain of my father's illness was one thing. The pain of my mother's sorrowful and solitary path through that illness was another. My mother, a fiercely independent and proud woman with a wonderful Irish wit and rich laugh, made the decision to take early retirement on her own, saying that she was doing so because of the stress my father's condition was causing for the family. We had not, however, expected or asked for her sacrifice.

She refused to admit, for a inordinately long time, that her husband suffered from an irreversible dementia and until the autopsy report, held onto the hope that it was almost anything besides Alzheimer's. Indeed, while she eventually (less than a year before his death) became convinced that it was simplest to tell people who asked about my father that he suffered from Alzheimer's — since it was a condition more people now understood, they would have a better chance of understanding her situation — it was not a word that ever came readily to her lips.

She decided that she would care for my father in their home for as long as that was possible (preferably for the entire duration of the disease) and she decided that she would do so without any appreciable help from others. She would not take advice and with few exceptions, deeply resented anyone suggesting she do things differently, even when she knew that advice was given with the best of intentions and her well-being in mind. And she built the kind of walls around herself that are invisible to the naked eye but virtually impossible to breach.

My mother was transformed by her husband's illness and I felt powerless to stop the change. I also watched the transformation in my mother with a sense of loss that was not entirely unlike the one I felt for my father, as odd, as absurd, and as selfish as that may sound, and for a period of time I grieved for them both.

At first there was the fear — fear over what was or wasn't happening to her husband and the immense implications. There was also an increasing weariness — weariness because she had to make yet another trip to yet another doctor in the seemingly endless search for an answer. There was the beginning of exhaustion — because in every waking moment she worried about my father, whether he was with her or not, whether he was having a good day or not, and because as time went on, she slept less and less, and when she did sleep, it was troubled.

These were the realities that initially erased the smile lines from around her eyes and mouth and replaced them with lines caused by tension and frowns. These were the realities that initially erased the laughter from her heart and from her home and replaced it with frustration, despair and intense sadness.

Fear, weariness and exhaustion were compounded by bitterness and anger that resulted from the impact of the disease but were directed sometimes at my father, sometimes at me, sometimes at a stranger, sometimes at life. She, together with her husband, had worked so very hard for so very long to provide what was necessary for their children, to help their own parents, brothers and sisters. They had sacrificed many things and now, when they should be able to enjoy each other's company, they couldn't — life was being stolen from them. With each realization that there had been another deterioration, with each example of a life changed forever, the anger and bitterness grew. But so did the desire, the commitment and the determination to be primary caregiver, to make my father's life as normal and happy as it could be, to ensure he would retain his dignity and self-respect. Love, anger, hope, despair, frustration, emotional exhaustion — conflicting yet ever present.

Deep depression hit when my mother finally admitted, at least to herself, that the condition was irreversible. The depression was so intense that we worried she was suicidal and struggled to find ways to ease the situation when any help we tried to give was pushed aside. I believe a large part of the credit for her surviving those months goes to Steve, whose abilities as both a medical doctor and an astute and caring son, enabled him to reach her when she'd blocked many others out. The intensity of the first episode eventually passed, a number of months after it started, but episodes of depression recurred, in varying levels, until and after her husband's death.

While the complex and warring emotions consumed my mother, our relationship began to change. At first we continued to do some of the things we had always done together, including my father wherever possible or arranging for him to have company, either at my house or his own, depending on where he felt most comfortable at the time. When my father was increasingly unable to leave his home (or uncomfortable doing so), she would leave him only on rare occasions with one of just a few people she believed he was comfortable enough with and who in turn, understood the stage of his illness and could handle any erratic behavior. Eventually, she wouldn't leave him at all, and the only break we could offer was to be in the house with her. She said she felt like a caged bird — even if offered freedom, she would fly just a short distance from the cage before being drawn back by forces she couldn't overcome. She withdrew from almost all aspects of life besides the care of my father. She could do no less; she could do no more.

My mother didn't involve herself with the kind of support groups to which many people turn. She went only once to an Alzheimer's Society meeting, but didn't return because the negative feelings of leaving my father were greater than any positive feelings she received from listening to others who shared a comparable pain. She also mentioned that most of the people were daughters and sons and couldn't really understand what she was going through. She took my father only once to a day care facility then refused to repeat the experience. Leaving him had been difficult enough and she worried constantly for the few hours she was away. But the look of relief and happiness in his eyes when she returned to him was overwhelming and she could not bear to leave him again. So she left his care to others only when there was absolutely no other choice. It was her way of dealing with the situation.

The other thing my mother didn't do was speak about her feelings a great deal. For the most part, she tried to hide any of her own pain from us the same way she would have hidden it from the family and friends of patients under her care throughout her decades in nursing. She didn't cry — at least not often. She didn't lean on others — at least not often. And she didn't ask for help — at least not often.

For my part, my role as daughter of both the victim and the primary caregiver was essentially to provide whatever support and help she deemed acceptable at the various stages. While advice was generally unwelcome, I didn't stop trying to advise. However, I learned when I could say things and when I couldn't simply from the sound of her voice when she spoke the first words over the telephone or from the look on her face when I entered the house. I made carefully timed suggestions and accepted the rejection when it was given. I became the supporter, because that's pretty much all I could be. It took me some time, but I came to realize the most important thing I could do to help my mother was simply listen when she wanted to talk and support her decisions — I could not make them for her.

Would I have done things differently had I been in my mother's position? Because I have not lived her life I cannot say for sure. Maybe I would feel exactly the same way. Maybe I would do exactly the same things. Maybe I would handle the situation exactly the same way. Maybe I wouldn't. Maybe I wouldn't have the strength.

The simple reality is that my mother did what she had to do and what she was able to do because she is the person she is — she committed herself, at any cost, to caring for her husband, in a manner that she believed shielded her children and minimized any impact on them. She did more for my father than any reasonable daughter could hope for. In so doing, she also became a victim, because as the demands of my father's care increased daily, she cared less and less for herself and her own needs.

Both my father's life and my father's illness taught me the same lesson. It's easy for us to look at how others are leading their lives or dealing with a particular situation and believe we could somehow do things better, that their way is wrong and our way is right. It's easy to blame or criticize or condemn people because they do or say things that hurt us or behave in ways that, from our perspective, seem illogical or inappropriate. By the time my father's illness required the kind of care that caused my mother to be a prisoner in her own home, I'd long since lost his counsel; but while he had lost memories of our times together, I had not lost my memory of my time with him. And so I tried to live as I believed he would have; I tried to inflict no more pain on my mother than life had already dealt her. I tried to understand when her pain was directed at me.

It is true that my father's disease changed my mother in countless ways. The illness is harsh, it is emotionally ravaging, and the people who are forced to deal with its path through a loved one's life cannot help but be ravaged themselves. The pain, at times, is that intense.

Friends and family of Alzheimer's victims are like the friends and families of others who are trying to cope with something that is almost impossible to cope with — they want to help; they try to help. If it were not for these people, we would be much less likely to survive and move on with our lives. I believe, however, that family and friends are most helpful when they give what is needed, rather than trying to impose what they think is needed on someone else. And that they are most helpful if they are forgiving when we block them out because we know no other way of coping.

I believe we each must do what we must do, what we can do. I believe we should fight against judging others for their actions or imposing our will on them. I believe those of us who are not the main caregivers of Alzheimer's victims must simply accept that while we may not be able to help in the way we would choose, we should try to help in the ways that are needed. And every individual — whether patient or caregiver — will have needs that are tied directly to who they are and who they were, before the illness.

I would have liked to do more for my father when he was ill. I would have liked to do more for my mother. But I know, because I have forced myself to look and analyze and have shed tears of inadequacy and helplessness, that I did what I could do, all that I could do, whether or not that was enough. And more importantly, I know my mother did all that she could do in the manner in which she wanted, and that when my father died, alone with her in the bedroom they had shared for so many years, she should have no reason for regret.

My mother did what she had to do. William did what he had to do. Thousands of husbands, wives, daughters and sons get up every morning and do what they have to do, whether that means being the main caregiver, or visiting the hospital every day or every week, or cooking meals, or buying groceries, or sitting, listening and holding a shaking hand. Despite this truth, many of us, perhaps most of us, will never really feel as though we've done enough. Even my mother.

Some months after my father's death, my mother finally found a phrase that described what the years with my father's illness had been like for her. She said the experience was one of *living with dying* and the disease was such that she couldn't forget what was happening, even for the briefest of moments. My mother has been irreversibly changed because of her experience with my father's illness and if suffering makes you strong, then she is certainly strong. But the strength was not without cost and the echo of the pain will be with her, with all of us, forever.

When all the care in the world,

when every effort in the world,

cannot change the outcome,

cannot heal the suffering.

Just do your best.

Then do everything you can

to believe it was enough.

16

Father of the Bride

On the night we were married, Peter and I danced our first dance in my father's garage. I was wearing a white taffeta gown I'd sewn myself. It was unlike most of the wedding dresses being worn at the time — there was no train, no lace, no plunging neckline. Instead it had a high collar, a four-inch band at the waist, a mid-thigh slit up the center of the front and was shaped in at my ankles. Peter wore black tails, white vest and bow tie, and we waltzed together to Lionel Richie's "Three Times A Lady", in a freshly painted garage that had been transformed, along with the rest of the house, for a celebration party that saw the younger guests dance the night away in the garage and driveway while older friends and relatives arranged themselves in comfortable groupings through other parts of my parent's home. Perhaps it doesn't sound odd, at this point in the story, to say our first dance couldn't have taken place in a more appropriate or perfect location.

The events that led to this October night had begun almost three-and-a-half years earlier. I was a nineteen-year-old university student who loved to dance. It was late April, exams had finished and my father would watch and smile as I'd model the latest outfit for him and my mother before I headed out for the evening. I was driving the little red car he'd given me for my seventeenth birthday and was at the end of a rather short relationship that had spent a couple of on-again, off-again, really-going-nowhere months.

I met my soulmate and husband on one of those warmer than usual spring nights — slid into his arms and danced with him for the first time. He was 6'1" with broad, strong shoulders. His skin was a medium brown, his hair was rich black and curly, and his dark eyes were veiled and deeply serious. He was from the island paradise of Trinidad, the place I knew from my father's stories, the island where my dad had bought the sandals a little boy had loudly called women's shoes when he was so shocked to see my father wearing them. A tropical island that, to me, was more fairy tale than real.

The best way to describe that night and that meeting is to say I knew, on some level, it was significant, much more significant than any other first dance. And so I went to my father the next day and asked him what people from Trinidad were like. It was actually a ridiculous question because I already knew what his answer was going to be, but I wanted to tell him I'd met someone from the island he'd visited so many times. Let him know there was a chance he'd be calling. Warn him, by mentioning this one particular dance, that something was different this time. And yes, to some degree, obtain his blessing for whatever may happen.

Peter and I saw each other again two nights after we'd first danced together and the simplest way to tell the story is to say we were together from almost that moment onward. Ours was not an uncomplicated relationship — I was, in many ways, so young. There were also other involvements to end and there were people who, for reasons of their own, did not want us to be together or did not think our relationship was wise. There were university degrees to complete, careers to launch, dreams waiting to pursue.

I'll never forget the night, just a week after we'd first met, that Peter came to my home to meet my parents. After the steak, baked potato, vegetables and apple pie had been finished, my father came downstairs to the den where we were sitting and talking. My father had never sought out boyfriends or dates to strike up conversations, he'd never grilled them on their intentions. But on that particular night he came to sit for a short time and converse about the islands, about hockey, about other topics I can't even remember. What I do remember with crystal clarity was how important it was to me that these two men think well of one another. I so wanted my father to extend the same level of approval and trust to Peter that he had always given me. And I wanted Peter to see in my father the qualities I had always seen.

I'm not sure I could have explained this at that time; in fact, I'm fairly certain I could not. Sometimes I think I have such a clear understanding of what my father meant to me and his importance in my life because through the years of losing him, I thought a great deal about exactly who and what I was losing and I revisited the shared past that was being taken from him. And I recall, on that night, sitting quietly in the room and wishing from deep within my soul, that they would get along with one another.

I have mentioned my father was a relatively quiet man in the sense that his actions more so than his words were the truest key to his feelings. My husband is like that as well, and their acceptance of and respect for one another was not evident so much in their words as in the relationship they formed from that evening on. Peter became part of our family and my father's friend. He became a frequent visitor to my father's garage; they constructed and painted fences, built a patio, found new fishing holes, picked blueberries, watched hockey, war movies and westerns, laughed and talked and shared. It was one of my greatest joys to see the respect and friendship between the two most important men in my life. To watch from the window in my bedroom as they worked together in the backyard, talking about whatever it was they talked about. To see them walk out of the garage chuckling, with the smell of grease cleaner on their hands, and wonder what mischief they'd been up to. To walk on Bellevue Beach holding Peter's hand as my father and mother walked hand in hand in front of us, watching the setting sun.

There was no competition between these men; there was no fear that the strength of my caring for one somehow lessened the caring for the other; there was no tension. They simply opened their arms, their hearts and their lives a little more to include the other.

Perhaps there is nothing remarkable in this acceptance — you must judge that for yourself. From my perspective, I'm not sure I can describe how it made me feel to know that I hadn't let my father down by opening my heart to someone else. That he was happy to let me learn about this other sort of love. That he had not just accepted my choice in a partner, but became a dear friend to him. That he never, not even once, made me feel that he wished he could hold me back, that he wished I'd remain the little girl who would call to him in the middle of the night when the nightmare demons invaded my dreams.

Instead my dad would leave a few dollars on my dresser in the morning before he left for work so Peter and I would be able to go to lunch or a movie that day. Instead, when I woke up one morning with the world spinning out of control because of a rather acute ear infection, my father went to Peter's apartment to pick him up and drive him to our house, so he could spend the day by my side, taking away some of the terror of this first-time experience. Instead, my father picked the fishing rod and accessories that would be Peter's birthday present as we added a new birthday celebration dinner to the ones our family had always shared. Instead, he accepted us and supported us in whatever way he could.

There was some concern, particularly on my mother's part, that a relationship between two people from different cultures, with different colour skin and different religious backgrounds might cause more problems than we were prepared for. And she says my father asked her once, very early on, if she knew if we'd already thought of all that, talked about it. We had, and since she'd expressed her concerns to me many times, she knew that. So she told him yes, we had talked about it and understood the implications. *Well, that's all right then,* was all he said. *As long as they know and they're prepared.* But never once did he say or hint that these issues really mattered, that they should somehow change the way we felt about each other. In fact, if there had ever been an instance when I thought my father did not approve of Peter because of the colour of his skin, the accent in his speech, the culture he had come from, I probably would have stood in shocked silence. For the man speaking would not have been the man I knew as my father.

Peter and I spent about two years together before the first big change. The degrees were finished and I'd been accepted into a master's journalism program that would take me thousands of miles from home. Peter was moving back to Trinidad to apply for landed immigrant status — our wedding would take place when he returned because we didn't want people to say the only reason we married was so he could stay in the country. A particularly blatant example of how young I was, that I would choose that separation over a marriage earlier than the twenty-four years I had been convinced was the 'right' age.

My mother said don't worry, if you're meant to be together, you will be. My father said nothing. He just accepted our decision, then helped us pack and hugged me tightly before we got on the airplane. My mother said she was worried that Peter and I would be living together for a few weeks before he left for the islands. My father said he was happy that Peter would be there, at least for a short time, to ensure I was taken care of and settled in before he left.

I don't know what my father felt as he watched me leave home, knowing the chances were I would be moving away permanently. I know only that he recognized I was following a dream, doing something that was important to me, and as always, I had his support and full confidence. He made no demands, set no limits, asked no questions that we couldn't answer. I suspect he understood, more fully than I could imagine, the path we'd chosen was going to be much more difficult than either of us realized. I suspect he understood loneliness more completely than either Peter or I did at that point. I suspect he knew that the next months would be a key part of my 'growing up'. I suspect he worried and perhaps he felt an ache in his heart.

I didn't realize it when I embarked on the journey, but I'd never really known loneliness before the day Peter left me standing on my way to cover the university's Convocation for a news writing class — turned to wave once then walked back to my apartment, called a cab and made his way to the airport. For all our plans that we would stay in contact, that this was just a short but necessary separation, I watched him go with the pain of not knowing what would happen, of not knowing if I would ever see him again. But the anguish of that first evening and the months of separation that followed are another story for another time, and the only point that matters now is that we'd been apart less than four months when we decided neither of us was prepared to endure the two-year separation we'd planned before we got married. We would become officially engaged at Christmas and then marry as soon as Peter's immigration papers came through, probably the following fall.

I returned to my parent's home about a week before Christmas — lots of time to buy Christmas gifts and prepare everything with my mother. Peter arrived on Christmas Eve, an engagement ring I hadn't seen in his pocket. He told me later that shortly after I picked him up from the airport, he asked my dad to come into my bedroom for a moment because he needed to ask him something. The question wasn't necessary, he knew that, but before he officially asked me to marry him, before he put the ring on my finger, he asked my father for his permission. And my father's answer was the kind of gift only he could give — he looked at Peter, told him there was no one he'd rather see me marry and hugged him. *He hugged me,* Peter told me later. *He really hugged me.* From my father there was no greater seal of approval, no clearer sign of acceptance and trust.

That year my mother, father, Peter and I attended a New Year's Eve Ball, and I think that was the second to last time my father and I danced together, the last opportunity coming less than a year later at my wedding. Peter and I stayed up almost the entire night — sitting on the couch in the den in my parent's home. He was leaving again the next day.

We made it through the next months; we suffered and cried and laughed and learned and had horrendous phone bills even though we wrote twenty page letters every week. We grew closer together; we grew farther apart. Somedays we remembered what love was about; other days it no longer made any sense. But we looked inside ourselves and each other and together knew completeness. And we also knew, without really understanding why, that despite the fact that we hadn't planned to return to the city where we'd met, that this was exactly where we must go to begin our lives together.

My mother says she wasn't married in a white dress because she was afraid she would have jinxed everything if she'd bought one, that something would have gone wrong and she would never have married my father. So her wedding photos show my mother and father in handsomely tailored suits as they stood in the church. I was married in a white dress, but the same sort of fear that fate would step in and keep Peter and I apart was strong in my heart, and I delayed the process of sewing my own gown until just weeks before the ceremony.

But at 2:50 p.m. on October 1ˢᵗ, the feast day of St. Therese, I found myself in the porch of the same church in which my parents had been married, my father looking handsome and distinguished in his black tuxedo. I found myself looking up the long aisle to the altar and seeing Peter standing there. After all the months apart, after all the struggles, despite the people who hadn't wanted us together, he was standing there and we were, after all, to be married. And I began to cry. Tears streamed down my face because I really couldn't believe something I had wanted so very much was finally and actually happening.

My father didn't know of all the forces that had conspired to keep Peter and me apart — no one did. Perhaps he was flooded with his own memories of waiting for my mother in that same church more than thirty years before — fully aware that wars and distance and fate could have kept them apart and as thankful as I now was that their story had continued. But my father did know how I felt that day, just as he always knew. We didn't discuss it; we didn't have to. He simply took my hand and held it tightly as I tried to stop the flow of tears. And as I linked my arm into his to walk up the aisle, he continued to hold tightly to my hand, calming my soul and pouring his strength, his support, his love, his pride, his understanding, into my heart. *Thank you dad*, I whispered. *Thank you so very very much.* And he kissed me and placed my hand in Peter's.

When I look at the photographs I have of my father from that day, I see a man who had not yet begun to show any physical signs of the disease that would soon ravage him. A man who was fully aware of the significance of this day in his daughter's life and the importance of his role as her father. We now know that the earliest stages of Alzheimer's had actually begun to manifest themselves during the previous year when Peter and I were away, and perhaps there are aspects of the wedding organization that my father was less directly involved in than he would have been if he was completely well. But none of that was obvious to us on this particular day.

From the moment he married my mother, my father devoted his life to his wife and children. He battled knee problems, bleeding ulcers, surgeries and the removal of part of a lung. But he still managed to be there for all of us whenever we needed him. Was it willpower that enabled him to stay healthy enough until after that day, until he placed my hand in Peter's and turned to sit beside my mother in the more than 100-year-old church pew? Did he ever say to himself, I can now begin to let go, my sons and daughter are fine? Did he sit quietly and say that he was now able to pay for the extra years he'd been given when the red rose showed our prayers would be answered and his lung and life saved? Did he look at the white roses Peter and I presented to our parents in the middle of the wedding ceremony, hold his own while we walked to the part of the church that held the shrine to St. Therese to place another white rose at the base of her statue, and ask, *St. Therese, give me strength for what is to come?*

I have no answers for these questions. Even though I've asked them many times since his death and listened for the responses in my mind and heart and soul — where his answers to my questions are usually found — I have found none. Instead, I see my father standing next to me in the foyer of the church, wearing his black tuxedo and holding my hand — his eyes light, his eyes bright, his smile gentle as my own tears flow. And I feel his love.

Even questions that have no answers
in logic have answers in love.
Even those things that cannot
possibly be known are known in faith.
In this world, even the impossible
can be possible.

17

A Particularly Empty Rocking Chair

We have a traditional style rocking chair in our home. It was one of the first pieces of furniture Peter and I had — given to us by my parents as part of our wedding gift. It stayed in the living room of our first apartment until Kenneth was born when we moved it to his bedroom. We — Peter, me, my father, my mother — read him stories in that chair, sat there to sing him to sleep. Peter and I spent many hours on many different nights watching over him from the corner of the room where the chair was located, nights when he would awaken from a bad dream, when his nose was stuffy from a head cold or when he was running a fever. When we moved to our first house, the chair found its way to our family room and there it became the place my father sat most often during his frequent visits.

The chair doesn't really match the furniture we've gathered over the years and lost its place in that particular family room when we acquired a new sofa set after my father's death. But unlike some of the other early items in our collection, it hasn't been left behind or given away. In fact, it came with us when we moved and now sits thousands of miles away in a new house in a new city. It has changed locations a couple of times in the new house. Urges I can't quite explain have caused me to lug the chair up or downstairs or from one room to the other, though most recently it has been sitting in the spare bedroom.

Now, rather than having the urge to move the chair, I'm driven to make sure that room — which had the tendency to become an area where things were not-so-temporarily stored and piled up rather chaotically until someone was coming for a visit — stays reasonably neat and tidy with easy access to the chair. Now I sometimes go into that particular room just to sit and rock slowly as my father did, feel his company in my home. Now I find myself pausing to look at the empty chair as I pass, half expecting to see my father sitting there with a book or magazine in his hand, or at least to see the chair rocking gently back and forth as it would if he'd been there just a moment before.

It surprised me, after my father's death, to realize the kind of significance something like a simple rocking chair could possess. It surprised me to realize this chair wasn't something I could leave behind with as little thought as we left behind other things. And it surprised me that I would see in the rocking of this chair, the motion of my father's illness — from the beginning until the stage when he could no longer visit our home.

In the beginning, the man who sat rocking slowly in his chair was still deeply involved in all that was happening around him. I've told you about that man — he could read stories to his grandson, sit as he watched him drift off to sleep. He could chat and laugh and enjoy his favorite dessert, a piece of apple pie. It made a difference what he ate for supper because he could still taste the difference between various foods. He still cooked breakfast every morning. He still drove his vehicle and wrote cheques to pay the bills. He still read and enjoyed the books we gave him on his birthday, on Father's Day or at Christmas. He still used his fishing rods and tools. In the earliest days he still recognized us.

Before too long, the man who sat in the rocking chair would look at his wife in the early morning and say: *If I don't get any worse than this, we can handle it.* And the woman who looked back at him would despair because she knew things were already worse than when he'd said the same words on another, earlier day. This was a particularly painful period for my father. He was acutely aware of what he was losing — knew that he was forgetting more and more — and suffered tremendously through the periods of lucidity knowing there were increasing gaps. His dependence on others steadily increased as he lost more and more of his ability to carry out everyday tasks. I don't know if he ever tried to inventory the things he knew and things he didn't. And I don't want to even try to imagine what it must have been like not to know what day or month or year it was. I can only see him sitting, sometimes relaxed, increasingly tense. As the chair rocked.

It was from this point onward that we never knew what to expect from one day to the next, sometimes from one hour to the next. My father still visited frequently — arriving either as a passenger in his own vehicle or ours — and generally enjoyed the time in our house. He'd carry his slippers in a white, plastic grocery bag that he clutched as if it contained his last and only worldly possessions. We would walk with him through the door to the back porch, the entry we always used, and wait as he bent to remove his shoes. Initially there was no problem making the transition from shoes to slippers, but with time that changed so that sometimes, but only sometimes, he'd manage to get his shoes off and his slippers out of the bag and on his feet without confusion. Usually, however, he'd take his shoes off and put them back on again, leaving the slippers in the bag and repeating the process until we could make it clear it was time to stop. Initially we didn't really have to wait with him to see that places for coats and caps were found. But that changed too and sometimes, but only sometimes, he'd know where to hang his coat and place his cap.

We'd watch and wait and try to help — his daughter, son-in-law or grandson — and sometimes he'd understand our instructions without difficulty. On good days, we'd chuckle together, able to see the humour in the sequence — *how did those slippers get back in the bag anyway?* On bad days, the air was filled with a pain and sadness so tangible it felt as though it could be gathered into your fist and crushed.

I came to believe that dealing with an Alzheimer's sufferer at this stage of the disease is something like dealing with a child who's somewhere between two and five years old, uncertain of his surroundings, unsure what's expected of him, and more than a little apprehensive. On the other hand, dealing with an Alzheimer's sufferer is nothing like dealing with a child. I would tell myself it shouldn't be that difficult for people who have dealt with children to understand the need for simplicity and assistance in the life of someone suffering from Alzheimer's, but even as I recognized a childlike need, I don't think I ever made the necessary mental adjustment — not completely anyway. No matter what my mind told me, my eyes saw an adult I knew as competent and loving. No matter what my mind told me, my heart saw and felt everything both of us were losing. No matter what my mind told me, my soul screamed for answers to the question that had no answer — why?

We tried to learn how to give the simple instructions that helped my father accomplish whatever task was being undertaken without adding to the frustration he was experiencing or without causing him embarrassment. We tried to rethink priorities, learning how to deal with his decreasing ability to self-direct his actions, learning when it was or wasn't important to try to correct an 'error', when it was or wasn't important to get the right answer to a question. Did it matter if he took ten minutes to get his shoes off and slippers on? No. Did it matter if he was in physical discomfort or feeling ill and having difficulty telling us? Yes. Were we successful in our attempts at making the necessary adjustments? Sometimes yes; sometimes no. Some visits were a joy; some were exceedingly painful.

Part of what was happening at this stage, though I don't know if I ever thought about it in these terms at the time, was that my father was slowly withdrawing from us. The process was both involuntary and voluntary. Plagued in the early stages by a fear of the unknown and an increasing paranoia, people with Alzheimer's will stop doing many of the things that were at one time normal for them — stop going places they'd always gone, seeing people they'd always seen, doing things they'd always done. They make conscious choices to withdraw from certain aspects of their lives because they fear they won't be able to cope. The circle is particularly vicious. The less they allow themselves to do, the more they lose and the less they are actually able to do. Eventually they aren't able to resume a particular activity because it's become another one of the things they've forgotten.

Anyone who's close to an Alzheimer's victim has seen the grief in the eyes of someone who sits helplessly because he can no longer remember what it is he could do to help. Heard the anguish or anger in a voice that's telling you *no she doesn't feel up to going out today.* Watched the desperation in the set of the shoulders as he escapes through a door in search of something, someone or somewhere. Felt the shame she tries to hide at her own feeling of uselessness. And anyone who's been close to an Alzheimer's victim knows one of the things you don't want them to do is withdraw any more than their illness demands, even as you recognize the inevitability.

Looking back, things weren't really all that bad when my father still felt comfortable in our house — when our house was still familiar, even if he did occasionally have trouble finding a particular room. Before his visits, we'd try to organize things so he could be involved in as many of the activities as possible. If I was going to be wrapping Christmas or birthday gifts, I'd arrange it so that he'd sit on the floor next to me, handing me the scotch tape when I needed it, using his finger to hold the first knot of the ribbon in place as I prepared to anchor it with a second. He helped fill loot bags for birthday parties, following the specific directions given. He handed me pins when I was sitting on the floor cutting out a new pair of pants or a skirt. Because Kenneth was old enough to direct play activities, he could play well with his grandson, even when the progression of the disease had become significant.

Watching my father's expression when he was able to help and participate in our activities was enough to convince us this involvement was vital in helping him maintain a reasonable quality of life, vital for anyone in his position. It's not always easy — to be honest, it's heartbreaking. But with everything Alzheimer's sufferers are losing, everything you can help them keep has great importance. An Alzheimer's life, in some ways, is a life in reversal. A child wakes up each day and is able to do a little more. A person with Alzheimer's wakes up each day to the very real likelihood of being able to do a little, or on the really bad days, a lot less. But the need to be involved, the need to be useful, the need to be needed, the need to be who you've always been, these things don't change.

One thing I didn't realize at the time was that these were still among the very good days — when my father still knew us, was still comfortable with us, could still follow easy directions, was physically well enough to do many things. I regret I didn't enjoy these days more; I should have felt less tension; I should have been able to say, *things aren't so bad.* But I found myself awash in the mixture of a past that was lost, a future that was unknown and a present that seemed too unfair, bombarded by not just my own feelings, but those I felt coming from both my father and my mother.

As time passed and my father lost more and more, as he became less and less comfortable away from his own home, visits were increasingly stressful. And his tendency, after the shoes, slippers, coat and hat had been dealt with, was to head immediately for his rocking chair. Conversation became a problem without a solution. While in the first stages of the illness, the only thing that was noticeable were his repeated questions or comments, as time went on there was increasing silence. My father's vocabulary decreased — words he knew one day disappeared the next and he'd no longer be able to complete the sentences he started. At first it was just a matter of helping him find the words he needed. In time, these attempts only frustrated and angered him. He seemed to retain his ability to answer simple yes-or-no questions for a long time, or so we thought. The only problem was, we didn't realize at first that his *yes* or *no* answer had little or nothing to do with reality in general or the questions we were asking in particular. We'd actually developed a habit of trying to interpret his actions, make guesses about his needs or wants, then phrase a question in a manner that would lead him to agree or disagree. My mother, in particular, would give an explanation then say something like, *That's right, isn't it Dick?* and he'd nod or say yes, whether it was correct or not.

By this point, our actual presence in the room with him also played an important role in his comfort level. With so much becoming unfamiliar, I believe we acted as anchors. We were faces he could still recognize; we represented caring he could still understand. These things weren't able to make up for the increasing strangeness that was becoming his everyday world, but they did help stave off the anxiety that would threaten to overwhelm him when we left him alone. Once we recognized his habit of getting up and leaving a room within moments of it becoming empty, a worried expression on his face, we'd try to make sure we never had to leave him alone. It would have been less imperative if he could remember our explanation of where we were going and our assurance that we would be back in a few moments, but he couldn't remember — or maybe he was frightened that once we left, we'd also be unknown forever. I'm not sure. In any event, we tried to have someone stay with him at all times — a friendly, loving presence.

One of the issues, at this stage, was the potential for him to wander off, to leave the house without our knowledge, and it's true that we were concerned that if we left him in the room alone, his panic would send him through a door to the outside world. Our house was on the corner of a reasonably busy street and there was danger attached to that possibility.

It was intensely saddening to lose my father's presence in our house, even though he was still physically with us. It was intensely lonely to sit on the couch beside his rocking chair, watching him gaze towards the television set without seeing the picture. To feel his inevitable silence and his isolation. To know that about the only thing we could do was sit there with him, ask nothing of him, and keep him company. But it got even more difficult when our presence no longer gave him any comfort, when he looked at us with the same sense of confusion that had previously been reserved just for the place, not for the people.

I don't remember the month or even the year, but I do know that the day he first stopped recognizing me was the day he stopped calling me 'duck'. And about that same time, he couldn't sit with any sense of ease in our house unless my mother was with him. It became so bad that he would actually become physically ill, his stomach paining or his head hurting. The first couple of times this happened, we weren't quite able to comprehend that the simple act of visiting us had now become a painful and terrifying practice for him. But then we'd take him home, in answer to that request agonizingly pulled from his lips in a one word plea. And as soon as we'd pull into his driveway, his colour would change from grey, the sweating would ease, and he'd smile.

I think one of the most challenging things was that we never really knew what the day would bring, whether the tricks and approaches that had worked the day before would work with the new sunrise. Whether the patterns could be repeated successfully, or if some new stage of memory loss was going to require a total rethinking. Whether the kind of care needed would be different. But even as we recognized this reality, there was a lag time between the changes in behavior and our ability to adjust to them.

The last few times my father sat in the rocking chair in my house, he no longer remembered he was forgetting. I recall telling myself, at this point, that this period was somehow easier on my father — the frustration of one moment could flow into the smile of the next without there being any memory of the discomfort. I remember thinking that it was easier because he was happy to do the same thing over and over again. I remember thinking that as long as we could ensure a reasonable quality of life on a moment to moment basis, make sure his needs were met, make sure he wasn't in pain or under stress, then he could be happy, if only from moment to moment.

I guess this rationalization was my way of dealing with the situation; it was easier on me, I suspect, if I could convince myself it was easier on him. But the truth was I had no concept of what it must be like to live in a world where the present is the only reality — where the thought of a moment before has disappeared forever — so I cannot really judge his level of happiness or unhappiness. And when I try to imagine what it must be like, it terrifies me.

On my father's last visit, we'd brought him to our house to spend the evening with us so that my mother could attend a wedding — not something she wanted to do but something she felt she must do because a dear friend of hers and my father's was remarrying after the death of her husband. We made sure everyone would be home so my father would never be alone and we made no plans, except to sit

with my father, have supper, and try to find a movie that would catch
his attention from time to time. Talk to him about whatever came to
mind. Walk with him if he needed to go to the bathroom or seemed a
little restless. Watch over him.

We ate supper together — something simple, though I don't
remember what — and as we sat together in the family room he started
to become agitated. We'd dealt with that before, calmed him. But on
this evening, he would not be calmed and he could not explain what
his needs were, because in his agitation there were no coherent words
left. An improvised form of sign language showed us he had stomach
pain. His moves to brush us away and head for the door to the porch
and then the outside, the way he trembled as he bent to reach for his
shoes, showed us he desperately wanted to leave and he didn't believe
we were going to help him in this effort. Peter managed to get him
to slow down enough to stop him from going through the door, took
him by the arm and moved him back to the rocking chair. Together
we managed to convince him that we would take him home — that he
could trust us to take him home if that's where he needed and wanted
to go.

I sat beside him in the back seat as Peter drove, Kenneth beside
his father in the front seat. I held his hands, rubbed them slowly and
gently to try to calm him — *It's OK,* I kept telling him, *we're taking
you home. Home?* he'd repeatedly struggle to shape the word. *Home,*
I'd repeat and nod. The ride wasn't long, but for him it probably
seemed like an eternity. He rushed from the car when we arrived in
the driveway, rushed with awkward, staggering, yet strangely certain
steps to the familiar door. Straight up the stairs. Shoes off. Slippers
on. Straight to his room. He lay on the familiar place on his bed, took
my hand. *Home,* he whispered. *Thank you,* he whispered. And he closed
his eyes, opening them every few minutes to look sideways at me —
the stranger sitting in the chair beside his bed and holding a book that

wasn't being read.

I stayed on the chair next to the bed for however many hours it was until my mother came home from the wedding — the passage of time is all a little foggy now. I stayed on the chair until my mother arrived and went to his side, eyes filled with concern and guilt for leaving him. I stayed on the chair until I saw relief fill his eyes — the relief of a child who believes he's been deserted then realizes he hasn't.

I walked over to kiss the man who was still smiling from the sight of his wife. And in a brief instant of awareness, he smiled at me and whispered *thank you, duck.* Then I left with my husband and son, all of us aware that coming to our house was no longer something my father could enjoy. Aware that being there now caused him physical pain and emotional anguish. Aware that from that moment on, our house would be a little bit emptier. Especially the rocking chair.

Life is full of beginnings and endings,

of meetings and partings,

of empty rocking chairs.

Treasure them and the times

before the emptiness.

18

And Finally a Grandfather

Kenneth was born nine months and nine days after Peter and I were married. Even though we'd planned on waiting for at least three or four years before starting a family, I'll be forever grateful that fate intervened to change our plans, that my father and my son were able to spend time together, getting to know one another and finding joy in each other's presence. My father was as wonderful a grandfather as he had been a father and he loved his grandson with the same intensity, the same quiet acceptance that had been so important to his own children.

I remember the night we told him I was pregnant; I remember his utter joy as he smiled and hugged me. I remember how he never made me feel fat or ungainly as the time before the birth grew shorter, how he helped in any way he could throughout the pregnancy. I remember how he arrived in the hospital room at 10:00 p.m. on the night his grandson was born, having just come from the nursery, a huge smile on his face. I remember him watching the tiny baby, holding him in his arms for the first time. Introducing himself to a tiny new individual, silently offering his respect and his love.

Alzheimer's had begun to affect my father, but it wouldn't start to impact how he would interact with his grandson for some years to come, and in the meantime, he had a lifetime of experience and lessons to offer.

At first my father was Granddad Dick, but in the manner of so many children before him, Kenneth chose to dispense with any formal title and began to call him Dick. He was still quite young when he decided to name his favorite teddy bear after his grandfather. We didn't even realize he had done so at first, until our questions led to an exasperated explanation. *No, THIS is Dick,* he said pointing at his teddy bear. *Uncle Dick Teddy, not GRANDDAD Dick!*

My father would sit for hours and play patiently with his grandson — through the stages from large building blocks to small, from washable crayons to permanent markers. From small squeeze toys to cars and trucks and wooden train tracks. My father built and organized and reorganized. His hand would rest on his grandson's chest or stomach, to sooth him if he fretted in his sleep. He talked on imaginary telephones, sat with his little man on his lap to read favorite books over and over again, emptied and refilled the storage compartment of a small white and blue space shuttle that was Kenneth's transportation around the apartment.

He and his grandson created huge parking lots, intricate wooden train tracks. He and his tiny grandson danced to the sounds of the Irish Rovers, watched their video tape over and over and over as Kenneth stood in the middle of the room with his own little guitar and whistle, joining the group in their performance. He picked his grandson up from day care, stayed with him, played with him. They watched *Sesame Street* and *Winnie the Pooh* and *Transformers*. They fished in the middle of the living room floor, using a home made rod with a magnet at the end of the line to catch tiny paper fish that had been anchored with paper clips. They created fleets of dories from small sheets of paper, my father's two large hands guiding his grandson's two small ones as a kind teacher guides a student. They made paper hats for one another and every stuffed toy in Kenneth's growing collection.

Kenneth and his grandfather had the opportunity to fish together, hunt through the bush on a warm September day to find a patch of blueberries worth picking, wander along the beach at Bellevue, the big man showing the little man how to choose the best rocks for skimming, then how to skip them along the water. Kenneth got to watch him make tiny sailing ships from pieces of driftwood and feathers found on the beach, then set them sailing out onto the huge sea. Together they wrote messages, slipped them into bottles, and sent them on paths to faraway shores.

Kenneth loved it when Dick would read him his bedtime story and stay with him until he fell asleep. He loved it when Dick would come shopping or stay for supper. We have dozens and dozens of photos of the two of them involved in one activity or another — their faces wearing special smiles of companionship and contentment, and their eyes radiating pure joy.

When he was thirteen, in an autobiography that was a school project, Kenneth wrote about his grandfather:

In 1994, I entered Grade 5. That was the year... my Newfoundland born grandfather died of Alzheimer's disease.

I remember the Sunday morning when I got out of bed, wondering where my mother was. When I asked my father, he explained that my grandfather had died. It was a crushing blow; despite the disease, my grandfather had always been my buddy, and much of my personality was affected by him.

His life in the Merchant Marine caused me to research the naval merchants of the Second World War, which led to my fascination with the rest of that war, which led to my study of history.

My grandfather always wore a khaki shirt and pants, in the naval tradition. I wear shirts and jeans like he did, and have since adapted the style to serve as a uniform-like set of clothes.

But most of all, he and I just spent a lot of time in his garage, building things out of cardboard and whatever else we found. That was the most profound of the times I had with him. He taught me about his career, and about how he'd built things around their home.

Now he was gone.

That grade was a little harder than the five before, but I managed. Soon I got back to normal and started becoming more like my grandfather had been.

Peter, my mother and I had witnessed the elements of Kenneth's life that seemed to have been most impacted by his grandfather — the preference for khaki pants and khaki shirts that always had two pockets. The talent for making things out of scraps others would have tossed aside as garbage. A fascination with history, starting with the wars his grandfather had fought in. The way he'd try to brush hair that wanted to fall forward back in a style more similar to his grandfather's. And when I read the words he'd written, before he submitted the assignment to his teacher, I allowed myself, for a few moments at least, to see the two of them in my mind's eye. Working quietly together in the garage, walking along hand in hand. Beaming at each other with the open expressions of love that held only joy and respect in each other's existence.

Named Kenneth Richard for his two grandfathers, my son is a lot like my father. There is little physical resemblance — that's not what I mean — but there is that same respect for others, that same way of holding himself with pride and dignity, a deep kindness in his soul mixed with a strength of character that enables him to follow his own beliefs, his own dreams, his own inclinations, without needing the approval of a large circle of people. Just as my father was happy puttering in his garage, fixing and creating things, my son is happy in his own space, building, repairing and creating.

Kenneth has his grandfather's Swiss army pocket knife. He also wears his grandfather's leather bomber jacket... as soon as the summer passes and the fall days get cool... pleased that it fits him for another year. He carries always in his wallet, a small photo of Dick at Bellevue. They are his special treasures. Special reminders of his particular and unique relationship with a man who taught him, above all, that it's OK to be who you are. Who despite his struggle with a devastating disease, was an incredibly bright light for my son. And my memories of the two of them together are of special significance, because in those times and days lie the last days of my father's aware life, before knowledge, memories, and eventually a personality, became locked within a prison from which death was the only escape.

In many ways we say goodbye to my father now, on this page. From this point on, he is essentially locked away from us. Trapped inside a mind- and body-destroying shell of human form. Still a father, a grandfather, a husband, a brother, an uncle, a friend, a kind and gentle man, but increasingly unable to be any of these. Unable to be himself. Trapped.

For a long time, I questioned why a man should bother to be the best he can be, to always do the right thing, to love with such freedom and intensity when at the end, it's all taken from him and his last days are of suffering in an isolation that I cannot even imagine. Why bother, I would think, when it can so easily and cruelly be taken from you, when you don't remember anyone or anything, when everything is erased as if it never was?

It haunted me, this question. It angered me. It stayed in my heart as a dagger. Until one day, I looked into my son's bright eyes, I retraced my steps along Bellevue Beach and realized that we were the reason — the people my father's life had touched in so very many ways. The people who learned from him respect for self and others, and the power of unconditional love. And we had a special responsibility — to live in a way that would make him proud. Every single thing mattered. Every story read, every boat built, every minute in the garage, every sacrifice, every tear, every smile, because they had given us so very much. Because a large part of who we are… quite likely the best part of who we are… is irrevocably linked with the life of this one man. And his love.

That is what we remember, that is who we remember, and that is who we ask you to remember with us through the remainder of his days and these pages. It is the only way to find some sense in the suffering. It is the only way not to cry.

When fate steps in to change the plans

you have made with the greatest of care,

have faith that there is

a greater wisdom,

a better path,

an unknown reason.

And walk bravely forward.

19

Missing Pieces

If a person's life is like a jigsaw puzzle, then for the person with Alzheimer's that puzzle is one where an unseen hand reaches down and, without warning, removes pieces. It's swift and silent, this hand, as it goes about its job of dismantling realities created over decades.

Sometimes the hand removes a single, seemingly insignificant piece — one small shape from within a large and complex setting that actually goes unnoticed until someone finds a reason to look closely at that particular location. The memory of one small section of a road infrequently traveled — gone. The memory of a well-loved, yet rarely seen face — gone. The memory of the taste of a fried egg sandwich during a Saturday night hockey game — gone as if it had never even existed.

Sometimes the hand removes a number of pieces at the same time — one from here, one from there, one from the present, one from the past — with no obvious pattern and no apparent reason. The feeling of watching a grandson catch his first fish — gone. The memory of watching a son win a soccer game on a rainy, windy Saturday afternoon — gone. The sensation of the Caribbean wind through your hair and the Caribbean sand beneath your feet — gone.

Sometimes, with even greater cruelty but no greater logic, the hand steals large groups of pieces in one quick motion. Important pieces as well as not so important ones. A daughter's house, once a second home — gone. The names of the months and days and seasons — gone. The correct steps for changing a tire — gone.

And sometimes, a piece or two gets returned to the picture, without warning, without explanation. The name of a neighbor forgotten for months — remembered. The location of a grandson's bedroom in a daughter's house — remembered. The importance of a birthday to a wife — returned for a few brief hours. But only for a few brief hours, or moments, as the hand hovers above the picture, waiting for the exact instant when it will swoop down again and take away for a second time, what had just been given back.

The frame around the puzzle, I think, is the physical body itself — the structure that shelters thought and feeling and enables action. The frame, or body, doesn't always exhibit the same kind of destruction that's occurring within, or perhaps it's just that the destruction isn't at the same rate. It seems those parts of the mind that control various mental and memory centres can begin to disappear long before there's a noticeable physical impact. But if you look at the puzzle as a whole, you will see pieces are missing from within the body of the picture as well as from the frame. And those parts of the mind that control the working of the body are also, eventually, erased.

What's it like if your own life is the picture from which the pieces are being removed? And what's it like if you are actually part of someone else's picture, and your piece is one of the ones that's been removed? The only answers I can give to those questions come through my observations of my father and through the experience of my personal disappearance from his life. For both, existence becomes less than it was; the picture loses some of its richness; important pieces go missing. For the Alzheimer's victim, the pieces of the puzzle become fewer and fewer until ultimately, so little of any one scene or location remains that there are very few places left to reside outside what has become a great and frightening void.

Unable to work because of the mental impact of the disease as well as the physical attacks that left him shaken and weak, and more and more uncomfortable in once familiar places, my father's life was increasingly lived in the house that had been his home for more than twenty-five years. At first, the pattern of the days was almost unchanged and as always, he would spend a great deal of time in his garage. As the disease progressed, however, there was a significant difference in what he did during the hours he spent there. He didn't, as my mother thought, do the regular maintenance and tune-ups on the Bronco or care for it as he had all his other vehicles. Instead he meticulously wrapped a wide assortment of things in towels or paper, held the wrapping together with elastic bands and sometimes masking tape, and filled the nooks and crannies in the vehicle's interior — by the side of the back seat, in the back trunk area, almost anywhere else he could find space. There were obvious reasons for having some of the items there; others made little sense.

His garage, always perfectly organized, still appeared so. But things could no longer be found — he sorted, often wrapped then rewrapped, then moved things around over and over again. And he no longer remembered where particular tools were kept, or even if they were still in the garage. He no longer remembered when items were borrowed by neighbors or family. Asking where something might be found only caused him frustration, as he would search frantically, still pretending he knew what it was he was looking for.

Because of my father's various health problems through the years, it wasn't unusual, when we were growing up, for my mother to send someone to check on him every so often if he happened to be in the garage by himself, just to make sure he was OK. She lived in fear, it would seem, of something happening to him. The intensity of this particular anxiety was heightened acutely as the Alzheimer's progressed. There would have been nothing more unnatural for my father than being locked out of his garage for his own safety and yet there was a growing fear that when he was alone there, he might somehow hurt himself, or begin to feel ill and not be able to call us. At the time these worries first surfaced, he was essentially behaving normally in the garage, but ultimately, whenever he was in the garage there were mixed emotions — relief that he was still able to find some comfort in that location along with fear that he may inadvertently harm himself.

It was difficult, and the difficulty was compounded by the fact that the more he needed us with him, the less he wanted us there. The beginnings of paranoia made him look at us with suspicion and distrust if he saw us come to check on him. At the same time, our own growing awareness of his situation made us all the more watchful, particularly my mother, who was with him almost twenty-four hours a day. And so the sounds of doors opening and closing, and the sounds and speeds of footsteps, took on new significance, just as did the sounds of silence.

When I look back on this period, I see a man who essentially escaped to the garage, I think at first in order to avoid the prying and watchful eyes of the people he no longer completely trusted. To find the familiar in the unfamiliar. To feel safe when there were fewer and fewer places where he actually did feel safe. It was wonderful that there was a place he could go. It was terribly sad that he needed one.

I can see him standing there now, by his desk, fiddling with things. I can hear my mother's barely controlled, tightly strained voice asking him a question she didn't need answered because what she was really doing was checking on him. I can see myself sneaking downstairs and peeking around the door, hoping he wouldn't see me. I can hear him muttering to himself at some unknown problem, then growing silent at the sound of approaching footsteps.

At some point the garage was no longer the garage, or at least that's how I'd describe it. I'm not sure what or where it was, though perhaps his hide-out was the best description, his fortress against the unwanted or the unknown. Sometimes I ask him, silently in my mind, what was it like? What did you think? How did you feel? Did you know where you were and who you were? What was it like from one moment to the next? I don't expect an answer. But there is an image that returns time after time. It's an image of a noose, hanging from the low garage ceiling — swinging slowly back and forth. And hanging from the noose is a package, a carefully wrapped, tightly bound package — one of my father's jackets wrapped in layers and layers of towels and papers. I wasn't the person to discover this on one of the trips to the garage to check on my father. I wasn't the person to pull it from the ceiling and unwrap it to discover the contents. My mother was. I know she was terrified by the sight, though she refused to give many details about the event. I think she was also angry, angry at what he'd done and what had possessed him to do it, though these are not words she used then or would even use now.

Alone in the garage that day, my father had made a noose and hung it from the ceiling. What impulse had caused him to do this? What impulse had driven him to wrap his coat in layers and hang it from the noose? Part of me believed, part of me still believes, that he prepared the noose for himself, but then either became confused or afraid or logical, and ultimately followed a different impulse to this particular conclusion. Whether an indication of violence that would be directed at himself, or violence that may have been meant for another, the reality of this noose is one of the incidents I see as a sign post along the disease's course, and from that moment on worries for his safety and that of my mother escalated.

Despite this incident, this sign post, my father's home in general and garage in particular, continued to be his comfort zone. He didn't exhibit the need to wander that many Alzheimer's patients do; he didn't seem to be searching for a house he'd lived in at some point in the past. He was, in this place, seemingly as content as he could be, at least for as long as the term content could be applied to any of his periods of wakefulness. We were lucky in this regard and we knew it. But we also knew that on any given day, at any moment, some unexplained urge could possess him and lead him out the door. And so his movements and activities were monitored closely. Doors were secured with new, unfamiliar locks so that by the time he could figure out a way to open them, we could be by his side to act as a distraction and keep him inside. One Christmas, my mother purchased a motion-sensitive wreath that would begin to play music when he even approached the door. I remember that wreath as being particularly ugly and I remember the song it played as being particularly annoying. It probably wasn't; more likely I was predisposed to think it ugly and horrid because of its reason for being.

Then there was the day my father disappeared. Despite all the safeguards and the locks he could no longer open, my mother went to look for him and he was nowhere to be found. It was a Saturday morning and she'd just come from the bathroom. Normally he would be waiting for her in the bedroom and she would help him dress for the day, but he wasn't there. When she couldn't find him, she checked the doors and they were still locked from the inside, so she knew he hadn't left. She was searching, she says, for what must have been fifteen minutes, calling his name but getting no response, going from room to room. All the rooms on the downstairs level of my parents' house are connected to at least two other rooms, so you can literally chase someone around and around. Children who visit love this feature, but on that particular morning, it wasn't exactly amusing. Finally, on one of her trips through the downstairs area, she saw my father dart in front of her, around a corner and through another door. Knowing that he was safe, her search became less frantic and she eventually caught up with him. We all laughed about it later — how she lost Dick in his own house. It was funny because it was something a little child would do, run giggling away from a parent to avoid the pajamas or the bath or the new outfit he'd been told to wear. And it was sad, because my father wasn't giggling and he wasn't a little child.

When a person has Alzheimer's, when the pieces are removed as though from a puzzle, all the normal codes of and explanations for behavior become irrelevant. People do things they would never normally do, behave in ways they would never normally behave. Sometimes you laugh at them or with them; sometimes you cry because of them. But the unwavering constant is that you watch over them because when you are caring for an Alzheimer's victim you have to. You have to see the things they no longer see, recognize what they no longer recognize. It's exhausting, this vigil. Maybe because unlike the process of watching over a healthy child who's developing along the normal course and will, as time goes on, become more and more independent, the loved one with Alzheimer's becomes more and more dependent — needs you more and more even as he or she wants you less and less. Maybe because you're trying to see through four eyes and hear through four ears. Maybe because of the wide range of emotions that fill you as you watch — fear, worry, frustration, anger. Maybe because you know how helpless you are.

There's one final image of the vigil in my father's house, the vigil that was held during the time when he was still well enough to move around somewhat normally, but when we were worried for his safety. It's of a small boy, about seven years old with dark brown hair and large dark eyes. He's sitting in the doorway of the kitchen. In his arms there's a worn dark brown teddy bear wearing a striped t-shirt. Sometimes there's a book or drawing paper and pencils on the floor beside him. He's watching and listening, this little boy, watching to see if his grandfather leaves the garage a floor below to move to another part of the house because when this happens his job is to tell his grandmother. A different but strangely symbolic kind of child-proofing.

Cry when you must.

Laugh when you can.

Accept your worry, your fear

and your anger.

And look for answers

but do not despair

when they cannot be found.

20
Just How I Feel

My husband says I carry with me an intense sadness. It isn't always obvious, he says, but sometimes more than others he can see it behind my eyes. *You're missing your dad, aren't you?* he asks, invariably at a moment when my thoughts have turned back in time to be with my father. Peter is the only person who understood and truly witnessed what the loss of my father did to me. He is the one who held me late at night when I would awake crying because of the intensity of the loneliness brought to the forefront by a particularly vivid dream and all the more poignant in the deep hours of a silent, restless night.

You see, most of the time, as I felt myself disappear from my father's life, I was able to focus less on how that felt to me and more on what needed to be done or coped with on any given day — on my father's needs as the patient and my mother's needs as the primary caregiver. But I wasn't always able to do this and at some point I admitted to myself that I was deeply hurt because I felt that virtually no one gave a moment's consideration to how I was, that no one remembered the countless hours I had spent in my father's company, and how close we had been, and that no one thought to ask how I was or if there was anything I needed. I was not proud of myself for feeling that way; I'm still not proud. It seemed and seems so terribly selfish. My level of suffering was so much less than either my father's or my mother's that I felt I had no right to mention my own suffering. But it was there.

Doesn't anyone even care? I asked Peter on one particularly difficult night. *Does anyone besides you realize that I was one of the closest people to my father, that he was an incredible friend, and the fact that I'm losing him hurts in a way I can't even describe?*

Peter knew of course. And a handful of people who would telephone (like Ann Marie, the person I called Hayes and my friend since Grade 7) or come to me in the office in the morning (like Michelle, who was as important a friend as colleague) and ask how I was. My mother, meaning absolutely no harm, would say: *Well, you're OK. At least you still have your husband. You still have someone to hold you during the night.* These words were an expression of her relief that I wasn't dealing with the situation alone, as she felt she was. And she was totally right, of course; I just wasn't able to hear the words correctly at that point.

Peter's particularly special gift to me during that time — apart from all the support he provided — was that he never thought I should feel any differently than I did. He never expected that his presence alone should somehow compensate for my father's absence or erase the pain associated with my father's illness. He knew, still knows, that my father is and was irreplaceable, just as he knows — I hope — that he is and always will be irreplaceable.

The thing to remember about the people who share the Alzheimer's experience with a loved one is that each and everyone will be affected differently, will feel differently. But I cannot imagine that there is anyone who will feel nothing.

The adult child who became 'friends' with a parent only later in life may feel terribly cheated when the disease strikes before they really have gotten to spend time together. The child who lives thousands of miles away may feel an exaggerated guilt and helplessness at not being close enough to help, or a quiet desperation as she wonders if her father will recognize her the next time she goes 'home' for a visit. The husband or wife caregiver who loses patience when there seems to be no way to get the once so independent spouse dressed in the morning may feel an intense guilt. The husband who looks at his wife and silently rages at the unfairness of life because he doesn't want to be married to this old woman, may carry that memory with shame. The friends who feel such an inability to cope with the erratic mannerisms of a person they now barely recognize, may increasingly avoid any contact and are haunted by their perceived weaknesses. The wife who broods over the absence of her husband's brothers and sisters, thinking they should spend more time with him, may not realize the reality of what they must witness brings a pain they have never learned to bear. The children who have no say over whether or not their mother is institutionalized, over whether day care is sought, or over the physical deterioration of their caregiving father, may feel anger or frustration or be deeply hurt.

And the list goes on. I met an incredibly vibrant lady whose mother was suffering from Alzheimer's during the time my father was and for her family, the coping mechanism was laughter. The stories she told about her mother were as hilarious as the look in her eyes was touching when she told them. *If you don't laugh,* she'd say. *If you don't laugh...* Some families are able to share their feelings, talk about them, laugh and cry together. Some families experience irreparable rifts as disagreements rage over caregiving arrangements, medical treatments, recreation activities, mealtime menus, sleeping arrangements — so many things can lead to arguments. Some families never really talk about it.

There are no absolutes in this world. There are no simple blacks and whites. The truth is that sorting through our own feelings and emotions as we cope from close or afar is complex and exhausting and whether we realize it or not, support and understanding are extremely important. That support and understanding takes different forms for different people, means different things to different people. But it matters. It matters a great deal.

A couple of years after my father's struggle had ended, I met someone whose father had died less than a year earlier. His story was completely different than mine. His father had traveled a great deal when they were young and so the person I'd talked to had never experienced the kind of closeness I had with my father. He'd felt cheated, he said, terribly cheated that now when they were actually becoming close, when there were grandchildren to enjoy, when there was time to do things together, his father was slowly taken from him. But he said he also realized that even in his illness, his father taught him things, showed him things, and he developed a new level of affection and respect for this man who would sit with him in a coffee shop, sometimes aware, sometimes less so.

I looked at him, after he'd finished talking, and asked. *So how are you?* He gave me the funniest look when I asked that question. He didn't really think about himself, he said, though he guessed he was OK. Actually, no he wasn't, but he was trying to be. He still didn't know quite how he felt or how he should feel. *I know,* I told him. *Don't be too hard on yourself,* I told him. *Don't think you have to feel one way or another way,* I told him. *Just remember to take care of yourself. If there are things you need to feel, be kind and let yourself feel them. Give yourself time. And don't be surprised if some days, even after this length of time, you walk around with the memories as vivid as if they had been yesterday. Don't be surprised if you need to cry, if you need to shout, if you wake up one morning and feel a grief more overwhelming that anything you felt at the funeral. Alzheimer's can do that to you,* I told him. *I know.*

I don't believe people should live their lives around the incidents of illness and death that have touched them. I don't believe lives should be defined by suffering or pain. I don't believe we can awaken every day dragging with us some injury from the past and dreading an injury that may happen in the future. I do believe, however, that we are deeply affected by our suffering and our pain just as, at times, we are deeply affected by the pain and suffering of others. I do believe that if we're willing and if we can find the courage, we can learn a great deal about ourselves and about others from these experiences, and in time, perhaps that knowledge can make us better.

My husband is right. I do carry with me an intense sadness that some days is acute and others barely noticeable. It certainly shouldn't be compared with what either my father or mother were forced to suffer, or with what my mother must still experience. And so I try to keep it in perspective. Also, I recognize in retrospect that if I felt hurt by the lack of awareness I felt from others through the worst part of my father's illness, I was the most to blame. So often I hid my pain from myself. So often I hid my pain from others. So often I appeared to be the person with everything under control — calm and cool in the turmoil. How, then, could I expect others to see deep inside my heart and offer any kind of support? That is who I was. That is who I am. That is how it had to be. Now I simply try to remember, when I meet someone who is living what I once lived, that the story of their experience may not be found so easily on their faces or even in their eyes. Sometimes people are able to share with us their needs and ask for our help; sometimes they're not. But we shouldn't assume the needs don't exist just because they aren't being articulated. And so I place a hand gently on a shoulder. I offer a hug, I listen, I question, I remember and I try to understand.

Every person is, in some way, a survivor.

There are fallen tears.

There are hidden scars.

And we should never assume

the life of another is easy

has been easy

because these are invisible.

21

The Journal

I didn't keep a journal throughout my father's illness, one that tracked the events of any given day and charted the progress of his illness. I can find words on computer disks, on sheets of paper in a binder, in hardcover journals — words that may or may not make reference to my father but that still bring me back to a particular time, place and memory. The recording of the events as they were happening was something I didn't really consider at the time. How then, I wondered, as I struggled to begin this chapter, was I to remember the episodes in my father's struggle that must be relayed? How was I to piece them together so that the exact date of their occurrence, the exact sequence, was less important than the impact? Was the story destined to be left unfinished because I didn't know what to say next?

Dad, I mentally asked, late one night as I lay next to Peter, struggling to remain still so that I would not disturb him, *what can I do? How do I continue? How do I tie all the remaining pieces together?*

I've read that our loved ones communicate with us, help us find the answers we need if we just remain quiet and attentive, if we allow ourselves to hear them. I've seen my father in stargazer lilies; I've woken late at night to feel his presence so strongly that I turn to the foot of my bed to smile at him, only to see nothing but the shadow of the night; I've asked him to help me find a way to lift a particularly heavy burden of sadness; I've felt his presence on a long and lonely drive. And on that particular night, the latest in a string of nights where the period from 2:00 to 4:30 a.m. seemed destined for sleeplessness, I found an answer. *Just write your journal now, duck. Just write your journal now. Write what you would have written if you'd been able. That's all you need to do. Write your journal now.*

I thought that perhaps I should turn on the light then, open the journal I keep in the drawer by my bed and at least record the idea, the answer that had been given to me. But no, I thought. This is not one of those revelations or phrases that seem so vivid at night but can't be retrieved in the morning. This I will remember. This I must remember. So I rolled over and slept, and the next day I remembered. *Write your journal now.*

***

Another first this morning. My father went to the kitchen for breakfast without combing his hair. Thing is, I never thought about the fact that I'd never seen him with his hair uncombed until my mom told me about this. I think maybe he always ran his fingers through his hair when he got out of bed. His military training perhaps. Respect for himself and for us. It was a particularly poignant reminder of what was happening to him, that so ingrained a habit had slipped by. She vowed, she said, that it would not happen again. From now on, she would see that his hair was always combed.

***

We sat in the restaurant in Sears today. By the fake fireplace mom likes. There was even a fire log. It crackled. We talked about how my father wasn't going to get better. How this condition of his would not be reversed. I know exactly what this means even though I have no idea... really... of how the coming weeks and months and years will unfold. Is that because it is better that I do not know, or because I cannot really comprehend? I don't know. It doesn't even matter. The only thing I am fairly certain of is that we will not speak of it often.

***

***

Dad no longer recognizes when his clothes need washing. He just puts them back in the closet at the end of the day and takes the same ones out in the morning. So now mom takes his clothes and puts them in the laundry. Lays out his pants and shirt in the morning so he knows what to put on.

***

It wasn't funny but we laughed anyway. Pajama bottoms don't work very well when treated as pajama tops. The arms of a cotton knit turtleneck are really too tight to stretch over feet and ankles. The process of getting dressed for the day or dressed for the night has altered yet again. My father can no longer handle these tasks without direction and careful guidance.

***

Rik goes frequently to the house to see dad, and he takes him out whenever he's well enough… to eat or to visit the house he and Sarah are fixing up on the Southern Shore. Today, he says, my father tried to take his shoes off and put his slippers on when they entered the barn. Today, again, he had no idea where he was.

***

Today my mother said, the people from the Department of Veterans Affairs came to assess my father. It was not one of his better days and they immediately recognized his deterioration over their previous visit. They asked him some questions, she said, anger, sadness, despair in her voice. They asked him if he had any children. He said no, even though Rik and Sarah were there. They asked if he knew who the little baby was, pointing at his granddaughter Mae. No, he said. But you do know what a baby is? Yes. And he points. They asked if he knew what season it was. Yes, of course, he said, but he gave the wrong one. And what is your name, they asked. Dick. And you have no children? No.

My father, I think, why have you forgotten me?

***

***

Today my father's keys were taken from him. He hasn't driven for so long that perhaps it shouldn't seem like a big thing; he doesn't even unlock the door to the house when they get home. But mom was afraid that he'd forget he no longer drove, get in the Bronco and be gone before she could stop him. Have an accident. Kill himself or someone else. Or just get lost and never be found. So she hid them. She says it's the hardest thing she ever did, sneaking his keys away from him. Hiding them where he wouldn't find them. Saying nothing when he said I don't know what I did with my keys. Watching him as he patted his empty pocket... confused.

***

My mother found him sitting on the couch, a huge smile on his face. She smiled back, wondering what had brought such joy to a face so often serious. I'm Dick, he said, Dick Barron. Don't you always know who you are, she asked. No, he answered, I don't. Then I understand exactly why you're smiling.

***

Steve is home for a two-day visit... the most he can manage... to see dad. I called him and told him if there was any way he could get here, he should really try to come. There probably wasn't much chance left that our father would remember him much longer. If he remembered him now. He's not well, I told him. I think you'd better come if you can. And so I watched dad watch Steve. I listened to him not answer questions or get involved in the conversation. And I felt a deep and sorrowful chill when Rik told me that dad had taken him aside, after the special evening meal prepared in honour of Steve's visit, and asked: Who's that fellow out there? An even deeper chill and sorrow when mom said later: I think Dick enjoyed seeing Steve.

I didn't tell Steve. What's the point of walking up to someone and saying dad didn't know you today... he asked Rik who you were. Especially since I suspect Steve already knew.

***

***

We have to be more careful at the grocery store now. If dad is coming along we have to make sure we go when it isn't crowded. People who are trying to move quickly through the too-narrow isles get agitated by his slow gait. And he doesn't understand when they ask him to move. It's even getting difficult to make sure he stays by the cart when we're at the check-out. But he still manages to help bring the groceries inside, even if he doesn't realize we've given him the lightest bags.

***

Kenneth made his first Communion today. Mom and dad came with us, but for my father the unfamiliarity of his surroundings seemed to overwhelm him. As nervous and as agitated as I've seen him to date. I doubt he understood why we were subjecting him to this event. I'm not even sure why we did. But at least he seemed OK when we were taking the photos.

***

Dad came with us today when we went shopping. He walks so slowly these days... like every step requires immense concentration. We walk slowly too, so that he doesn't lose sight of us. He doesn't say anything, but I think he would be terrified if we disappeared from his view. Sometimes I can almost see the lifeline between us.

***

I had to use the Heimlich manoeuvre, she said. He tried to swallow then started to choke. The piece of food, it flew out of his mouth and across the room, just like it does on TV. I didn't want to tell you but thought you'd be upset if I didn't. You're his daughter after all, and you have a right to know. The swallowing mechanism is becoming inconsistent, it would seem. The eating process less certain. Sometimes I think he forgets to chew enough and just swallows. Or maybe he can't recognize when the food is ready to be swallowed. Now mealtime supervision is important, not just to ensure he stays and eats enough... otherwise he'd lose interest in what he's doing and wander away... but because there is increasing danger while he's eating.

***

Your mom called, Peter told me when Kenneth and I came home from shopping early this afternoon. And something in his voice made my heart lurch. Dad? I asked. Yes, but he's OK, he answered. They were shopping and he started to look quite pale. Pointed to his stomach and chest area as if in pain. They left immediately but on the way to the Bronco he collapsed in the parking lot. Fell down and couldn't get up. Wasn't unconscious, but was very very weak. Your mom refused the help of a passer-by and finally got him up herself, then took him to Uncle Jim and Aunt Flo's. It seems they convinced her to take him to the hospital.

They kept him in only for the length of time it took to run the necessary tests and see things looked normal. No evidence of a heart attack. But something certainly happened.

What's scarier? That he collapsed or that mom seems to think that picking him up off the pavement herself instead of calling an ambulance is somehow a normal reaction. If it had been a heart attack and he'd died while she was driving along, she would never have forgiven herself.

One thing's sure... dad's walk through the mall today was his last one. He has become too weak to risk taking him there again.

***

Certain small things remain unchanged. The glass case in the left shirt pocket. The wallet in the back pants pocket. But he wears turtlenecks under his long sleeve shirts now, because he is cold even when the temperatures are warm. A friend of my mother's comes to the house to cut his hair, because he can no longer go out. Sometimes he wears cardigans, because they keep him warm and he no longer remembers that he never liked them. His eyes are watery and wide. He stares without seeing at the pictures on the TV screen, no longer able to name the actors and actresses, the hockey teams or players, as he had once so easily done. He moves the food from his plate to his mouth with a robotic rhythm. And when you look at the books and magazines he's reading you notice he's holding them upside down. But his foot still taps to the rhythm of the music on a favorite tape. And his hugs are full of trust and love.

***

The phone rang just as I was getting out of the shower. I had a hair appointment in a couple of hours. You'd better come... it was my mother's voice. Your father's not well. He collapsed in the hall; didn't make it to the bathroom. Ursula's helping me clean everything up. I got dressed as quickly as I could and flew down the road. Dad was lying on the bed when I got there. Conscious but weak. Grey and sweating. He acknowledged my words but without understanding. Shouldn't he go to the hospital? No, I don't think so. His blood pressure is OK. He just seemed to have very bad stomach cramps and they seem to have passed. I stayed for a while, did what I could, then went to have my hair done. Couldn't help but think I needed it done anyway, particularly if there was a funeral to go to. I'd given my mother the phone number and kept expecting someone to come tell me there was a call. But there wasn't and so before I went home, I went and bought new face cloths, towels, and a waterproof mattress cover for the bed so that the mattress wouldn't be destroyed if there were any accidents during the night. Brought them to my mother. Things had returned to normal by then, as normal as they ever were these days. This vacation of mine has been nothing but one phone call after another. This vacation has been a waiting.

***

It's funny. It doesn't matter what else my dad forgets. He still goes to the kitchen to do the dishes after supper and he always puts the garbage out on garbage day. Without being told or prompted.

***

***

He was sitting in the white wooden lawn chair when I pulled in the driveway. It was sunny and hot — a wonderful summer evening — but he wore a jacket. My mother sat next to him. Used to be that he'd come to the door or the gate the minute we arrived. Ready to greet us with a smile that was full of welcome. Today he just sat there... able to offer only a confused nod as I walked towards him. I smiled brightly, walked over to him and gave him a kiss.

***

While I'm at the office my mother is at home bathing my father. For a while all she had to do was remind him to take a shower; then she would help him take a shower... passing him soap, reminding him to wash his hair. But then he started to have trouble standing up for the length of time it took to finish the task, or he'd start to get out before things were finished. So showers turned into baths with the same kind of supervision. But now she bathes him while he sits there quietly. Too weak or unaware to notice.

***

There will be a funeral. Aunt Trix died suddenly in her bed two nights ago. Mom is shocked and devastated... the other family members have arrived and that is somewhat of a help. But dad has no idea why there are so many people in the house. He does not comprehend what he has been told. And my mother longs for the comfort he would once have been able to provide. She longs for his arms around her.

***

Whenever I was sick when I was growing up, dad would come home with a six-pack of soft drinks. Root beer. Ginger Ale. Coca Cola. In bottles. He'd hold the cardboard case by the handle as he walked into the room to see how I was. His first stop before he even took off his coat. It always made me feel better, this treat. I wish I could do something, anything, for him now that would mean as much as that root beer did to me. But there seems to be nothing.

***

***

Mom finally got respite care today. My aunt, staying with my dad for a few hours. I took a long lunch. We ate in a restaurant in the mall, then did some shopping — for shoes. She said she felt like a bird set free from a cage, and kept looking at her watch, waiting for the time to go home. Respite care is supposed to be good for the caregiver. I have no idea if it helped her in the slightest.

***

The night was particularly bad... my father in a unusually foul mood, pacing and refusing to rest for even a moment. It started when mom was talking to one of her sisters on the phone. The call was long distance, but Ursula stayed on the line for hours while mom walked with dad, so mom could pick up the phone if she needed her.

***

My mom's friend Pat was at the house this afternoon when I stopped by to visit. I feel like I'm waiting, she said. Though I don't know what for. There is a sense of anticipation in the house these days... as if some unseen presence is controlling the roll of the nights and the days. There is death in that house. And I am waiting too.

Feelings trapped inside
can find release in words.
But sometimes the very things
that would help us ease our pain
remain locked away.
For even the words are too painful.

22

The Long Night

One of my greatest fears during the last year of my father's life was that I would call my parent's house for my early morning check-in and the phone would go unanswered. Having slipped into a reality of his own, having lost sometimes his ability, sometimes his inclination to communicate, we could never be sure of his emotional stability. My mother, afraid he would wander during the night when she was sleeping, decided she must begin to shut the door of their bedroom, believing the squeak of the door as it opened would awaken her in time to stop him from going anywhere. When she realized he sometimes moved so quickly she might not be able to reach him in time, she decided to lock it, using new locks he was unable to master.

I was waiting for the paranoia and aggression that is a symptom of Alzheimer's to hit my father full force while continuing to hope that perhaps extreme symptoms of this sort would never actually materialize. While my mother remained convinced my father would never hurt her, that he wasn't dangerous, I was haunted by the incident with the noose and his increasing tendency to look suspiciously at people he once knew and trusted. I also felt shivers run down my spine every time I'd find him standing in front of the mirror in the bathroom, the bedroom, or over the piano — leaning towards the glass so that his face almost touched — speaking quietly and quickly in words that I couldn't hear but with an agitation that was palpable.

It wasn't so much the fact that he was talking to the reflection in the mirror that worried me so, though this was disturbing enough; it was the way he would end his conversation the instant he saw anyone watching him, then slide furtively and suspiciously away.

It was increasingly obvious that my father was becoming less and less comfortable, even in the one place where he had always been comfortable. He did not recognize the person in the mirror as himself, or if he did, he didn't know how odd it was to be talking to his reflection. So I wondered. What would happen if he awoke in the middle of the night and found himself locked in a room with someone he didn't recognize but perceived as an enemy?

It is true that I'd never heard or read about Alzheimer's sufferers fatally injuring their caregivers in fits of unexplained rage. It is true that I'd never heard or read about anyone like my father physically harming their caregivers or family members. But I believed that given his military background and his tendency to slip back into war-torn times, violence from this man was indeed possible.

Medication hadn't been recommended at this point, but my worries didn't cease and my morning check-ins became a ritual. I didn't make the telephone call before I left for work because I didn't want to disturb them if they were still resting. Despite her conviction that the sleeping arrangements were appropriate, my mother was actually getting less and less sleep, and if she happened to be out of bed at their normal time (around 7:00 a.m.), she was likely occupied with the tasks of getting my father ready for the day. Interruptions at this time were inconvenient at best *(I'll call you back; I'm dressing your father)*, dangerous at worst *(I can't talk; I'm afraid he'll fall)*. And so every morning sometime between 8:30 and 9:00 a.m., after I had arrived at work, hung up my coat and switched on the computer, I'd telephone my mother's house and count the number of rings. I'd ask how things were this morning, how the night had gone. I'd gauge the mood by the sound of her voice, and having satisfied myself that I didn't have to leave instantly for the house, I'd hang up and begin another work day, feeling a mixture of relief and guilt that whatever task I faced would be easier than what my mother was doing.

I must have effectively hidden my relief at the sound of her voice each time she answered the phone because she was surprised, some time after my father's death, to learn that I worried about the things that could have happened in the darkness. That I went to sleep at night and awoke in the morning worried for her safety. I had thought my concerns were clear, but they were not.

In any event, as her level of exhaustion grew, my mother was eventually convinced that sleeping pills for my father were unavoidable. Even if it was not a problem for him, his habit of sleeping for a short time, then waking up and walking around until he could be convinced to return to bed or decided to do so himself, left my mother with no period in the day when she could herself rest for any extended stretch of time.

Medicating a person with dementia means trying to find the drug and dosage that will have the desired result while not exacerbating the confusion and disorientation. The mild sleeping pill that was prescribed worked wonderfully for a short time, giving my father, and therefore my mother, a few hours of uninterrupted rest. But its effectiveness soon became sporadic, sometimes working for five or more hours, sometimes for just one or two, sometimes working quickly, sometimes taking more than an hour to have any effect. At first he swallowed the pill without argument. Soon my mother would be forced to hide the pill in a spoonful of jam or some other food. And the nights again became longer and filled with the potential of unknown dangers.

In addition to being the period when the first signs of paranoia and aggression appeared, my father's final year was a period of continual and devastating physical deterioration. He was noticeably slower in his movement, noticeably more unsteady. He was in discomfort more often than ever before. He seemed to be experiencing pain or some other sort of discomfort in his hands and feet, though he was unable to explain what was going on. He would break into a sweat; he would be unable to finish meals; he would bend over as he held his cramping stomach. He became physically unable to handle the few outings that had been left to him — a short stroll on the harbour front, a short drive. He stopped spending time in the garage — he no longer had the strength to walk up and down the stairs, or even to sit or stand there. Every so often, when he was having a particularly good day, something would be arranged — a short trip to a nearby rugged beach where all he had to do was move from the car to the beach chair that was waiting for him a few steps away. But these occasions were rare.

Another aspect of the deterioration during his last year was the loss of control over bodily function. Like a little child still being toilet trained, there was no guarantee my father would be able to recognize when he needed to go to the bathroom. When he was at home being closely monitored, you could make reasonably accurate guesses and guide him there. But there was no guarantee he would or could tell you he needed to use the washroom, or if he could, there was no guarantee that there would be time to get him to one after he'd made that point clear. Partly because he might not understand where you were trying to lead him, and partly because of his increasing tendency to grow agitated and annoyed when you tried to lead him anywhere.

My mother did not believe we should rush into having him wear protective underwear; she wasn't even sure she'd be able to get him to keep them on if they were uncomfortable, fully suspecting that he'd remove them the moment she turned her back. In the meantime, Peter and I researched what was available, obtained samples and prepared for the day when we would be buying them.

These are the things you adjust to when someone suffers from a dementia. Most people I've spoken with who have witnessed the same kind of deterioration speak with deep regret about the person's loss of dignity. An aunt who was once so careful about her appearance, now fighting with anyone who even tried to help her dress, walking around with her hair in disarray and her clothes dirty as she obsessively dusts her house. The uncle who had always been so polite and loving, sitting in a corner swearing at anyone who comes near, pushing out his hand to drive them away. The father who hides the soiled tissues from his trips to the bathroom in the nooks and spaces of the baseboard heater in that and other rooms. The mother who braces her arms against the door frame when encouraged to enter the bathroom but refuses to wear a protective undergarment.

There's a frustration associated with the daily and hourly task of dealing with these unnatural behaviors. There is also a sadness bordering on heartbreak, because you know how the person you see before you would feel if they were aware of their own behavior. They can no longer feel the embarrassment or humiliation they would normally feel; so you feel it for them. And if you're like my mother, you also do everything in your power to ensure her husband can retain his dignity for even longer than is humanly possible.

Of course, there are also other reversals. Individuals who were once aggressive and extremely vocal become gentle and quiet. People who never showed emotion become overly emotional. And this causes its own sort of pain for the family members who see a person so unlike the one they always knew.

For us, despite the deterioration that was constant, we were grateful for many things. My father didn't run out of the house partly dressed, as some fathers have done, though he did attempt to walk around without his pants from time to time, my mother not knowing whether to laugh or cry. He didn't sneak out of the house in the middle of the night, to be found the next morning wandering aimlessly as he searched for home, but maybe he would have if the bedroom door hadn't had double locks. Or perhaps that's because by the time he would mentally have been at the stage where these actions seemed necessary to him, he was physically unable to do them.

During my father's last spring and summer, he ventured rarely to the grounds around his home, and even more seldom to anywhere off the property. He was watched closely while he ate a limited diet of food that needed little chewing because of the danger that he would choke (at worst) or simply forget what he was doing and get up and leave (at best). He grew terribly terribly thin, as quiet as death, nervous, agitated and suspicious. He lay on his bed a great deal, sat in the wooden lawn chairs when the sun was warm enough, sat in a chair in the living room with the same cassette tape playing over and over in the background. It was the one Rik, a musician and now a children's entertainer, had recorded and my father's obvious favorite. On good days, when someone came to visit, his watery red eyes would fill for a time with joy. Sometimes he would smile at the children, even as he'd look with wariness at the adults. Once he danced happily with his little granddaughter Mae.

If care had been required twenty-four hours a day prior to this period, it was required thirty-six hours a day now. Constant watching. Constant wondering. An even more constant worry when we had already thought it was not possible to worry more.

I have two distinct recollections that stand firmly in the midst of a wash of unfragmented images of my father during this period, sitting shakily in a chair, at the table with a spoon or fork in mid air, holding a set of prayer beads.

The first involved the realization that when I thought things were as bad as they could be, when I thought things couldn't get worse, they did. Cruelly and inevitably something previously unthinkable would happen and the safety net I'd wrapped around myself would be ripped open. After a time I stopped hoping for the adjustment time I'd grown accustomed to, during which we would learn to deal with the new behaviors or conditions. Coping and adjusting became a minute-by-minute necessity.

The second recollection involves conversations with my mother. She would all but implore me to agree with her when she said that my father wouldn't need to go into a long-term care facility, that she would be able to take care of him for as long as necessary. And I would answer in total honesty that I didn't see my father going into a hospital or a home, even as part of me logically knew that if he continued to deteriorate, it would be impossible for his care to continue at home. It was a contradiction within myself that I didn't fully understand until I sat beside his bed one evening, watching his seemingly deep sleep, wondering when he would wake up, sit up suddenly, stand shakily and move to escape when he noticed my presence in the softly lit bedroom.

It occurred to me in the dim light of the room that I had been watching my father sleep in that bed since I was a wispy-haired little girl. After most of his stomach had been removed when I was two years old, he needed to lie down after the evening meal, to let his food settle before he headed to the garage. And I would often lie or sit next to him, a small but almost constant shadow, watching his chest and stomach rise and fall, rise and fall. Making sure it didn't stop. It wasn't that I was afraid, I was simply watchful. Even when I was older, I would stop my studying or my homework, or whatever I was doing and go quietly to the bedroom door and watch until I was sure his stomach was rising and falling. And if his nap was longer than usual, I would check more that once. I never told anyone I did this. I certainly never asked myself whether it was normal behavior. I just did it — year after year after year — because it is what I felt I had to do.

I didn't think I could control his breathing; but I did watch it.

And on this night, I suddenly came to realize my belief that my father wouldn't have to be institutionalized was directly tied to my expectation that he was going to die in exactly the place he had laid for all the time I'd watched him. On that night I was certain he would die peacefully in that bed. The only thing that remained, I thought, was to see if my preconception would be proved true.

I believe there are things we know

have always known

will always know.

Even when the

laws of the universe

tell us this is impossible.

23
A Light Extinguished

After a spring and summer of taking life one moment at a time, watching my father fade physically and mentally at a rate not witnessed before and hardly believable, my mother approached her birthday on September 8th with exhaustion and more than just a tinge of bitterness.

Just ignore my birthday, she insisted. *I don't need presents or cards. I don't want them. How can I possibly celebrate my birthday when Dick doesn't even know if he's in the world?*

I ignored her and arrived after work with birthday cards and gifts. I was alone, something I felt was a significant enough concession in a family where birthdays had meant special suppers with all family members in attendance, home-baked cakes, candles, gifts and cards. The important thing, I thought, was to try to give her some indication that even if my father no longer knew he was alive, she must remember that she was. The important thing, I thought, was to do the least of what my father would have wanted, would have expected.

It was warm and bright, a beautiful Indian summer evening. My father, when I arrived, seemed brighter and stronger than he had been in months. It surprised me, this change. There was awareness in the eyes, though of what I cannot be sure. There was almost an eagerness as he stood looking out the window. *You want to go outside?* I asked him. *Yes,* he answered. And so I told my mother I would take him outside. We walked carefully downstairs and stepped carefully over the doorstep leading to the driveway where I walked beside my father. The pace was painfully slow, but he was obviously pleased to feel the fresh air, the warm sun. He ran his fingers gently along the side of his Bronco, looked with interest at the yard. I seem to remember making comments about something or other, though I don't remember exactly what I said. When my mother decided to join us, he looked at her with the kind of mischievous smile I hadn't seen in what seemed like forever, bent to kiss her, and linked her arm through his, taking her hand as he did so.

I looked at my father, the light in his eyes. I looked at the smile on his face and his hand holding my mother's. I looked at my mother's surprised delight and realized I was grinning. *I think you two would rather be alone,* I said and turned to go inside, where I sat in the kitchen chatting with the friend who had also come to bring birthday greetings. Pat, the woman who'd been married the evening my father last visited my house, was one of the handful of people my father would still smile at, some sense of safety or acceptance in his eyes, one of the few friends from whom my mother accepted the support that was offered.

We laughed, pleased that I'd had such an overwhelming feeling my father wanted to be alone with my mother, to enjoy with her the bonus summer day as they walked outside their home, amused that I had been in the way. When they eventually came inside, perhaps ten minutes later, we asked my father if he'd like to sit with us in the kitchen. Though this was something he rarely did any longer, he sat smiling in the chair we pulled up for him. Answering questions with understandable, if short phrases. Seeming to follow the conversation and enjoying the company.

I'll never know if something enhanced my father's awareness that day and he truly understood it was my mother's birthday. I'll never know if he intentionally gave her the only gift he could — a quiet walk around the driveway, through the front yard and back, stopping under the wild apple tree before they made their way to the back fence, across to the stretch of land where blueberries had once grown. I'll never know why or how on this day he managed to speak to us in words that were understandable and relevant. The physical weakness aside, it was absolutely wonderful to see and feel him with us again, a precious gift not just for my mother, but for all of us — the wife, the daughter and the friend — who would hear his laughter for the last time as we sat that evening around a table that had suddenly become festive, despite the absence of the birthday cake.

The next day we each questioned our own recollections of those few hours as my father slipped cruelly and immediately back into the no-man's land that had been his prior existence. In fact, if we hadn't been able to ask each other whether or not our memories were true, we probably would have begun to doubt them as nasty tricks of wishful or wistful thinking.

Our private hopes that something had changed, that my father would continue in this somewhat larger sphere of reality, were dashed with the abrupt realization that September 9th was a bad day, maybe even a little worse physically, mentally, and emotionally, than any that had gone before.

I came to suspect that on some unrecognized or unconscious level this walk with my mother, her description of things that had been done with the Bronco, the yard, the fence, the house, were an important element in my father's final inspection. A personal and private goodbye to the place he had called home, said in the presence of the woman he'd first met in her bedroom so many years before. The only but most significant gift he could give her. A dying man's last smile.

Less than a week later, a week during which my father's condition had remained at this new lower level, I was scheduled to take an afternoon flight for meetings in Prince Edward Island. Shortly before noon I called the house to learn my uncle was there. My mother had called him because she'd been unable to settle my father down. He wouldn't sit. He wouldn't eat. He wouldn't stop pacing even though he was staggering and bumping into things. When she'd tried to approach him to clean him after he'd soiled himself, touched his arm to lead him to the bathroom, he turned on her with rage in his eyes and spat out: *Don't touch me!* He growled. *I don't know you.* He'd even managed to trap her against the wall, and she panicked when she realized she didn't have the portable telephone she now carried in her pocket. When she did manage to get to a phone, she called my uncle. She needed someone strong to help her, she said. She didn't want to bother me or Peter, she said. We were at work and she didn't want to bother us. She could manage, she said.

By the time I got to the house, the man who'd been thrashing about a short time before was lying quietly on the bed, exhaustion from his exertion having finally taken over. The rage had passed; my father had been cleaned and changed; my uncle had left. The house was eerily quiet.

What do you do in a situation like this? How do you get on a plane and carry with you questions about what might happen while you're gone, the guilt at being absent? What do you say to a mother who pushes you away so firmly there's a physical sensation of pain? How can you make yourself heard by someone who refuses to listen? How can you bear to leave? How can you bear to stay? How do you reconcile the fact that when help is needed, really needed, someone else is called? Are you that useless? That unwanted? How are you supposed to feel when someone says they're trying to protect you, trying to let you have a normal life, when there's no longer any such thing? How do you recover from the feeling that your father, on some level, must feel as if you've abandoned him, even though you know this is illogical? How can you deal with the intense pain that is being caused by someone's determination to spare you pain? How can the home care continue? Where do the answers come from?

I made a number of phone calls. I talked to Peter, I talked to my office, and I finally gave up and got on the plane. The rationale I used was that of all the places I could be going on this afternoon trip, this one was oddly appropriate because it was the island to which Rik, Sarah and Mae had moved some months before. Rik was to meet me at the airport, we were to have dinner together, then he was to drive me to the small resort town where the meetings were being held. Just in time to have dessert with the group who'd arrived before me. In the meantime, we would talk.

The news I brought was not good. Our father had deteriorated significantly since he'd last seen him during the summer. Physically weaker, periods of aggressiveness, inconsistent sleep patterns, loss of control over bodily functions. Unless things stabilized, I didn't see how he could continue to be cared for at home, and yet we both knew my mother would resist putting him in hospital or a home with every ounce of her being. We were in an awkward position, brother and sister, not knowing what tomorrow or even that night would bring. But knowing that certain decisions might have to be forced, even if there were those who thought the decisions were not ours to make.

The stage my father had entered could be brief, or it could be lengthy. He could stabilize and slip back to more manageable patterns, or his aggressiveness could increase. He could die tomorrow or live for years in this state, or in a much more vegetative one. We had no way of knowing. In the meantime, it was clear that even as my mother professed her ability to cope, she was on the verge of a collapse she refused to acknowledge. If we had to we would find a way to do what had to be done.

My brother dropped me at the hotel where the meetings were

taking place at about 9:00 p.m. I met the small group of colleagues who were waiting for me in the restaurant and ordered dessert as planned. White linen tablecloths, flowers and candles, the low lights and buzz of animated yet private conversations, in my state of mind I thought them surreal. I told my colleagues enough of the situation so that explanations would be shortened if I was forced to leave the meetings early, and I ate strawberry tort with a rich chocolate sauce.

The next morning, I awoke before dawn and ran in the cold, drizzly autumn air of the seaside town, without the proper clothing since I'd been too unfocused to pack it.

Things are going OK, my mother would say when I checked in. *No, you don't need to come home. Your job's important so you should stay there and work; your father wouldn't want you to come home. He wouldn't want his illness to interfere with your work or your life. There's nothing you could do anyway. Nothing you could do.*

I did not see my brother again before I left the island, but my mission was clear to me when I returned home. Even while part of me still believed my father would never have to be hospitalized, even while part of me could not visualize him in a hospital bed with me sitting beside him in the vinyl covered chairs that only look comfortable, that eventuality still had to be addressed. My mother must be made to see that while there was little choice but to accept that my father was dying, the stress of caring for him was killing her. And she had to somehow understand that while losing our father was devastating, the possibility of losing them both because she killed herself caring for him was too cruel to comprehend. If she would not admit what she was doing to herself, perhaps she would eventually acknowledge what she was doing to us.

Was this likely? Probably not. My mother had always been incredibly strong-willed. I remember when I was nineteen and her own mother was in hospital. Having suffered a number of strokes, it was uncertain whether she would live or die. My mother, the health care professional to whom all other family members turned in times of crisis, snatched only a few hours of sleep here and there over a period of days that stretched to weeks. She stayed up all night then went to work in the morning. She refused advice. She refused help. When it was all over and my grandmother had been buried, I watched her crash. And as I watched her with my father, I knew a crash would come. Only this time it was doubtful she would recover.

We did talk when I returned home — a number of times through different sets of uninterrupted minutes while my father rested for brief pockets of time. Whenever I could make her listen. This can't go on indefinitely, I told her. If there was no improvement, if there was no stability, she physically couldn't continue to deliver the kind of care she was committed to delivering. No matter how much she was determined to do so, no matter how much she wanted to do so. And if she could not make the decision to put my father in a home if that became necessary, I told her, I would make the decision. I would relieve her of any responsibility and feelings of guilt and take them upon myself.

It's bad enough I'm losing my father, I said, *but I can do nothing to stop that. I'm not prepared to lose both of you.*

Of course she would not allow me to take the decision from her and said that if the time came when she felt she could not handle my father, she would make the call. She would make the decision. It was hers and only hers to make.

I didn't shout. I didn't argue. I never have. Instead I accepted with silence that despite her protests, if I had to remove my father from his home to save her life and ensure he was cared for in an institution, then I would do that. And I prayed for them both.

My father was in his own prison. My mother was in hers. And I had found mine.

Sometimes the uncertainty is
hardest to bear —
a day of hope followed by
a day of hopelessness.
Yet the days of hope
and the moments of happiness
remain eternally as bright lights.

24

Picking Flowers

The exact point at which the decision was made is unclear, but between the beginning of September and the middle of October, my mother made the telephone call that put my father on a waiting list for a bed in the long-term care facility that specialized in caring for veterans. He was not first on the list; there were others who were deemed to be more needy. And there was no estimate on the length of the wait — all the beds were full and there was just a single way one would become free.

This was the same period during which all the anger my father must have ever felt seemed to surface at unpredictable times and last for inconsistent amounts of time. Sleeping medication worked for a short time some nights; barely at all others. Periods of relative quiet would end suddenly and for no apparent reason there would be intense anger and a swing of a surprisingly strong arm towards the offending object or person. Strings of barely understandable words would be spit out in the direction of a perceived threat or annoyance. Sometimes my father would sit in what we began to call 'his chair' — perfectly still, slumped forward a little, the music from Rik's cassette seeming to hold him there. When he wasn't doing this, he would pace constantly — back and forth, back and forth, bending down to pick up the flowers that were part of the pattern on the living room rug. Picking at them, flicking them away. Sometimes he'd let you hold his arm to steady him because day after day he became weaker, but increasingly you would have to walk a step or so behind, ready to catch him if he fell. Occasionally he would lie on his bed, or sit on the edge, staring at his own reflection in the mirror.

We never knew when he would become angry or violent. We never knew when he would sit and fall into a semi-sleep. We never knew when or where he would try to go to the bathroom. I would go to my parent's house in the evening and often at lunch times to give my mother some company and walk with my father. *Watch him,* was the direction. *Make sure he doesn't fall; try to guess when he wants to go to the bathroom.* I'd do this, completely unable to imagine how she coped on her own for the long hours of the night and day.

The physical habits that surfaced in this period were difficult enough to watch. I cannot quite describe the fear or dread with which I entered that home each day, a fear and dread that shamed me because I felt these emotions somehow betrayed him. This was the man who'd made the sandbags I used to exercise my leg after surgery, who had gotten up in the bleak darkness of a storm-blown winter to gently begin the process of my physiotherapy so I would suffer less when I arrived at the hospital. This was the man who had set the table every night before bed so it would be ready when he arrived in the morning to cook breakfast for everyone, who had made me poached eggs on toast and cut them into the bite-size pieces I liked so much. This was the man who had gently lifted me from the car after I'd gotten car sick without scolding or taunting me.

But I was not prepared for it the first time I saw my father try to open his pants to urinate in the living room. I was not prepared to see him sitting totally unresponsive in a chair then rising as if woken by some startling dream and start to pace. I was not prepared for his strength when he forced me away from him, or the wild, watery, angry eyes.

Nor was I prepared for the sense of frustration and unrelenting pain that emanated from him. I had seen my father suffer when he agonized over what was happening to him. I had seen him suffer when the gaps in his periods of lucidity became longer and longer but were still obvious to him. I had seen years of physical and mental distress. But I had never before seen him feel so confined, so caged. It was as if he was embroiled in a battle for his very life, unable to live but unable to let go. He was trapped in a mind that denied his very essence and a body that was wasting away.

And so when he paced, we paced with him, trying to adjust to his uneven, staggering gait. When he bent to flick away the flowers on the patterned rug, we bent with him, holding our breath for fear he would fall. When he sat in the chair, we sat sometimes on the arm, sometimes on the couch or in the other chair, whatever seemed most acceptable. When he lay on the bed, we sat next to him resting against the pillows, or in the chair under the window, watching for the first sign of movement. Always ready to begin the pace.

Sometimes, when he sat on the side of the bed, clumsily trying to rub one of his hands with the other, he'd let me take his hands in mine and rub them gently. *Are they cold?* I'd ask. *Cold,* he'd whisper. *Do they hurt?* I'd ask. *Hurt,* he'd answer. And so we'd sit, side by side, and I'd massage his fingers and the palm of his hands as best I could. He would smile a little then and I would say a silent thank you with my prayer.

One night we had taken a break from our pacing to sit on the couch. Pat was visiting and she sat in my father's chair. My mother sat across from her. And I sat beside my father facing them both. I started to rub my hands — it was fall and they were cold. Or maybe it was that I felt cold all over. My father, silent until then, looked down at my hands then across at me. I smiled a small smile. *Cold?* he asked. *Yes,* I answered. *Cold.* He smiled back at me then — a quiet, warm smile — and took my hands in his and started to rub them just as I'd rubbed his so many times before. *Thank you,* I said. *Thank you so very much.* And I looked across at my mother, my eyes directing her glance downwards. *He's rubbing my hands just as I rub his. He's rubbing my hands.* And I lowered my head a little so he would not see my tears.

We sat there for a long time that evening. The friend who was visiting, the same one who was present on my mom's birthday, always seemed to be good for my father. He still smiled at her, still seemed unthreatened by her. And for a time we could sit calmly in each other's company. At one point, after he'd stopped rubbing my hands but was still holding them, he lifted up one of my hands and looked directly at my mother. *Look what I have,* he said with a huge smile. *Look what I have.* And then he started to rub my hand again. He knew me again, in that instant. It was so brief it was poignant, bittersweet, and a particularly precious gift all in one. I treasured it, and the gentleness with which he rubbed my hands to make them warm. And as I came to realize it would be the last such moment, I came to treasure it even more.

Later that night, after I'd left, the pacing continued, the night was restless. Soon anti-psychotic medication could no longer be avoided and since he could not go to the doctor, the doctor came to him. The first prescription, which was to help sedate him and curb the psychotic tendencies, was a tremendous relief. It would quiet him, help him relax, help him rest, help us ensure he didn't fall or hurt himself, and ease our fears over my mother's safety. He could be on this kind of medication for weeks, months or years, my brother Steve explained when we discussed it. There was no real way to predict the speed with which the disease would progress, though the next stage would see my father enter a vegetative state — unable to feed himself, unable or unwilling to walk, sitting or lying all day with no communication.

Steve was incredibly helpful throughout this period, a continual source of information and assistance. No matter what time of day or night, if I needed him all I had to do was call his cell phone, leave a message, and as soon as he was finished with the patient he was seeing, or could free himself from his hospital rounds, or make it from his bed to a telephone where he would not disturb his own ailing wife, he would return my call. He was the person I called when it became clear just a short time into the first prescription, that the medication wasn't working. If anything, my father had become more uncontrollable and more aggressive. The question — what do we do now?

I was at my parent's house the evening the doctor made his second house call to look again at my father. It was clear to him, just as it was to us, that he was actually more agitated than he had been a week before. More suspicious. Throughout the visit, my father was urging me to walk with him back and forth through the living and dining room and into the kitchen. I'm not sure who I was this particular day, but I certainly wasn't his daughter. He spoke in hurried and almost nonstop whispers, waving at me so that I'd bend my head close to his. Most of the words were unintelligible, but the gist of the warning was clear. There was someone on this ship and this someone was the enemy. We were either trying to find the person or hide from him. I'm not sure. We walked back and forth, stepping over the same imaginary rise in the floor between what should have been the kitchen and the dining room. We swayed with the movement on the water. We stopped quickly and turned away, crouching low in chairs. I was relieved that in this drama I could not quite understand, I was a comrade and not an enemy. And so while the doctor and my mother talked, I played my role and listened. And when it was obvious he expected an answer, I repeated the parts of my father's phrases that I understood, fearing that if I veered too far from his words, I may say something to make him angry. And that anger would be directed at me.

I had some questions for the doctor, the most pressing one being what happens if the new medication doesn't work.

It will, he said.

But what if it doesn't and it's 3:00 in the morning and my father can't be controlled? Is there a different medication we can get now to try in that event? Do I call an ambulance? What advice can you give? Do we give him another pill? I remember my mother and I having quite different approaches to this medication problem. She was willing to accept the new prescription and the assurance that it would work, and was a little impatient, I think, with the fact that I had questions. But I'd gone through that once and now wanted contingency plans. We received advice on the frequency of dosages, but were told that this medication should quiet my father considerably, relieve his agitation and allow him to sit quietly for extended periods. The anxious, unsteady pacing, the intensity of the hallucinations — these should now be controlled.

There was a definite improvement at first. My father didn't sit for the extended periods predicted, but he was more manageable. There was less of a struggle getting him washed and dressed, less of a struggle getting him to eat, less aggression. Then something snapped and the only way I can describe it is to say the medication and anyone trying to give it became the enemy, and my father fought with every ounce of strength and wit we didn't know until then that he had left.

Inside each and every one of us

there is a love

so much larger

than our mere physical form,

so much stronger than any barrier.

If you doubt this truth

imagine a couch, a father and a daughter,

and cold hands being warmed.

25
When Things Can't Get Worse

My mother was forced to move out of the bed she had shared with my father fifteen days before his death. His medication was offering only brief and unpredictable respites, and so she had taken to dressing for bed in loose sweat pants and shirts so she could be ready, at the first sign of his stirring, to deal with whatever the need or mood was at the time.

In reality, the only difference between night and day was that my mother felt her isolation at night even more acutely than during the day. While the world slept, she sat beside my father, did crossword puzzles and watched. When she became overwhelmed by tiredness, she would close her eyes and doze, usually in the same erect position. Partially asleep or awake, she was conscious of even his slightest movement or change in breathing. She was nervous sitting there, silently keeping track of the hours and then the minutes before the dawn. And with every sunrise, she was more worn and more tired than she had been the evening before.

On this particular night, as she sat beside my father in bed doing her crossword puzzles, he stirred and made an anguished noise in his sleep. Instinctively, she reached across with her hand to touch him gently and soothe him. But instead of being calmed, he came awake instantly. Glared at her with fire in his eyes. Shot out of bed and began to pace, staggering on weak legs. Came around to her side of the bed. Took the book from her hands and looked at it — confused. Gave it back and returned to his pacing, his body rigid with something — tension, fear, anger? She made herself as small as she possibly could, she says, heart racing, praying the rage would pass, heartbroken because in that instant she knew he did not know her, devastated because in that instant she knew that he could hurt her. And she felt total isolation.

My father tried to open the door but couldn't and she continued to sit as quietly as possible, trying to be invisible. He eventually got back in bed, but she would not sleep that night. We didn't find out about the incident until the morning — it was not my mother's habit to call us in the middle of the night. By then she had come to the conclusion that staying alone in a locked room with my father was no longer safe and she would move into my old bedroom. It took a little longer to convince her that she could not continue to stay awake virtually all night, every night — now sitting in my bed and listening for every movement in the room down the hall as she frantically completed crossword puzzle after crossword puzzle. No one knew how long my father would live, or what the next day would bring. But it was obvious my mother would collapse before too many more nights, unless she allowed someone else to stay awake as she slept.

While overnight home care was being arranged, Peter spent the nights there. He'd make a futile attempt to sleep for a few hours after work in the evening then leave for their house at about 11:00 p.m. to spend the hours from midnight to 6:00 a.m. sitting in a living room chair with his book. He'd return home in the morning in time to shower and go to work.

The patterns of our days and nights were ruled by the psyche of a man who no longer had any idea he was controlling anything or anyone. There was an intense sense of asynchronicity, as if everything and everyone was out of alignment. At times I would find myself sitting behind my desk at the office, furiously trying to meet the latest deadline, and feel an overwhelming sense of absurdity. Absurdity that things like news releases and magazines must still be completed. Absurdity that the calendar and the clock controlled anything, even hours of work. Nothing in life seemed to fit.

It was somewhere around this point that I went to my employer. I told him my father's condition seemed to be deteriorating in unpredictable ways and at unpredictable times, and there was an increasing likelihood that in the weeks to come, until a space was found for him in a long-term care facility, I might have to leave at any moment of the day. The individuals who might answer my phone were told that if my mother called, I should be interrupted, even if she insisted there was no need. Michelle mixed special kindness with efficiency, helping me meet the demands of the office with an air of normality. Michelle is one of the first people to hear me say *when you think it can't get any worse, it does.* She listened when I needed to talk; she talked when I needed to listen. She took care of Kenneth in the evening when going to the house with us became too much for him. She helped me cope.

She knew where I spent my lunch hours and how I would sometimes close the door to my office for a few moments when I returned. She knew where I went after work and why I would be so tired in the morning. She knew the changes in my father during those last two weeks...

I am there now, in that house. I can close my eyes and see how things had changed and I can feel the racing of my heart, the pressure building in my head.

My father is in his pajamas, he has refused to get dressed again. He is pacing back and forth, staggering really, and we are with him. Me and our neighbor from across the street, another Pat. We are trying to get close enough to hold his arm, steady him, but he won't let us.

Pat didn't wait for my mother to call, he was there because he knew she needed him. My father needed him. He remembered even the smallest of past kindnesses and repaid them more than 1,000-fold — he and his wife Nora and their daughter Leanne.

By the time I would arrive in the evening, my mother would desperately need a break from my father's fight and we'd take over, trying to give her some space perhaps to eat or at least have a cup of tea. We would walk back and forth, the hardwood floor cold under our feet. Wherever my father went, we followed. When he sat in the bedroom we sat with him. When he tried to go out the door to head downstairs, we would block him. When it was time for his medication, we would guide him to the kitchen table.

When I close my eyes, I can see him stagger to the table and push our hands away when we tried to steady him into his seat. I can see the head bend forward, his face just inches from the bowl of porridge, his limp grey hair falling into his confused eyes. The fight with my mother as he tried to push away the spoon that contains his nightly mediation mixed in with jam. The effort to move the spoon from his bowl to his mouth and the clumsy swing of his hand if anyone tried to help.

Sometimes all motion would stop and his head would simply hang there for seconds at a time. Sometimes my mother would gently smooth the hair back from his eyes. Sometimes she couldn't touch him. Sometimes he'd look up at us, eyes narrowed in suspicion. Sometimes the only expression would be no expression at all. And from the moment he realized that there was medication hidden in his food he would either refuse to eat, or spit out the food as soon as he felt the pill. It would be late at night by now, perhaps 10:30 or 11:00. We'd be trying to time the medication so he would get at least a little sleep. But he did not want the medicine, was suspicious of it perhaps. When he realized we would keep trying to give him his pills if we were aware he'd refused to take them, he actually became skilled at hiding the medicine until we were out of sight then spitting it out or taking it from his mouth and putting it somewhere. Funny how he retained that piece of his awareness. And so sleep, or what little there was, usually came because he was too exhausted to push himself even an inch further, and even then it usually took all three of us to get him into bed. After that, on a good night, we'd just have to wait for the home-care worker to arrive for the shift change, and Pat and I would go home, while my mother tried to sleep in my small bed.

Around this time my mother bought a new chair for my father, a recliner. Expecting the medication to calm him so that he'd be content to sit during the waking hours of the day, a call was made to a furniture store and a description of what was needed given — my mother wouldn't leave the house to choose it herself. A friend went to the store to take a look at the chair and delivery was arranged. My father was meant to be comfortable in this chair, much more comfortable than he appeared to be on the occasions that he sat in his chair or on the couch, his head falling backwards with no support. The new chair was moved into the living room, and the one it replaced moved to the dining room to stay there for a few days before it would be moved to the basement. But I don't think my father ever sat in the recliner, not even once. Sometimes he'd walk to the old chair that was now so out of place in the dining room and try to sit there for a few seconds — a resting place on his journey. Instead the recliner became the place where the home-care workers sat. Where my mother sat. Where I sat or Kenneth sat or Peter sat.

These were the nights when my father first bent over to the floor in his bedroom, fell the short distance to a sitting position, and wasn't strong enough to get up. These were the nights when he swung out at us from his sitting position if we tried to help him and swore at us if we didn't. These were the nights when Pat and I laughed and chastised my father for remembering so many foul words when he could barely speak any others. They're vivid, the images. My father in his pajamas sliding along the floor at the foot of his bed. Muttering. Stumbling to get up. Kicking and swinging if we got too near. All kinds of strength to push us away but none to support his own thinning weight, his mind frustrated enough to be angry but unable to control his body. Anger and frustration the likes of which I'd never seen. Anguish and pain. Such intense anguish and pain.

Peter was out of town when these episodes began and didn't return until after they'd finished. My mother couldn't bear to be in the room when they occurred — she had seen so much already — and so she stayed in other rooms with people who had come to help, including a sister who had arrived for a short visit but stayed when she saw the situation. While Pat and I tried to keep my father from hurting himself or someone else, tried to catch his head before it hit the corner of a desk, or his leg before it jammed into the edge of the bed. Covered him when he curled in a tiny ball on the hard, cold floor and somehow slept.

It was on one of these nights my father would say his last lucid words. After the hours of pacing and then sliding along the floor, after the late night supper of rolled oats and the struggle with the medication, my mother, Pat and I led an exhausted man to his bed. He'd become gentler than we'd seen him in days. Cooperative almost. We helped him sit, raised his legs to ease them onto the mattress, fixed his pillows behind his head. My mother leaned over and brought the bed covers up to tuck under his chin. His eyes were already closed, but before she was able to speak her usual *Good Night and God Bless,* he opened them. Bright and clear they were as he smiled my father's smile and looked deeply into her eyes, aware and awake. *I love you,* he said. Then he closed his eyes and immediately slept.

My mother maintains she would not have believed what she had heard or seen that night if we hadn't been there to tell her it was so. Indeed, we would not have believed what we had heard or seen if it hadn't been for the fact that we all shared exactly the same memory. But daughter and friend were intensely grateful for this bittersweet moment.

It was on one of these nights that Kenneth spent the evening across the street from my parent's house with Pat's daughter Leanne, playing Monopoly I think. We called him home after his grandfather had settled and Kenneth sat in the new chair, the energetic tale of his evening becoming quiet as his brow furrowed, his face paled. *I don't feel well,* he said. We got home as fast as we could, before his stomach began to rebel against his own emotions. I sat with him through the wee hours of the morning, made the trip from the bed to the bathroom over and over again. Cooled the cloth for his forehead. Held his hand. Rubbed his head. Told him it was OK when he'd say he was sorry for getting sick. *I'm sorry Mommy.*

I didn't think very much as I sat on the floor by my child's bed that night. And yet I felt my small son's anguish as if it was my own, felt how little I had left to give him, how little I could do to help him cope with his grandfather's deterioration and the speed at which it was occurring. When Kenneth dozed, I let my head fall forward into my hands. Eventually, when he had been sleeping peacefully for some time, the intensity of his own exhaustion being eased, I tiredly shuffled to my own room and fell asleep.

The next day, as word began to travel about how sick my father really was, people arrived at my mother's house. When I got there in the afternoon, I found my mother sitting on the couch, my father leaning against her in his pajamas. She was holding his hand, rubbing it. His head hung low, his chin resting on his chest, his hair falling in disarray over his face. Body so thin, face so grey, a shadow of my father. His brother and sister-in-law looked at me in shock.

We didn't know how sick he was, they said. *We had no idea. We would have come more often, done something.*

It's OK, I answered. *This part... it's been very fast.*

He'd been pacing, as usual, my mother at his side, but when his legs had begun to buckle under him, she'd managed to get him to the couch. He fell into the sitting position with her by his side, and for as long as he slept she would not move. As darkness came and visitors left, my father began his pacing again and his sliding along the floor. He managed to get himself stuck between the desk and the bed in his room. Such anger. Such anguish. He would not let us touch him but we couldn't leave him. We carried on a running conversation, Pat and I. Talking to each other. *You're making sense tonight, aren't you? But you're not being very nice, are you?*

I had to go home, I knew. I had to take Kenneth home and let him get to bed early enough so he would sleep, so he wouldn't get sick again. *I cannot leave,* I thought, *and yet I cannot stay.* I went to the bathroom. I went to my bedroom. Closed the door. Sat at the foot of my bed and sobbed. *I can't watch this* — my thoughts. *I can't watch this anymore. I can't do this anymore.* Until I grew angry with myself for such utter foolishness. *All you have to do is sit there,* I chastised myself. *Your suffering is insignificant and if you can do anything to help your father, anything, you get in there and you do it.* And I returned to the room for a while longer. We couldn't get my father up before I eventually did have to leave, but he had quieted a little by then and Pat would stay with him. Help my mother get him into bed.

Dear Pat. So kind.

Once he lay down that night, my father did not get up again. Pat says that shortly after I left, it was as if my father experienced a momentary but sharp pain while he sat slumped on the floor. After that he became quieter, no longer violent but also unable to find any strength to help the people who were now able to reach under his arms to lift him and carry him to the bed. They thought he had finally worn himself out and perhaps it was as simple as that.

There was no more wandering this night. There was no medication fight. There were no more words. Except the words of prayer that the suffering of this man be somehow eased.

We think we know how much we can take.

We think we know

when we have reached a limit

and can go no further.

But we do not know until we have tried

because not trying is unacceptable.

26

Sometimes We Forget

On Monday morning we get ready for work and school as we would during any other week. Except it isn't just any other week. Kenneth's grandfather is gravely ill and the tiredness in this young boy's eyes acts as a dark reminder of the impact it's having on him. But it isn't until the evening that I remember to ask Kenneth a question I should have asked weeks earlier: *Does your teacher know what's going on with Dick?* I feel a deep sense of shame because I had not thought of that sooner.

No, he says, *I haven't said anything.*

You should tell him, I point out.

I don't want to talk about it.

Do you want me to write him a note?

Yes please.

And so I do.

Peter is finally home from the squash tournament that had been arranged months before for the team he was coaching. I have detailed for him the changes in my father over the past five days, but he is still visibly shocked when he first sees him lying in the bed, semi-conscious. There is a look on his face I have never witnessed before, as if he is seeing the past and the future and struggling with what he knows he must accept in the present. He is deeply affected by my father's moans, the sharp intakes of breath and unidentifiable mutterings. His brow is tense. But within minutes, he is in control. He is calming my mother, he is changing my father's diaper and helping move him in the bed to minimize the chance of bed sores. I do not watch this process; my mother insists I not see this happen and so it is now my turn to leave the room. And I do not learn until sometime later that Peter talks to my father while he cares for him, quietly and gently. That he tells my father he can rest if he wants to, he can relax, he can finally let go, because he will take care of us now. He tells my father that he does not have to suffer any longer. Pat, as always, is there.

I am also trying to finish the monthly publication for teachers that I edit, even though it seems as if the normal things in the world should have stopped, and I go to the office the next morning thinking about Kenneth and knowing what it is I have to write. I start, for once, with a title — *Sometimes We Forget.*

For the past six weeks or so my father, who has been suffering from Alzheimer's for a number of years, has been deteriorating severely and steadily. The last seven days (I am writing this article on October 27) have been particularly difficult, and his ability to communicate has all but disappeared. Alzheimer's is a horrible, devastating, heartbreaking disease.

I tell you this not because it's easy to write or talk about, and definitely not because I think it appropriate to write editorials on one's private sadnesses. But it occurred to me only last night, that while my husband and I have tried to ensure our son's home environment is as sane and supportive as possible as he tries to cope with the sadness and uncertainties of his days and nights, I never thought to tell his teacher, the one person who is probably more responsible than anyone else right now, for giving him something to focus on, for keeping his mind busy and for making him laugh.

I'm sorry, Mr. Collins. I should have thought of telling you sooner. I should have warned you that if you see sadness in my son's eyes, or hear irritation and frustration in his voice, it may have nothing to do with you, or school, or his studies. And everything to do with the "buddy" he has slowly and painfully lost over the last five years.

There's a lesson in this, as there is in most of life's struggles. As parents, we send our children to you each and everyday, and we trust you with their minds, their hearts and their souls. But we all too often forget the kind of support, even basic information, we can, indeed, should provide you with. You see, while there's lots of talk about parent-school partnerships (and this talk is very important), I now realize I've fallen into the trap of seeing the partnerships more as group to group, institution to institution, not individual to individual, parent to teacher.

I'm glad I thought of it last night, though, and I'm glad I wrote a note explaining the situation this morning. Now I'm going to see if there's some way... I can help remind other parents to tell their children's teachers when life gets difficult. Help you do what we trust you to do. In the meantime, if you could write, call, fax or e-mail me with the kind of things you really need to know, it would help me with the list I've started. I just wish I could tell my dad about it.

(Reprinted from *The Newfoundland & Labrador Teachers' Association Bulletin*, November 1994.)

I ask Michelle to read this for me, tell me if it's too personal, if it's inappropriate. She goes to her desk then comes back to my office with tears in her eyes. She tells me not to change anything, to use it. And she quietly closes the door when she sees a tear begin to travel down my cheek, leaving me to my own thoughts.

I cry for my father, in the next few minutes. I cry for my son, for the loss he is enduring. I cry for myself, for my failure to be as good a mother to him as I should have been, for not seeing something that now seemed so obvious. I cry for what has happened and what is yet to come.

By lunch time I am at the house again, any evidence of tears having long since been repaired and a morning's work between my feelings and the midday activities. I help my mother spoon some food and liquid into my father — a slow process as we half prop him up on his pillows, half hold him up. For a man who looks skeleton-like, he is amazingly heavy. Although he is barely conscious of our presence, there is some reaction and mostly he is able to swallow. I sit by his bed, listening to the noises he is making, watching the covers move up and down as he breathes, watching his anguish as he tries to move but finds he is unable to.

This is the pattern of the final week. People come and go from my mother's house; we feed my father as best we can, even though late in the week he spits the liquid out at us across the bed. First weakly, then with increasing strength, so that it streams through the air in a carefully formed arc and lands on my sweater. It's as if he's telling me something. It's as if he's saying *don't give me anything else. I don't want anything else. Just leave me alone and let me die. It is over. The fight is done. I want to be free.* I feel this from him so strongly it's as if he has spoken clearly and loudly.

Sometimes it seems as if he is peaceful, the breath flowing in and out easily. I feel this is when his spirit is finding a way to free itself and he is floating perhaps a little outside the prison of his body and mind. When spirit and body reunite, there are moans again. He is shrinking before our eyes in the bed and yet we still do not know if he will live for days, weeks, months or even years. I, for one, cannot look beyond the next hour, sometimes the next minute. The body is his prison and he is in agony.

His clothing is changed frequently. The pharmacist-owner at the drugstore where we've shopped for as long as I can remember — Parkdale, it's called — takes the time himself to come to us with hospital gowns. He picks out ones in colors he knows my father would like best, and drives to my mother's house. We are surprised and deeply touched that he does not send the delivery person, but takes the time to come to us himself. He will not come into the house, staying in the driveway for a few moments to talk. He knows it is no longer possible to entertain guests and he knows we would try to do so.

The priest comes to visit, the doctor. My father exists in a semi-coma. My mother washes him and tries to keep him hydrated. She worries constantly that she is not doing enough to ease his discomfort. She sits beside him on the edge of the bed. She holds his hand. When she smooths the hair back that has fallen into his eyes, he no longer struggles against her touch. Peter and Pat change him and move him again. The hospital gowns are removed, cleaned and replaced.

Peter and I go to work everyday. Kenneth goes to school. My father's immobility makes certain things easier — I am no longer wondering whether he will harm himself or my mother. The house always has two or three or four or five people with my mother. The kettle is always boiling. Food is being prepared, and sometimes even eaten. Relatives come to visit and sit by my father's bed for a time, having their own kinds of conversations. My mother and I describe the path of the illness and the recent weeks in particular. He seems to be in less pain, now, we tell them.

When we aren't in the bedroom, we are close by in the living room. My mother's sister Sheila is a bright star that shines and makes us laugh as she helps us share memories of years gone by. I see Hayes when I'm running errands. *I've been going to call you,* I tell her, *but I just haven't been able to get to it.* She is not angry at the delay — she just hugs me and says she'll go see him. And she says call me if you need anything, anything at all.

I talk frequently on the phone with both my brothers. *Is he dying?* one asks. What can I say? The answer is yes but I have no idea of when. *Should I come?* Their struggles are different than mine because they are dealing with distance. But they struggle just as much or more.

The weekend is welcome. Sheila had extended her visit as long as she could but must return home. Another aunt, Margaret, is scheduled to arrive on Monday — she had planned to visit during the summer but told my mother she would come when she really needed her, when she was alone. I talk to Margaret on Saturday night as I sit in my father's new recliner, conscious of the silence in his room. *Your father is not suffering as much, now,* she tells me. *There are many people gathered around him, and his spirit, it is travelling.* I believe her.

It is late when I leave for home, but not as late as it has been on other nights. Friends and family have visited. We have chatted. But now the house is empty except for me, my mother and the nurse who will spend the night. My father is quiet, my mother needs sleep. I go to my father's side, look down at the gaunt and ravaged face. I slowly smooth his grey hair back over his dry, leathery forehead, rest my hand there for a moment, then bend down to kiss him.

Have a good rest now, I whisper. *I love you.*

Focused so intensely on one part of our lives

it is all too easy to neglect another,

to be blind to the obvious.

We are, after all, human.

27

A Spirit Set Free

Sometime near 4:00 a.m. on Sunday morning, the nurse wakes my mother. He tells her my father's breathing has changed and that she should go to him right away. She is by his side within seconds.

Minutes later our phone rings and Peter moves from the bed to the dresser across the room to answer it before the second ring. *Your mother says you'd better come now,* he tells me quietly as I sit up in the bed, shivering and clutching the comforter to my chin. *No, he isn't dead but she says you should come right away.*

My mother holds my father's hand. She recognizes the breathing pattern — she has witnessed it many times over the years in dying patients. She knows that it often lasts for hours, but she has never seen anyone recover from it. She says the *Our Father* aloud as she holds my father's hand and his prayer beads. She kisses my father and tells him she loves him. And then he dies. Just as simply as that, after all the struggle, he stops breathing without any additional anguish or pain. Alone with the woman he loves.

At about 4:30 a.m. on the morning of October 30th, 1994 my father's death, after all, is a simple thing.

I have dressed quickly and driven to the house in the dark. My hands are shaking, my entire body is shaking, and I'm thankful that there's no traffic, that the drive is less than ten minutes. I pull into the driveway and run into the house. I am not thinking. As I walk into the

living room, Pat and Nora are there to meet me. My mother comes
from the bedroom as soon as she hears me arrive.

Is he... gone? I ask. There is the briefest pause.

I think someone nods, or perhaps I know the answer before I ask.
A sob erupts from me even though I do not expect it, had not thought
I would have any tears for this moment. I do not know exactly why I
am crying, if it is in relief for an end to the suffering or in pain because
of the immense loss of this early morning and all the years that have
passed or for both those reasons. But I slow the tears with a number of
deep, silent breaths, calm myself and walk to the bedroom to see him.

There are a multitude of images and feelings from that morning.
There is an intense sense of peace, of the end of an interminable road
of suffering. There is a sense of freedom. There is a new silence.

I had always been frightened by the prospect of seeing someone
who had died. Given any choice, I would not go to wakes and on
the rare occasion they were unavoidable, I would not sleep for days
afterwards. But I am not afraid of my father. I kiss his forehead as
I had the evening before; I stand and look down at him, and the
emptiness of the body in the bed. It somehow does not seem real as I
take up my position in the chair beside his bed and watch him. I have
no idea how long I sit there, then I think I see the blankets that cover
my father move. It is an odd game my mind is playing on me, an odd
game perhaps born of all those years of watching. They do not really
move, of course; it is the change in the light as the day moves more
fully towards dawn. But for an instant I want to cry out — *look, he's not
dead.*

Nora is sitting with me, keeping me company. We are talking
a little, though I don't know about what. All of a sudden, on this
otherwise still morning, as dawn arrives, the curtains in the room
billow. It's a huge, flowing movement and it startles us. We look at
each other. There is a sense of joyous freedom in that movement of

air, a joy we cannot explain even though we both sense it.

I think my dad just left, I smile. *Where do you think he'll go first?*

My father is finally free — that is the overwhelming thought in my parent's house that morning and with it comes a deep sense of relief. Death at the end of an Alzheimer's struggle does that. Death is the freeing of a spirit.

At some point I have called Peter and he will have the task of telling Kenneth. My mother and I start making the other calls. I knew he was dead, some of them tell us. Sheila, the aunt who had returned to her home the day before had woken moments after his death, noticed the snow outside her window and wondered when the call would come. My brother Steve's ill wife, Glenna, having suffered through an unusually bad period, was overcome in the earliest hour of the morning with a sense of peace, an ease in suffering and a deep sense that my father was with her in the room. She'd looked at my brother, told him to remember the time, and ask her later about my father. Our friend, Pat, who'd been so kind to both my mother and father, said she'd seen him the night before. He'd been in her living room, wearing a suit, which was significant because she'd never seen him in a suit and had wanted to. Said he'd looked so well and his smile had filled her with hope and peace.

Of course, we said, if my father was free he would go to all of these places and see all of these people. He would show those who were willing to see and hear that he was with them again. He would offer thanks and peace and hope and an ease in suffering.

The doctor comes to the house and prepares the death certificate. He does not have to do this, but he makes the effort for my father and for my mother. My mother approves the ordering of a partial autopsy, telling the doctor that my father's children will need to know the final diagnosis of the dementia. She is right, of course, though I am completely certain in that moment that I will not suffer my father's fate. They talk for a time, and then he leaves. At some point I move my car from our driveway across the street to Pat's so there will be room for a hearse.

The funeral director arrives around 7:00 a.m. It is the same person my mother had spoken with a number of weeks before, when she'd called the funeral home to make some preliminary inquiries. I meet him as he steps through the doorway from the porch into the kitchen and moves into the dining room. He is wearing the official uniform of his profession, something I had not known to expect, and the professional, business-like approach cloaked in a gentle and kind mannerism and voice, is a relief. I do not even know how tense I still am until I feel an overwhelming relief that there is someone here who can take care of my father.

My mother takes him to the body. Somehow a stretcher materializes in the living room. I am told to go downstairs. *No I want to stay.* But my mother insists I go downstairs because she does not want me to hold among the other memories of my father, one of him being lifted, naked except for his diaper, nothing more than skin and bones, onto the stretcher and removed from the house. I still want to stay, but I allow Nora to lead me downstairs and we sit on the couch together, she holding my hands. My mother does not know that despite her efforts, I will hold in my mind an imagined vision of my father's last move from his bedroom to the living room.

I had seen my father taken away on a stretcher, through the same door, many years before. It was the day Steve had seen my stricken face, and as only he could, had taken the moment to turn to me and tweak my chin, smile at me and gently say, he'll be alright. Steve is not in the house this morning and there are no such words to offer. I am experiencing both the past and the present as I run upstairs in time to stand beside my mother and see the hearse pull out of the driveway. We stay there for a moment, arms around each other, without any idea of exactly what to do next. But even as the body is being taken, even as my father is leaving his house for the last time, I feel the deep sense that I have my father back, that I can talk to him again and he will hear me. That I can seek his help and that he will be there to give it to me. That I can walk again with him on Bellevue Beach, drive with him beside me in the car, feel his presence in my life, and be deeply happy he is there.

No, there is no illusion that he is still alive; but there is the certainty that his spirit is with us. That it is travelling and flying and rejoicing in the freedom of being released from the body. That after so much suffering, he is whole again and happy again. So long unable to communicate with my father, so long lonely, I feel a quiet joy from a new and different connection. And so, as the hours pass, I look at people and tell them: *Today I got my father back.*

A body dies

but can you ever really accept death

when the air is filled with the joy of

a spirit set free.

28
To The End

During the twenty-four hours that follow my father's final moments in his house, we are focused only on the things that need to be done in preparation for a funeral.

I tell my mother I will take her to the funeral home that afternoon, to the 2:00 appointment that had been arranged, and then I head home to shower and change. Kenneth and Peter meet me as I open the door. Peter has already told our neighbors. That is a relief.

After I clean up and try unsuccessfully to eat, I pick up my mother. She is concerned about what she should wear. It is easy for me to pull work clothes from the closet, but she has been house-bound for so long she feels as though she hardly remembers how to dress.

There's no problem preparing my father's clothes. They've already been chosen — the black blazer and grey pants he'd worn on precious few occasions when the illness still allowed him to attend, if not always enjoy, events like weddings or other special celebrations. As for the shirt and tie, I'd bought them for him during the summer, driven by some unseen force. My emotions were mixed, looking through shirts and ties for something he would like, something he would have chosen himself or worn with pride because I had chosen it for him. Something he would never really see. These are waiting in plastic. It's a little harder to find a photo, one that would show how my father looked before the illness, the particular style of his hair. But my mother finds one and places it in her purse.

The meeting that afternoon teaches me things. It teaches me that you can be just as concerned about how a person is treated after he is dead as you were before. I had not known that. It teaches me that there are such things as the perfect flowers, the perfect casket. You can choose this type, we're told, but it isn't exactly waterproof. Or you can choose this one; water will not penetrate it. I would not have thought it mattered, until those words. Until I think how I could not bear to imagine my father's body resting in a place where cold, maybe muddy water could seep in around him.

I know it is only his body, I say, *but we must not give his spirit any reason to fret because his body is resting in water. We must keep him as dry and safe as possible.* So we choose green, because of his preference for green Land Rovers, and the copper model that will not leak, so he is not reminded of a dark and cold ocean and a terribly lonely life raft. So his physical remains can be as safe and warm as possible.

There is a book I am given, for a child to say goodbye to a grandfather. I take it for Kenneth. We have talked a great deal about my father by the time we leave — about a man who loved unconditionally, who never judged, who was gentle and kind. It is difficult knowing he is there now, that he will be alone all through the night, that we will not see him until late the following morning.

People start arriving at my mother's house early in the evening. I help her choose the clothes she will wear for the next few days — she does not think she will be able to make choices each morning. She has called her hair stylist to arrange a special appointment. I take her and sit in a nearby chair, watching the skillful work with the blow dryer and curling iron. The shop is the only sign of activity in a building not accustomed to seeing light until Monday morning. Like many things that day, it is dreamlike. My head is pounding and my stomach is churning, but I am somehow holding off the grip of exhaustion.

I am finally at home and in bed sometime around midnight. *The world is changed, nothing will ever be quite the same* — these thoughts carry me into a surprisingly deep sleep. In the morning, as unbelievable as it seems, I have to report for jury duty. The summons had come weeks before, and the fact that my father was suffering from Alzheimer's was not sufficient enough reason to be excused. So at 8:30 in the morning, I am lining up along a cold downtown street. I talk with the woman in front of me. She is a writer, I learn weeks later when I see her on a newscast talking about her book. That morning all I learn is that her father had also died of Alzheimer's.

There is no coincidence in this world, I think. *I could have stood by anyone at all, and here I am standing by a woman who has been where I am today, who helps without even knowing it.*

I eventually make it to the place where I must explain if there's any reason I can't serve. *My father,* I tell them. *He died yesterday morning. The wake starts today and the funeral is on Wednesday.* The official tells me to leave. I don't even have to show the death certificate. The truth of my words must have been etched on my face.

Kenneth is at school — he has chosen to be there for at least part of the day. He needs the company of his friends, the support of his teacher. He needs to tell them what has happened. Peter and I need to find some clothes for him to wear to the funeral. The pants we find will be too long, but I can hem them before Wednesday. There's a vest that will suit his white shirt. And there's a tie. We are home in time to change for the opening of the wake.

Changed, ready to see my father again, we go to the funeral home. We are led to the locked room and allowed to enter. My father is there, lying peacefully in his green casket, looking so much like my father that my eyes fill with tears. *Thank you,* I whisper across the room to the funeral director who is standing in the doorway. *Thank you for doing this for my father.*

The people start to come — so many familiar faces, so many strange ones. *I'm sorry about your father,* they say. *Thank you,* I answer. *He's free now.* There are hugs; there are tears; there are smiles and laughs and the exchange of old stories.

Everyone in my mother's and father's families come for the funeral — all living brothers and sisters, and some cousins I have not seen in years come from both near and far away. Some stay with us throughout the long day and night, others come and go. People bring food and drink. Rik arrives Monday night, Steve late on Tuesday. I cannot eat and sometimes the effort just to stay standing becomes too great and I find a place to sit for a moment. Peter and Kenneth are my strength. Michelle and Hayes are my strength.

Certain things stand out — Rik not being able to go into the room to see my father, and finally being helped in by cousins who support him. Steve asking for a few minutes alone with him when he arrives at the funeral home for the first time on Wednesday morning. Kenneth writing a farewell to his grandfather and placing it with him in the casket. People reading his words and crying. Hayes bringing the single white rose her little daughter Amy had insisted she buy for *Grandpa Barron,* because he'd look out of place with all the other angels if the rose was any other colour. The aroma of the flowers. Kenneth meeting and chatting with cousins he's never met before. Standing beside the casket and touching his grandfather's hand. Peter's arm around my shoulder. Feelings of guilt over wakes I have not attended in the past because now I realize how precious the words of comfort and presence of sympathizers are. Trying to understand what was being said about the funeral mass by the representatives of the church. Trying to eat but being unable to do so. Being encouraged to leave the room for a break, but wanting to stay by my father. Feeling as if time is passing both too slowly and too quickly. Thinking perhaps the world outside must have become perfectly still.

We close the room Monday and Tuesday night at 10:00. I alter the skirt that I'm to wear with my black suit — the lengths have changed since I made it. I cut and hem Kenneth's pants. On Wednesday morning I locate the hat I am going to wear; it is dented from sitting too long in an awkward position on the shelf in the closet of the spare room. And so I put it back. I slip into my heeled pumps and put flat shoes in the car — I'll need them for the cemetery.

When we arrive at the funeral home, my mother wants to know where my hat is. I think I tell her it doesn't look right with the suit, or that it is dented, I don't remember. I feel that she isn't pleased. I have let her down somehow. I walk into the empty room next to my father's and collapse into a chair. I have not really cried since that brief period on Sunday morning, but I cry now. Peter and Kenneth have followed me. They hold me and shelter me from others who have come to see what's happened. They ask for privacy and close the door. They tell me what I know already but need to hear — *Your dad wouldn't mind that you don't have a hat today. He wouldn't mind a bit. You aren't letting him down.* All I can think is that today is the day my father is being buried and my mother is worried about my hat. My mother, I will learn later, doesn't even remember her question and is appalled she would ever ask it. *Mom, it's OK. Really it is.*

There are prayers. Everyone gathers in the room with my father. I am at the far end, with Peter on one side and Kenneth on the other. Rik and Steve are on either side of my mother. I do not take my eyes from my father. When the prayers finish, the funeral director says he's closing the casket. People begin to leave. Rik says he cannot watch this and moves outside. My mother follows to comfort him. Steve leaves also. Peter and Kenneth look at me. I have not budged. *I can't leave him,* I say, *not until I see that everything is done correctly.* He would not leave me. I will not leave him. And so the door closes and Peter, Kenneth and I stand guard over my father, tightly holding each other's hands, and say another goodbye as the casket is closed and sealed. I don't remember if I cried when it happened, but I am crying now.

My mother wants to know why I didn't come out when everyone else did and so I explain. Then there is the process of getting the casket from the downstairs room to the hearse; the pall bearers are gathered and organized. Things are explained. They are a solemn group; they do my father a great honour. Then as if he is watching all the solemnity and sadness with the mischievous twinkle in his eye, the morning that had been grey but rain free changes and the skies open up. There is no hope for the people trying to get from the door of the funeral home to their cars. We laugh as we sit in the car watching — *you're doing this aren't you dad? You figured it was time enough for a joke.*

The weather cooperates by the time we reach the church. The parking lot is packed. I cannot even explain how happy I am for my father, that he can look on from whatever location he has chosen and see that so many people have taken the time to show their respects. He would not have expected it, but we wanted it for him. *Thank you,* I whisper, willing every person inside the church to feel my gratitude.

We are organized into whatever order is appropriate and follow the casket down the aisle. Steve and Rik are on either side of my mother; Peter and Kenneth with me. Rik will not be speaking during the ceremony — he knows he will be too emotional. I have a reading, though the delivery is uncertain and I am only able to get started after I imagine my father standing beside me. Steve finishes with his own special tribute, not permitted during a Catholic ceremony but sometimes permitted at the end. He has practiced it over and over again, he tells me later, so that he will make it through without too many tears. He talks about things familiar to the people who knew and loved my father. I am laughing and crying at the same time. I do not remember the readings; I do not remember the hymns; I only remember the intensity of the feeling in the church. Then it is time to leave. We follow my father to the parking lot. We share embraces with people who offer them, thankful for their strength and presence. We thank people for coming.

There is an honour guard at the cemetery. The area is roofed by a temporary awning and it is blowing in the wind. But the skies have cleared and the sun is even beginning to peak through the clouds. The casket is resting on strong straps, waiting to be lowered. I can hardly imagine my father rests there now. Forever.

Peter and Kenneth are by my side, my mother standing again with Rik and Steve. Close friends, cousins, aunts and uncles. I look across at Hayes and Michelle with tears in my eyes; they will stay with us through everything. The prayers are said. *The Last Post* is played in honour of my father's war service and I look up at Peter to see tears streaming down his face. He brushes them away. Nothing needs to be said. People start to move away, except, again, for the three of us. We stay back to find out what happens next. The casket will be lowered into the ground. Sometimes this happens after the family leaves, we're told, because it can be hard to watch. We will wait; we will see the process through to its conclusion. We will not leave my father until we know he is resting safely. My mother has rejoined us, and Steve, I think. Some others are also close by. The funeral director turns to my son. *Would you like to do it,* he asks. *Would you like to help lower your grandfather?* Kenneth looks surprised and startled for a moment, then nods seriously. *Just press this button,* he's told. He bends over, presses a button as instructed, and the casket lowers slowly into the ground. *Rest now dad,* I think. *Be free and happy now.* We gently toss a deep red rose to lie on the dark green, shiny casket. After one last look we turn together and walk away.

Kenneth, when he sits in the car, finally begins to cry. Such heartwrenching sobs. He has not really cried until now, when the goodbye seems so final. He cries and cries and cries, all the way to my mother's house for the traditional post-funeral gathering, a flood of emotions released. We stay there until mid-afternoon, until there are no more words left, no more energy left. Until the need to be anywhere else is too great to ignore. Then we leave for home.

After three days I had come to realize the importance of the wake and funeral process, about its role as a transition and a closure. I was glad for the bridge from past to present, but I also knew that whatever feeling normal had been, it would take longer than this to return.

You honoured us each and every day

by your presence and your care.

And I will honour you

I will celebrate you

and I will love you forever.

29
Standing Tall

As I reflect on the days, weeks and months that followed my father's death, I honestly can't tell you whether I grieved as would be expected after the loss of someone as precious as my father had been, though I suspect I didn't. I think, if anything, the life he had led, the suffering he had experienced, the months and years of no recognition, had ultimately ensured I was ready to let him go. I did wonder what it would have been like to come home one day to find he had died suddenly — in a car accident or from a heart attack perhaps — and the imagined shock was almost incomprehensible. I don't know how I would have recovered, as a child or even as a young woman, had I been faced with his sudden removal from my life. I would have raged at the unfairness of so good a man being taken so quickly. I would have been lost. But after ten years of watching the slow changes and the final months of absolute anguish, I could not wish him alive and in such intense pain.

You did not leave until you knew we were ready to let you go, I would think. *And I will not do you the dishonour of wishing you were here physically, just because it would be a delight to sit with you to watch a movie, to hear you laugh with Kenneth over some shared joke, to watch you skip stones over the waves at Bellevue Beach.*

I missed my father, I missed the hugs I could give him, but I was happy for his freedom and felt his presence so strongly through my days that I knew and know he is still with me, still one of the greatest strengths in my life.

There were adjustments. Concern shifted from both my father and mother's wellbeing, solely to my mother. What would happen, I wondered, after the visitors had left and her house was empty? Afraid of being home alone for as long as I could remember, it didn't seem possible that she would be able to sleep even one night alone in her home. Exhausted beyond comprehension, would she find a way to get the rest she needed? Never one to cook meals only for herself, would she eat anything beside toast and tea? Never one to accept help or advice from anyone, was there any way to reach her?

My mother's life had been completely driven by the need to care for my father from the time she had retired — with that purpose removed, the pattern of her days was drastically changed. Her anguish was not short-lived; her adjustments were difficult to make. Indeed, I could not compare my own life or my own adjustments with hers. As she would point out, I had lost my father, not my husband. I wasn't really alone; she was.

People have different ways of coping; people are willing to accept different levels of help. And so my mother is, in her own way, finding her path in this world without my father. And I am trying to do as I think he would have wanted — allow her to do as she believes is right, support, encourage as necessary, never judge, and most of all, wish her every happiness in whatever path she chooses. Try to offer smiles in the times they seem impossible. And be thankful on those days — now increasingly frequent — when her voice sounds so like it did when I was a young girl and she was happy.

In the meantime, my father's presence in my life is as strong as ever, his influence no less important. His laughter is alive in our hearts when we watch movies we know would light his eyes. His habit of continually caring for his house, and yard and fence is alive in my action when I walk to my fence with a bucket of stain and a brush, and stroke up and down as he taught me, when Peter and Kenneth mow and rake and arrange rock gardens, when we plant roses under our window. His ability to be happy with what life dealt him and not to look elsewhere with envy, lives on because we strive, each and every day, to be like him. We try to do as he did.

Now, when there is a question I cannot answer, when there is help I need, I can ask my father. Sometimes there are stargazer lilies. Sometimes there are answers where none seemed possible. Sometimes there is just an unexpected smile. Sometimes I look at my son and feel with all my heart, my thanks that there was time for him to know his grandfather, and smile at the honour he does him in the way he dresses, the pocket he uses for carrying his pens, but most of all his kindnesses and the depth of his soul. Sometimes I look at my husband and feel with all my heart, my thanks that he was a dear friend to my father and my father to him. That he understands how and why I loved and love my father so intensely, and refers to him with respect and gentleness. Sometimes I look at the photo of my father on the dresser that is reserved for mementos — a photo of him walking along Bellevue Beach in his khaki shirt and khaki pants, grey head bent looking at the rocks — and allow myself to be a tiny girl again, skipping along beside him.

It wasn't so long ago that I was in a crowded gymnasium, waiting along with everyone else, for the start of graduation ceremonies. The chairs immediately in front of me were empty, but the row ahead of that was inhabited by an older man sitting between two women, one of whom was in a wheelchair. I paid no real attention until we were asked to stand for the singing of the national anthem. I was busy watching the camera person manoeuvre his way through the crowds to obtain the shots I'd requested for a video news release. He was another grandfather in a room filled with proud and happy grandfathers. But when he stood, his shoulders were square and strong, his arms held carefully by his side, every bone in his body portraying respect and dignity. The emotion came first, the words later. I wasn't seeing the man who was standing there, I was seeing my father. When the song was over I turned to the back of the notebook I would be using to record words from the various speakers, things that would need to be discussed at later meetings, and wrote... *the man who stands tall. My father.*

My father was an incredible human being. He didn't look longingly to the possessions of other people but was able to find happiness with his own life. He was, in health and in sickness, the greatest teacher I will ever have. And the greatest honour we can give him is to live our lives in ways that we believe would make him proud. To be as much like him as we can be, even though he would never have asked it of us.

If you never knew my father, it is my sincerest wish that you know him now. That some of the power of his life impacts on yours, that some of the gifts he gave me become yours. It is my sincerest wish that if you are coping with the loss of someone you love to a tragedy like Alzheimer's and past joys are being blurred by present pains, my father's story will help you remember the laughter and smiles of years gone by. And now as I end this story, I think not of my own words, but those of my brother who, on my 38th birthday, ended his note to me with words that seem so appropriate. Steve had celebrated his own birthday just four days earlier.

My birthday present to myself, he wrote, was to see the foundation being poured for my garage — which will be dedicated to dad's memory. We were really lucky to have had him as our father and I really do miss him at times.

I couldn't agree more.

What wonderful memories
you have given us.
What a wonderful legacy of
strength, respect and love.

Afterword

Richard Joseph Barron,
born in Holyrood, Newfoundland, on August 8th, 1922,
to Mary (Butler) and Michael Barron, wasn't famous or well-known.
He wasn't a CEO or an astronaut or a politician; he didn't make
movies or build empires;
he didn't fly first class and he could walk down a
street in most cities of the world,
without anyone ever recognizing him.

But Richard Joseph Barron,
my father and extremely precious friend,
was a remarkable man who understood equality long before it
became a household word or a concept to be bandied about in
election campaigns. Who not only understood the immense power
of love, respect and trust but whose life reflected that understanding.
Who was an incredibly powerful and courageous teacher,
even in his suffering.
And who will be with me always.

I love you Dad.

STANDING TALL

Twenty-One Days In May

The measure of an
extraordinary woman.

JACQUI TAM

Mary Louise Barron

Prologue

Words are such powerful things. Right words... wrong words... unspoken words. Words we never have the chance to say. Words we wish we'd never uttered.

The last thing I have ever wanted to do, with my words, is to damage a treasured relationship.

The last thing I wanted to do when I wrote a book about my father, our relationship, and the heartbreaking journey that is Alzheimer's, was to hurt my mother. I didn't want her to feel that I had somehow betrayed her, or shared moments too private to ever be shared. But I knew there were sections of the book that would potentially do just that, and I feared their impact even though I knew there was no other way to tell the story.

I was so concerned she'd be upset that immediately after I packaged up a copy of the manuscript and couriered it to her in Newfoundland from my then-home in southern Alberta, I took my own copy and marked with yellow sticky notes every paragraph I thought might upset her. Then I counted the days until she would have received and read it, and waited for the telephone to ring.

I stood leaning against the kitchen counter in my home when I answered her call, my gaze directed towards the window that looked out onto our deck and the farmer's field beyond. The manuscript with sticky notes was on the counter beside me, though I had no idea what I could say about it if she challenged my memories of how she had been.

As soon as she spoke, I could hear the tears in her eyes… they were in her voice as well.

I was really like that, wasn't I? she asked.

Yes, was my quiet reply.

Don't change a word, through the tears, her conviction was firm. *Not a single word. People need to know. People need to know that's what Alzheimer's does to the loved ones. People need to know…*

I had not expected that. Perhaps I should have, but I had doubted that my mother would be willing to let others know how much pain she had suffered, and how that pain had affected our lives.

Despite being outgoing, Mary Louise Barron was an intensely private person. Her role in my father's story was one of intense devotion and love, but the experience of caring for him ravaged her and left scars that never healed even though she hid them well. In *A Daughter's Gift*, I wrote about the changes as I had witnessed them — talked of depression and anger and many other things. I had relayed some of the most intimate and heartbreaking moments of my father's later years — moments that had caused all of us incredible anguish.

But despite the pain she felt reading the manuscript, and despite its honest account of her suffering, she didn't ask me to change a word.

Not a single word.

That she didn't ask me to hide her suffering because she believed its truth could help others was, I thought then, everything that needed to be said about her courage, about her character, about the measure of this extraordinary woman.

But I was wrong.

There is more to be said. There is more to be remembered, in love, about the woman who will be with me always.

The Days After and Before

On the morning of my 46th birthday, I awoke in a hotel room, my husband at my side. There are sometimes moments between sleep and wakefulness when whatever may have been haunting you the night before is suspended... forgotten. When you can simply appreciate the first moments of consciousness without any sense of what has passed or what is to come.

Not on this particular morning.

Peter may have already been awake, or he may have woken when he heard me stir. I don't recall. He wished me happy birthday, kissed me gently, and then quietly got out of bed, pulled on pants and a shirt, and went to the front lobby for a newspaper.

I stayed in bed, waiting.

He returned to the room a few minutes later, silently handed me the folded pages. *Yes, it's there,* was his response to my unspoken query. Dread mixed with anticipation and a feeling of disconnected realities as I opened the paper, then turned to the obituaries and scanned for my mother's name. Began to read.

On May 27th, 2006, the morning of my 46th birthday, in a hotel room in St. John's, Newfoundland, the beloved city of my birth, I read my mother's obituary. Unbelievable, inconceivable, and yet somehow inevitable.

When I pushed the hotel bed linens aside, shivering even though it wasn't cold, I consciously reached to the back of my mind for the image and the sound of my mother struggling for her last breaths just two days before.

I ignored my memory of the silence that had followed in the private Intensive Care room… the sudden emptiness of her always so vibrant body. I thought instead of the people I had not yet been able to reach with the news, who would be reading the paper this morning and sitting, grief-stricken in their chairs. I silently rehearsed the story of twenty-one days in May, getting ready to tell it as often as it needed to be told, to all those who would be gathering in disbelief and grief. And I prepared to wrap myself in the safety of an outfit my mother would have liked, so I would be the daughter she could be proud of as I helped to give her a fitting farewell.

The story of those twenty-one days is neither unique nor unusual. Few stories truly are. As much pain or shock or loss as one family is experiencing at any given time, other families are going through so much worse. But my family and my mother's many friends somehow thought she would live forever, or at least for as long as anyone else who needed her was alive.

The thought that she had been incapable of rallying against the fluid buildup in her lungs after surgery, dying just twenty-one days after her cancer diagnosis, seemed impossible. But it wasn't impossible; it was real. And the fact that we would be gathering at a funeral home in just a few hours, in a room that would undoubtedly be filled with flowers, was a stark reminder of that.

If you have previously read *A Daughter's Gift*, you will know already that flowers — roses and stargazer lilies especially — have immense meaning in my life beyond what would sound logical. Pink roses assured us that the bone cancer I had been diagnosed with was not bone cancer at all. A red rose carried the message that my father would be fine, despite his lung cancer diagnosis. And beautiful stargazer lilies connected my father with me across time, space, and the incredible loss that is Alzheimer's.

But in *A Daughter's Gift,* I did not share the story of my mother and her older sister, Lillian. I remember Aunt Lillian as a tall, regal woman who suffered greatly with arthritis, migraines, and as time went on, a myriad of other health problems. She lived with her husband and five children in the heart of St. John's, in a stately home with high ceilings, a tall staircase, and no front yard. As much as anyone, she was one of the reasons I existed — her then-boyfriend Vince had introduced my father to my mother when she was bedridden with tuberculosis.

My mother and Lillian were extremely close — much closer than I ever realized as a child. Lillian was sister and friend, and almost a second mother as well. As they both aged, and as it became increasingly likely that one of the illnesses my aunt was fighting would claim her, the two sisters made a pact. Whoever died first, they agreed, would send the other sister a sign to prove there was more to existence than this one life, and reassure her that she'd arrived in another place happy and all was well. They would tell no one about the pact — they could only trust the sign when it appeared if no one else ever knew of their promises.

I have no idea how long after that conversation Aunt Lillian died, though I do know it was much sooner than either of them would have hoped. I also know that it was still in the period before my father's death, when I would attend funerals only if I had absolutely no other choice. In those times, I avoided funeral homes and wakes at all cost — I could not bear the sight of death.

It was out of character for me, then, to be so determined to not only attend Lillian's wake, but to arrive at the funeral home as soon as it opened on the first morning. Surprised, but willing to go along with the feeling that I was doing what I needed to do, I cleared the hour between 10 and 11 a.m. in my schedule, and left my office to go to the florist in the shopping mall across the street. Convention under these circumstances would have been to order flowers and have them delivered, but the same strange conviction insisted that I bring them with me.

The discussion with the lady in the flower shop should have been unremarkable as I tried to figure out what I wanted to order, but when I finally decided on a half-dozen white roses, she told me that I'd have to wait for the florist to get them ready. The arrangement therefore couldn't be prepared until early that afternoon, at which point it could be delivered direct to the funeral home.

But I have to bring something with me, I told her. *I have to.* She tried to convince me that the delivery would be fine — better in fact, and normal.

She was right. The logical thing would have been to leave for the funeral home, knowing the flowers would follow. But I couldn't. I knew I simply couldn't walk into the wake empty-handed.

So I thought for a moment before shrugging my shoulders: *OK then, just give me one white rose. Yes, that would be perfect, just one white rose. Wrapped in paper. And the half-dozen can come later.*

Tears filled my mother's eyes when I walked into the funeral home a short time later, holding what she recognized immediately as a flower wrapped in paper.

You brought it, she said. *You brought one white rose, didn't you?*

Aunt Lillian's sign. She had promised she would send one white rose. And I delivered it for her.

Time stands still, just for an instant, in moments like that.

My mother never doubted that the rose I placed in her outstretched hands was from her sister, and I never doubted that my aunt had somehow compelled me to deliver it for her. Why else would I have been so determined? There could be no other explanation for insisting I had to bring something so specific to a place I would never normally have gone.

Aunt Lillian had promised my mother a rose, a white rose, and she didn't waste any time sending it.

After this, it was inevitable that, on what we both knew would be her last morning, I would ask my mother if she would send me a sign. She had refused any additional medical intervention, and we knew her time would be measured in hours. Speaking was torture for her, and I regretted not having had the courage to raise this question earlier, but I leaned over her bed anyway and asked whether there was a sign I should look for... a sign like the one Lillian had sent her... one that would let me know she was with my father and all was well.

Pulling her oxygen mask away, she held up the index finger on her left hand, and struggled for an instant to gather enough air.

One red rose.

A pause, her finger moving back and then forward again

And one white.

Her voice was like gravel.

One red rose, and one white? I wanted to be sure.

One red rose, and one white. She confirmed with a nod, before my hand and hers returned the oxygen mask to her face.

One red rose, and one white. Aunt Lillian's white rose, my father's red. Together. This was my mother's sign.

Others came after she told me this — the steady parade of people she wanted to see, making their way to her bedside. I slipped out to the soft lights of the private waiting room that sheltered families who were coming to terms with the truth that there would be one fewer living member when they left the hospital.

I told the aunts who were gathered that she'd told me what to look for, that there would be a sign. But I would not tell them what it was. I would only tell them after I'd seen it, not before.

I was not thinking of any of this that morning in my hotel room, though. I did not think of signs. I did not look for roses or wonder where or when or if I'd see them. Instead, I wrapped myself in the protection of appearances, coping beneath the armor of a black suit that my mother would have thought appropriate.

Peter and I arrived at the funeral home before anyone else so we'd have time to ensure everything was as it should be... entered the room and moved to stand beside my mother's casket. She rested there, the mother of my memory, in her white nurse's uniform and navy blue cape. But things weren't quite right: her instructions had been very precise — she had wanted her Registered Nurse's cap, with its black band striking against the white, beside her in the casket but not on her head. They had affixed it to her head, leaving us with the decision as to whether or not we should risk removing it — messing the carefully arranged hair — or leave it in place. But she had wanted it off, so we removed it.

Such small things become so important in moments like those. You drink them in — lock them, and the emotions that go with them, into your mind and heart. Then, as you begin to absorb everything around you, you start to consciously register details that had previously gone unnoticed.

It strikes me as odd, in retrospect, that as important as the flowers on my father's casket had been, I barely noticed the ones on my mother's. I cannot recall the arrangements, or even the process of choosing them. But I suddenly noticed the room was overflowing with them. They were everywhere.

As I turned my back on my mother, of course my eyes were drawn to one particular arrangement: lilies, carnations, other flowers I don't recall... and in the midst of them all, one single red rose, and one white.

A physical jolt. Part joy, part agony. Profound and intense.

That's her sign, I told Peter. *This is what she told me to look for.*

When I read the card, my eyes filled with tears: the flowers were from Esther and Jeanie Buckley. Just as I was the right person to bring

Lillian's rose to my mother, Esther was the only person who could
have sent my Mom's roses to me. Thirty-two years prior, when I was
fourteen and facing a bone cancer diagnosis, she was the dear friend
who had first given us reason to understand that roses were messages.

Then, the roses had come to tell us that I was, unbelievably,
cancer-free. Now, they came to tell me that my mother and father
were reunited, and that all was truly well.

For the next two hours, while talking with the family and friends
who came to pay their respects, I watched the door for Esther and her
sister Jeanie. When they arrived, I excused myself and went to them
immediately. I brought Esther to the arrangement, I told her about my
mother's sign, and I thanked her. For the second time in my life, she
had made possible a message that was beyond logic and reason — a
message that mattered so much.

For after three heartbreaking weeks that somehow captured
everything I understood about her and our relationship, my mother
had sent me the sign that all was well.

Day 1

Friday, May 5

It was a Friday when my mother called — about 3:00 in the afternoon.

Normally, I would have been at my office at Wilfrid Laurier University, in Waterloo, Ontario. However, this was my first week back to work after having had surgery, and I was still much more tired that I expected to be. So I'd packed my briefcase at noon and gone home to sleep.

Mom and I had been talking two, three, four times a day that month — my surgery had been without complications of either the immediate or long-term type, but she needed to know how I was recovering, and I needed to hear her continuing reassurances. We had not connected on the previous day, though — I was on the mend and it was simply a break for both of us. Or so I'd thought.

She asked first how I was feeling, and I explained that I was doing okay — that I'd just come home early to sleep. She asked next after Atlas, our much-loved German Shepherd who had been diagnosed with lymphoma on February 15th, and who was fighting a valiant battle.

Then she said: *I have news, but I don't want you to be upset.*

A pause came next — a pause that in hindsight seems the type that was meant to give me the slightest warning that everything was about to change forever. I don't know if I said anything after she spoke. I remember only the pause, and the three words that followed.

I have cancer.

The rest came out in a rush. A trip to the family doctor the day before to have what she suspected was a hernia in her right lower abdomen checked... an immediate call from that doctor to a specialist... a CT scan that same afternoon... a visit with the specialist the following day — this first day. The diagnosis.

I imagined what it was like for my mother to receive such news alone. I pictured her in the clinical setting — always so terrifying for me, always so comfortable for her — and felt her isolation acutely, even though she probably preferred that there were no witnesses to her reaction.

I couldn't help but wonder how she had felt as she walked to her car in the hospital parking lot. How she managed to drive home — alone — with the knowledge she now carried. What she did in the minutes and hours before she picked up the phone to start making phone calls.

I wondered all those things, but as was her way, she was already offering only the information she wanted me to have.

I have surgery next week, and then I'll have treatment if needed, she continued in a rush. *Chemotherapy. It's just one tumor, so they'll get it all. And I'm still coming to Kenneth's graduation in June. I'll be well enough by then. I'll probably have lost my hair but I'll get a wig.*

One should feel something sharp at moments like this; I felt only numbness. One should probably cry, like I did when I had called her to tell her about Atlas's diagnosis. But my eyes remained completely dry.

She sounded strong, and in absolute control — as always. Her weekend was all planned out: she'd be cleaning windows and curtains. I was her daughter, so she needed just as much control from me. At least that's what I think she needed. Because I had learned such control from her, and now it was what I could give back.

I don't know what my next words were. I don't know how long the call lasted. But as we said our goodbyes, I remembered distinctly what she had said to me a few weeks earlier, when the doctor had told me my ovarian cyst had been benign. That I didn't have cancer.

Cancer, she had said, *that one word changes everything, doesn't it?*

Yes, I was thinking, *it changes everything.*

When our call was over, I stayed sitting on the step until my then twenty-one-year-old son Kenneth arrived to check on me, and to ask why I hadn't moved after the call had obviously ended.

That was Mary, I told him. *She had news.*

But she doesn't want us to be upset.

Day 2
Saturday, May 6

My mother returned to work as a nurse when I was two-years-old. My paternal grandmother — Nan Barron — had come to live with us. She would be able to care for me and my brothers, Steve and Rik, who were eight and five respectively, while my mother was at the hospital.

My mother's Monday to Friday work schedule meant that housework as well as other chores and errands mostly had to be tackled on the weekend. Laundry usually got started on Friday night. In the early days that meant hours spent running clothes through the now antique wringer washer that was set up in our basement, where rows of lines had also been installed so clothes could be hung to dry. Housework was usually done on Saturday morning, and through as much of the afternoon as was needed. Sunday morning, after church, there was the ironing, while the Sunday dinner cooked.

Our treat, as I grew older and we were able to get all or most of the housework done on Friday evening, was to go to the Avalon Mall to browse. Always in the morning (because we didn't like the afternoon crowds), we'd visit our favorite stores, hunt for bargains, study the latest styles, and then treat ourselves to lunch in the Mall's tiny café. I'd have a small plate of French fries and a soft drink. My mother would usually have a bran muffin and coffee, and one or two of my fries. I'd watch as she reapplied her lipstick after we'd finished.

If we knew we still had housework to do when we got home, that fact would hang over us. Still having the housework to do ruined the morning, my mother always said.

Decades later, this pattern of activity still guides my weekends. Housework and errands are mostly reserved for Friday night, Saturday, and Sunday. Saturday morning shopping — before the crowds — is still a treat. And if housework still needs to be done when we get home, that continues to hang over me... not as strongly as it once did, but there nonetheless.

On this particular Saturday morning — May 6th, 2006 — I found a strange comfort in the routine of housework. In that routine, I could find a modicum of control in a world that had fundamentally shifted.

Peter hadn't been home when my mother had called the previous afternoon, because he had been in Toronto refereeing at a squash tournament. We expected him home sometime between 10:30 p.m. and midnight, and Kenneth and I agreed to wait until then to give him the news. Navigating Highway 401 between Toronto and Waterloo was challenging enough; there was nothing to be gained by distracting him with such news.

In the meantime, Kenneth and I had discussed the few details my mother had provided. The single tumor was in her lower stomach, and she was having surgery on Thursday, May 11th. From what she said the cancer was localized, but they would likely do chemotherapy to ensure no other traces remained. And she would still travel to Waterloo in the first week of June, for his graduation from university.

We both knew, of course, that the twenty-four hour turnaround between the appointment with her family doctor and the booking of surgery meant there was a great deal to be concerned about. The system only moves that quickly when it is imperative that it do so, and sometimes not even then. But some truths are best not spoken.

That night, our telephone was busy. I made calls to my mother, who took them while sitting in the chair she always occupied when talking on the phone — the chair at the heart of the house she'd lived in for more than forty years. I spoke to my brother Steve, who lived just outside Vancouver. To other people I've since forgotten.

We checked my office schedule for the coming weeks. We checked flight schedules. I would go to St. John's to be with her for the surgery, of course. Steve, who would know how best to care for a post-op patient at home, would arrive about a week later, when she could expect to be discharged from hospital. Kenneth decided he would travel with me — so soon after my surgery, I wasn't quite ready to handle luggage on my own, but more than that, he would not send me to face this alone. Peter needed to stay at home with Atlas to manage his cancer treatments, but he'd come later if he had to.

And so on Saturday, in addition to the regular, now comforting chores, we booked relatively convenient mid-morning flights out of Toronto that would see us arriving in St. John's late in the afternoon of the day before my mother's surgery.

I started an inventory of my wardrobe, sorting through clothes that would be appropriate for the hospital so I could determine if I needed to sew anything before we left. I checked in regularly with the woman who had decided that, in addition to her own regular housework, it was time to wash her curtains. I heard the sense of purpose and direction in her voice. I marveled at how that voice could be so strong and calm — happy even.

But I'd grown up with my mother. We knew each other well. I understood why the last thing she would do on that particular weekend was let things slide. I understood what her purpose was and exactly why she was cleaning the curtains.

And happiness didn't even enter the equation.

Day 3

Sunday, May 7

With newly laundered curtains reinstalled and smelling fresh from their hastily-planned spring cleaning, my mother tackled her closets on the second day after her diagnosis. This even though I didn't recall them being particularly disorganized or messy on my previous visit.

Through all the years of my childhood, the closet in my parents' room had always been neatly organized — my mother's clothing taking about two-thirds of the space, my father's the rest. In the years that had passed since my brothers and I had permanently moved out of the house, the closets in our rooms had provided additional space for my mother to utilize. My dad's passing had further lightened the burden, and over the years, off-season wardrobes and clothing that wasn't yet ready to be passed along had been allocated to new locations.

Coats. Hats. Shoes. Bits and pieces that needed a home. This Sunday wasn't about cleaning, it was about bringing further order to contents most people would have already thought totally organized.

A few days after this, I would have reason to question whether the impression my mother had given me of her activity-filled weekend had been accurate — even for the young and healthy, cleaning curtains and organizing closets can be tiring. But on that Sunday, I heard only confidence and strength in her voice when she explained her purpose, and I believed what she told me. Or perhaps I chose to believe, knowing that was the role we both needed me to play.

In my own home some 3,000 kilometres away, I sorted through my closet to find the right outfit for traveling. The right outfit to wear when taking her to the hospital. The right outfits for hours or days with her at the hospital. The right outfit to wear when bringing her home. If you did not know my mother and her attention to appearance, this particular focus might seem out of place under the circumstances. But in my mother's presence, the right clothing for the right occasion was essential. At all times, and especially in times of extreme stress, standards had to be maintained.

But my selection came up short. I was well equipped to deal with my regular needs — I had a healthy selection of business clothes and some casual wear for the weekend. But neither would suffice in the circumstances.

So while my mother cleaned closets, I searched through my fabric stash and patterns, and began to sew — black wool bootleg trousers, and a black-on-black print poncho out of a heavy brocade-like fabric.

I could wrap myself in the poncho, I thought. Sitting in the vinyl covered chairs of hospital waiting rooms, I could at least wrap myself in fabric I loved.

Day 4

Monday, May 8

The thing about the kind of news my mother received on Friday, May 5th is that it completely changes everything. There is no part of life that isn't impacted — even the small things, like how to answer the inevitable Monday morning query about your weekend.

I remember no specifics about returning to work that Monday morning. I'm sure I shared the information with whoever was necessary… made arrangements to take time off again beginning on Wednesday… began the process of organizing files and sorting out the deadlines I would not be able to change.

There were also logistical challenges. My mother didn't own a computer. We'd wanted to get one for her, or at least give her one of ours that was being retired, thinking she'd enjoy email and the internet, but she was never interested in entering that world. Her preferred communications methods were telephone and face-to-face, so her home had none of the technologies that would be necessities for us as we stayed in touch with my office, or prepared the summer releases for Iceberg Publishing — the company Peter, Kenneth and I had established four years before.

We'd therefore need to stay in a hotel where we'd have internet access, and where my mother would have no reason to feel guilty for keeping us from our work. She would also be under no pressure to prepare meals or provide clean sheets and linens, and she wouldn't have the stress of us suggesting we do those things for her. Most importantly, I would realize after I arrived, there would be no need for her to keep up appearances — she wouldn't have to pretend to be feeling stronger, better than she was.

But to be completely honest, there was another reason I don't think I could have handled staying in my childhood home on this particular trip. Returning to 37 Penetanguishene after my father died and we'd moved away had grown more difficult with every trip back. It was as if the very floors and walls were imbued with a deep regret and pain. On rare occasions I could feel my father's presence; most of the time it seemed that nothing of his spirit remained. In the house, I felt a deep sadness.

The house didn't remind me of all that had been wonderful about my childhood, and there had been much. It reminded me of loss, and emptiness, and lives grown smaller as time moved on. Best not to try to deal with those emotions and everything else as well. Best to find an escape.

And so a hotel was booked — the hotel that became something of a second home, with my cousin Nikki at the front desk, the best hot turkey sandwich (Newfoundland style) on the room service menu, a view of St. John's Harbour and Signal Hill, and the kindest staff you could hope to meet.

Then, on Monday evening, before one more day at the office and my final packing, we celebrated Mother's Day in my house. I have never liked to celebrate special occasions before they arrive. It seems a tempting of fate and I carry enough of the superstitious Irish heritage to make me fear a jinx — as if the fates are watching for one slip-up, where they can catch you and pounce, blurt *I'll show you*, and ensure the day being celebrated early never arrives.

But in 2006 we made an exception — we changed the date and I had my own personal Mother's Day celebration.

Atlas, in another stage of treatment for his aggressive cancer, sat smiling by my chair in his usual spot. I can hear his breathing even now. I can see his large smile, and the eyes that somehow put laughter and joy before the pain that would have been his constant companion. There were gifts, including an iPod because I would need music for writing, for calming, for intermittent escapes.

It was good that I had it.

Day 5
Tuesday, May 9

I sometimes think that packing for trips would be so much less complicated if the trips themselves were uncomplicated, or if they were for the single and simple purpose of enjoyment. If you didn't have to worry about what or who you were leaving behind, or what you needed to bring 'in case', or what you would face while away. I can't remember the number of times I've packed for trips, but there have been relatively few times that the packing has been truly uncomplicated.

May 9th was not an uncomplicated packing experience. Every outfit worn in my mother's presence would be assessed, head to toe. My mother's sense of style was impeccable, and it was impossible for her to look at her daughter without taking stock and determining if she approved of the choices made. I didn't want to let her down, especially not under these circumstances.

In the hours available to me between Friday afternoon and Tuesday night, after I'd completed all the other tasks that needed doing prior to the trip, I'd spent sufficient time at the sewing machine to add the new items that could be combined with existing clothes to provide outfits for the anticipated number of days and situations. And so I began laying out everything on the bed, 'visiting the house' clothes... 'hotel room' clothes... 'hospital' clothes...

Everything was planned as carefully as possible. And yet I agonized.

Then there were the required files from work — human resource challenges being dealt with, communications plans around the issues and initiatives of the day, projects that had already suffered from the three weeks I'd been missing for my surgery, and three Iceberg Publishing titles in various stages of preparation for release in July.

Three books for the summer later became standard for us, but this was the first time we would be attempting that many — the fifth book in the *Equations* series, and the first two books in an entirely new series called *Defense Command.* Editing still needed to be done, so hundreds of pages were packed into various suitcases. There were questions about how to bring along electronic files — we hadn't had to travel with those before. Two laptops, hundreds of pages, and an iPod that would serve as an external hard drive — everything essential from our two offices was traveling with us.

In the years since, we've turned traveling with manuscripts, books, and event displays and supplies into something of an art form, but at that time, it was still fairly new to us. Systems that later served us so well were still in the process of being developed.

It's interesting that as I write this, I feel like I did when I was packing that night. Not quite going around in circles, but *almost* — and experiencing that same anxiousness in the pit of my stomach, a fear that I'm somehow not going to make it work. Like those bad dreams where you're convinced you'll never actually complete a task, or reach your destination... or that you will arrive, but everything you need will be somewhere else. Or you'll be in your pajamas.

I was haunted, too, by questions of whether I'd be able to cope with what I was soon to face. Honestly, I questioned everything. And then I got angry with myself, because packing was so much easier than what my mother was facing.

Eventually all the suitcases, briefcases and other carry-ons were filled. Eventually, I slept. A troubled, heartsick sleep.

Because while I was not alone in my home, my mother was alone in hers. Totally and completely, except for her fears and her courage, and feelings she would never share.

Day 6
Wednesday, May 10

We were in the air when my mother underwent a colonoscopy that caused her doctor to shake his head in puzzlement and make the decision to delay her surgery. He had expected to find the cancer in her colon, but didn't. Deciding then that the problem must have been in her uterus, he advised a delay so he could have a surgeon more experienced in that area join him. My brother Rik had driven her to and from that appointment; we would take a taxi from the airport to her house when we arrived, so we could see her before retrieving her car for our stay. She wouldn't be using it, after all.

In all the times I'd flown into that particular airport, this made for a strange first. In St. John's, only business travelers from elsewhere usually have no one to meet them at the airport; if family or friends lived even remotely nearby, you could always bank on being picked up. It was tradition to find a small crowd watching as the plane disembarked, waiting to welcome people home — because even if they lived away, Newfoundland was still and always would be *home*.

So there seemed a particular significance to knowing that on this occasion my mother would not be waiting at the entrance to the baggage area — that instead she was at home, watching the time but waiting for us to come to her.

The afternoon was sunny and the temperature pleasant when the taxi dropped us off and unloaded our luggage onto the paved driveway.

There was no need to bring the suitcases inside since we'd be moving them into my mother's car for the journey to the hotel, so instead we left them there and approached the back door. My mother was not by the door as I expected her to be — *she must not have heard the taxi arrive,* I remember thinking — but the door was unlocked, so we let ourselves in.

The ranch style house I grew up in has two front doors, one of which we called the back door. The back door was driveway level and immediately to the right of the large garage door; it was the everyday entrance for family members and friends. The front door was situated up a short flight of stairs roughly in the centre of the house between two large windows; it was reserved for special occasions and guests.

This back door was added along with the garage after the house had been built. When you entered, there were doors to the garage on the left, and a flight of stairs going up what would have originally been the outside of the house on the right. The door at the top entered immediately into the kitchen, and in addition to room on the landing for coats and shoes, the area provided space for a refrigerator that had, when I was a child, been much smaller and in the kitchen.

My mother was standing in the kitchen doorway at the top of the stairs. I have no memory of what she was wearing, or even her expression. What was so striking was the fact that while she had obviously heard us arrive, she had stayed at the top of the stairs instead of coming down to greet us.

The next realization was how desperately thin she was. My mother had vowed as a young woman that she would never succumb to what was at the time known as 'middle-age spread'. She may not have agreed, but those who knew her would have said she was most successful in that regard — trim and attractive always. However, on Wednesday, May 10th, I suddenly realized that when she'd happily told me a couple of weeks before that she'd *lost a little weight*, she had in fact been managing my expectations.

She'd said she was about 130 pounds. If she was 100, that's as much as she could be. And the doorframe was holding her up as surely as it held the door itself.

Communication is as much about what is not spoken as what is spoken. I did not tell her how thin she looked; I did not need to. I did not remark on how fragile she felt when I hugged her. Again, I did not need to. Instead she explained that the surgery had been delayed, and that it was good news because it meant we had time to do some things together that we wouldn't otherwise have done.

And, as I think we both knew in that moment and on that day, we would never do again.

Day 7

Thursday, May 11

They say memories are stored safely in our brains, that even when we cannot remember specifics, they somehow still exist. I don't know if that's true. I just know that I don't remember the specifics of the afternoon of Wednesday, May 10th in any great detail.

We arrived at my mother's house and quickly adjusted to the revised schedule for the week that would follow. We left for the hotel, checked in, navigated the unfamiliar but thankfully small car into the underground parking lot, rode the elevator to our room, and began the process that turned the room with two double beds temporarily into our own personal space.

We'd buy our supply of breakfast and snack foods and bottled water later, but placing our manuscripts on the desk, shoes along the wall, toiletries in the bathroom, and clothes in the closet, achieved the very necessary goal of making the space feel a little less impersonal and a little more like ours. Kenneth and I were alike in that regard: our first task in any hotel room was to make it somehow ours. Then we returned to 37 Penetanguishene at the appointed time, to pick up my mother and take her for a pizza supper at the same restaurant we'd visited together on our last trip home.

I'd realized how thin she was when I saw her earlier in the afternoon. What I hadn't realized, because she hadn't moved from her station in the doorway, was that thin also meant frail. Even in the most difficult periods of her life, even at her thinnest, she would never have been called frail. Even when sick with pneumonia, or suffering from intense vertigo, or beyond exhausted while caring for my father during his decade-long struggle with Alzheimer's, there was a core strength that somehow superseded the illness or the fatigue.

Had she not been so intensely focused on keeping her footing, I'm sure she would have recognized my shock when I first saw how gingerly and slowly she moved down the stairs, and out into the driveway. Just as I'm sure I would have seen her discomfort when she realized her difficulties were being witnessed. But her eyes were cast downward, and by the time she looked up again, my expression was schooled. As was hers.

I don't actually recall if I was ever told about the importance of maintaining appearances when growing up, but there is no doubt it's a lesson I learned as I watched my mother through the years and learned to model my behaviors after hers. No matter the grief, no matter the pain, it was important that the appearance of calm and strength be maintained.

My mother was clearly in pain that evening. Intense pain. Indeed, every action seemed to require extreme concentration, including the simple movement of fork to mouth. Still she smiled. Still she did not admit to anything beyond her happiness at our presence — how lovely it was we could have dinner together because surgery was delayed, and how convenient it was that there'd be pizza left over for us to take back to the hotel for tomorrow.

We all ate less than usual that evening, my mother especially so. And even though we had talked about doing something together afterwards — stopping at a favorite store in the same area and then taking the short drive to Middle Cove Beach so Kenneth and I could feel the rocks beneath our feet and breathe the rich salt air — we didn't do any of that with her. My mother explained she was tired after the exertions of the day, as of course she would be. But as we drove back to 37 Penetanguishene and dropped her off, I knew exertions were only a small part of the reason.

The sky was crystal clear blue, no clouds in sight, when Kenneth and I drove in silence without her to Middle Cove. Between 6:05 and 6:07 p.m. we captured images on my camera — rocks and ocean, and a classic seagull image set against the backdrop of blue. We didn't stay long, no more than ten minutes in total, but it was enough to ground us. Then we returned to the hotel where we unpacked the supplies we'd picked up at the grocery, and Kenneth connected his laptop to the TV so the DVD of a Corrs concert we'd brought along could be played.

On Thursday morning, after our breakfast of grocery store muffins and bananas, and after I'd arranged to change the date of our flights back to Ontario, Kenneth stayed in the room to write and edit, and spend time drinking in the view. He took photos from the window of the mist covering Signal Hill, and of the cargo ships making port to unload their containers. I went to the house to pick up my mother for one of our Saturday-like shopping trips.

There are two particularly strong impressions from that day. The first was the slowness with which my mother moved. A night's sleep had in no way eased the tiredness or reversed the frailness of the evening before. She had dressed stylishly as she always did, her hair was done, her make-up applied, and perhaps people who did not know her well would see no difference in how she carried herself. But it was glaringly obvious to me that her movements were incredibly studied and her pace so very slow.

The second was that she had absolutely no interest in looking at anything for herself. She'd always bought for others before herself — that was not unusual. Indeed, I distinctly remember asking her, when I was quite young, why she never bought anything for herself when we went shopping… and her just smiling and saying she didn't need anything. It wasn't until I was older that she explained she could only afford to buy for the children.

On this particular day she didn't say she had everything she needed for whatever time was left to her, but I knew that's what she was thinking. Instead she wanted to buy gifts for me, for Kenneth, for Peter. This also was not unusual. My mother regularly gave people gifts on days other than birthdays, anniversaries, Christmas — though of course there were presents at those times as well. She called these unexpected presents 'happy day gifts', intended to make your day happier and remind you how much you meant to someone.

She bought me two jackets that day… a reversible black fall jacket with a stand-up collar that I've worn only a few times but always remains in my closet, and a casual red windbreaker that I could wear when Kenneth and I visited Cape Spear. For Kenneth there were dry-fit golf shirts, for Peter some neckties.

I did convince her to buy deep brown lounging pajamas for herself, forcing myself to ignore the feeling that she was really only buying the outfit to humor me. They were distinctive, and the top had a collar that could stand up. My mother, you see, loved collars that could stand up. Hers always did. She also loved dark brown — it had been her signature all through my childhood before she made the switch to black after I'd begun wearing that color in my late teens. The pajamas would be appropriate for the hospital, we agreed, after the surgery when she was ready for visitors. And for home as well.

It is a distinctly disconcerting feeling to shop with someone who believes they have everything they need for the remaining short term of their lives. Someone who maintains the pretense that everything will be fine, but whose actions convey the opposite message. Someone who buys something for herself just to humor you.

I had expected a morning of shopping followed by lunch that day, but we made it to only two stores before I brought her home. She did not have the energy for more; indeed, that much activity had already been too great a drain. I stayed for a short visit, admiring the new living room furniture she'd wanted for so long and finally bought a couple of months earlier, then eased out the door.

She'd never admit that she wanted me to leave, but that is what I felt, because when the door closed and she was alone, she would be free to feel whatever it was she felt, act however she needed to act. She didn't have to put on a strong or calm facade for her daughter or grandson. If she was in pain, and clearly she was, she didn't have to try to hide it. If she needed to stop and rest as she walked from the kitchen to the bedroom, which clearly she did, she could do so.

With no one there to see, no one there who needed to be reassured that everything would be fine, she could simply be. There wasn't much I could give her, but I could give her that.

What strength my mother had. What amazing, incomparable determination.

And pride.

Day 8

Friday, May 12

I am reminded, as I relive the experiences of my mother's last weeks, that as outgoing and talkative as she was — she could talk for hours, to anyone, and no matter the circumstances, always found the right thing to say — she was also intensely private, and rarely asked for help or support. Adored by many, inside the family and out, at home and at work, she was the person everyone turned to when they needed help, and she offered all she could give of herself.

When I was little, she'd be called at all hours of the day or night when someone in the neighborhood was sick, or had fallen, or cut themselves. There'd be a knock at the door and someone would ask: *Is your mother at home? Can you ask her to come? We need her.* And she would go, spending much of her limited free time cleaning wounds, taking temperatures, sending people off to hospital when necessary. The Penetanguishene nurse.

When there were illnesses in our own family — on her side or my Dad's — she would spend all night at the hospital by someone's bedside, then go to work in that same hospital when morning arrived. She could somehow last for days on little or no sleep. It wasn't until I was a teenager that I began to realize the toll this took on her, but she couldn't have acted any differently — this was who she was.

The years she spent caring for my father as he battled Alzheimer's were perhaps the longest-running example of both how much she would give, and how little help she would accept, despite the cost to herself. I'd lived that experience with her, and it had taught me many things, one of which was how to judge what assistance she might be willing to accept, and when.

By the third day of our visit to St. John's, I had a much better sense of how little energy she had and the limits of what she was able to do. There would be no more shopping trips, and no physically taxing outings... On this day, day 8 since her diagnosis, we would simply have a quiet lunch and talk.

The restaurant we chose was relatively new, with a simple menu that specialized in chicken and rib dishes, with excellent fries and desserts. It was rare that my mother could go anywhere in St. John's without seeing someone she knew, and this day was no different: a former student of hers, who had later become a colleague in the School of Nursing at St. Clare's Mercy Hospital, spotted us at our table just after we were seated. My mother's answer to the inevitable 'how are you?' question was by now well-rehearsed, though this did not soften its impact on Bernadette, who was going through many challenges of her own. The two women parted with a hug, and the promise to extend many prayers for the challenges they'd both face in the days to come.

When we were alone again, my mother asked if I'd mind if she ordered a glass of wine. She knew that I rarely drank alcohol — with the exception of the first weeks of my convalescence after knee surgery, when my dad would pour his 14-year-old daughter a capful of brandy to help ease her shaking and settle her stomach so she could try to eat something before physiotherapy — I'd never turned to alcohol for assistance in coping with anything.

But her question struck me as almost absurd: of course I wouldn't mind. I remember thinking that she could drink the whole bottle if it would ease the shaking of her hands just a little, and soften the lines of pain on her face.

We ordered our lunch, and began to talk about nothing of consequence. I had intended that this outing be light, the conversation about regular things — a normal lunch during an anything-but-normal time — and much of it was. However, my mother had something significant she needed to discuss with me.

Her words, as I remember them:

I know you don't want to talk about this, and maybe you won't have to worry about it for a long time, but I have to tell you something. I want to be buried in my nurse's uniform. And my hat, I want that with me but not on my head. It should be near the top of the casket and off to the side. But the uniform I prefer has short sleeves, and my arms are so thin now. I don't know what to do about that. They'll look so thin. And I'm afraid with everything being white, I'll look too pale as well. There'll be no color whatsoever. And I don't know what to do about that.

I know these conversations are necessary, and I am my mother's daughter, so while inside my mind I screamed for her to stop talking about her final outfit — for the clock to turn back and her cancer to magically go away — I simply looked at her. Because as much as it broke my heart to be even thinking about this, I knew I had the perfect answer. I knew this was one problem I could actually solve.

You should wear your nurse's cape, I told her.

The red-lined, navy blue cape would cover her arms, and she had always looked so beautiful in it. In fact, for me, the cape with the white uniform, and the white hat with black band, was the attire that best captured the essence of my mother — her warmth, her caring, her class, her style, her pride, and her strength.

The dilemma was solved, and she smiled with relief as the load was lifted from her shoulders. I have no idea what kind of expression I wore in that moment, or what kind of expression I wore later, when we returned to the house and she took me to my bedroom — with its white walls, red shag carpet, red bookshelves, desk, and *Vogue* graphic mirrors on the wall. She needed to show me where everything — uniform, slip, and undergarments — were hung inside plastic, waiting for the day when I would need to access them. The box on the shelf held her stockings and perfectly polished shoes. And there was space beside the uniform where she would hang the cape.

I can see it as clearly now as if I was standing there still; the closet that had once been packed with my clothes and shoes, where we would hide with my young cousins when it was time for their visits to end so we could delay their departure... totally empty except for the garments my mother wished to wear to her grave.

Clothes that perhaps we would not need for many years to come.

Day 9

Saturday, May 13

My mother stayed at home for the entirety of Saturday, May 13th. It was another beautiful day — the weather was uncommonly good in St. John's for that time of year — but the week had been immensely draining for her.

For Kenneth and I there was a Mother's Day present to find, and a quick visit with my best friend since seventh grade, Ann Marie Reid. Her daughter's high school graduation was that night — a formal dinner and dance in the same hotel where we were staying, and my friend Hayes (her maiden name and my name for her to this day) wanted us to come see 'Miss Amy' in a dress that was the color of sunshine. We tried to convince my mother to come with us as well, but she declined, standing in the kitchen doorway and waving us away. She was happy to stay at home, she told us, and we didn't insist that she do otherwise. How could we?

The visit with Hayes was relatively short. The afternoon and evening would be busy for their family, and Kenneth and I had a mission to complete. I had bought a Mother's Day card back in Ontario before I knew Mom was ill, but in the turmoil of getting ready, I had forgotten to bring it with me. Her gift had already been sent and received — a new set of luggage for her trip to Kenneth's graduation in June, ordered and delivered directly from the store. Locating her black suitcase among all the other black suitcases on the luggage carousel had always been something of a frustration; on this trip she would have handsome gray plaid bags that would be easy to spot, and a fashion statement as well.

But items delivered in advance of Mother's Day when we were thousands of miles apart in support of a trip that might not happen were not sufficient gifts under the new circumstances, so finding something else — even something small — was important.

It actually took less time than I anticipated to discover *A Mother's Daily Prayer Book*, by Elaine Creaseman, June Eaton, Margaret Anne Huffman, and Marie D. Jones. The cover had a beautiful pink rose, and each spread had a prayer and a verse or quote, illustrated by a flower or two. I'd been searching in vain for stargazer lilies since we had arrived in St. John's — hoping for a sign from my father that everything would somehow be fine — and I remember even now how Kenneth and I paused and looked at each other as we opened the book to the date of her diagnosis, then the date of her surgery. But there were no stargazers on either day. Instead we found that flower on May 15th, one day before her surgery.

Kenneth dubbed May 15th stargazer lily day, and we quietly contemplated what message my father was sending. We also found a card which, I didn't realize until I returned to Waterloo some time later, was the exact one I'd purchased and forgotten to bring. Finally, there was a second card — a stargazer lily on the cover and blank inside, so I could write a message to her.

I don't remember what I wrote in that card, and I can no longer find it. Perhaps one day it will appear again, perhaps it won't. I do have the book. It normally has a place on one of the sets of shelves in my home but as I write this it is beside my keyboard, open to May 15th, and to the Fran Caffey Sandin quote that spoke volumes to me at the time: "I have felt assured that I do not have to fear the future because God is already there."

Yes Dad, I thought, *I know what you are telling me. With this lily, this quote, and the card that is blank inside. I should not be so certain of the outcome of the days to come. I do not want to be so certain. I want to be surprised and amazed and able to tell a different story. I want to believe there will be another miracle. And so I shall... or at least I shall try to...*

But mostly I will try not to fear the future.

Day 10
Sunday, May 14

At 6:03 p.m. Newfoundland time on Sunday, May 14th, 2006, Kenneth and I were atop Signal Hill with dozens of other visitors and locals who had come to watch the breathtaking image of the fog rolling in after what had been a beautiful sunny afternoon. It's a view you never grow tired of, no matter how many times you see it, and if you've lived away for a decade (as we had by then) it's an experience you treasure even more.

I know the exact hour and minute because of the time stamp on the first digital photo we took there. Then, in the sixty seconds between 6:04 and 6:05, I took three photos of Kenneth that remain among my favorites. At 6:08 he took one of me in a black turtleneck, the black poncho I'd sewn the weekend before, and dark glasses, looking out over the expansive ocean. Both of us were getting lost in the sight of the fog, both of us were letting the brisk ocean air, the wind, and the purity of the place, soothe us. I didn't recognize it at the time, but later I would come to realize that everything we experienced on the trip was somehow captured in those photos, even though much of it was still yet to occur.

We had asked my mother to come with us to Signal Hill, but of course she said no. The part of the day that was significant for her — the part she'd requested, and left the house for — was already behind us. She was again completely exhausted.

We had spent the afternoon at my brother's house — mother, son, daughter, grandchildren and dogs. My brother Rik, a musician who'd been living away from Newfoundland since before our father died, had moved back to St. John's a few years prior. He lived with his wife (who was traveling at the time), two daughters, and their dogs, in a beautiful, upper class, period home in the downtown area. It was the type of home my mother admired, even if she would not have chosen it for herself. Kenneth and I had not yet seen him on this trip.

The afternoon passed as these afternoons do — what's happening on the surface masking the story that rests just beneath.

Rik's youngest daughter, Rose, and their two dogs were determined to entertain. There were tours of bedrooms, playrooms, and studios, and detailed explanations of special toys. Rik spoke of plans to someday purchase the adjoining home from the musician who owned it, and then knock out the wall in between.

We watched my mother watching the dogs, as she sat wrapped in a dark green fleece sweater on the couch. We took photos... our last captured images of her. As much as I treasure them they are heartbreaking too, because it's impossible to miss the pain and the intensity in her eyes, and the lines etched more deeply in her face, which had grown too thin.

Rik ordered Chinese takeout. There were jokes about the chicken balls with their sweet and sour sauce not being real Chinese food. There may have been dessert.

The meal complete, we drove a tired mother home, after a brief stop at a pharmacy to pick up something she would need the following day. She did not want to have to go out again on Monday.

Then Kenneth and I went to Signal Hill, because the fog was rolling in despite the sun that was, in that moment, shining.

Day 11
Monday, May 15

May in Newfoundland is not normally shirt-sleeve weather, especially at Cape Spear, the most easterly point of North America. That particular location can be bitterly cold in the middle of summer, when just a few miles away the sun is shining brightly and the temperatures are comfortably warm or even hot. But Newfoundland is more than capable of surprising you with exactly the kind of day you need exactly when you need it.

We woke early on Monday, ate breakfast in our room, layered in warm clothes meant for short hikes over uneven ground, and for sitting on rocks atop hills. Despite my obsession with packing all the right clothes, I had failed to include a warm, causal jacket, though I forgive myself that omission. I had not expected such an outing, and it was really only the delayed surgery that afforded us the opportunity to visit this favorite spot. I was therefore wearing the red jacket that had been one of my 'happy day gifts' from the abbreviated shopping trip the day after we'd arrived.

We had asked my mother to come with us before we dropped her home on Sunday night, but she had of course refused. Again, she did not want to leave her house on Monday.

That morning, Kenneth and I took turns sitting on the first bench you encounter on Cape Spear's cliff-side path, each of us staring out over the North Atlantic while the other took photos. The water was the deep blue that marks the ice-cold waves… the rocks their dark gray and brown. Both land and sea were incredibly beautiful and incredibly dangerous for any unwary person who ignored the warning signs. It was chilly enough at first to keep our jackets on, but by the time we crossed the rocky terrain up to the lighthouse, stopping to lean against the fence that needed a new coat of white paint, our jackets were tied around our waists.

There is nothing to do on these cliffs besides stand or sit or walk. You take in all that is underfoot, all that lies in front of you, all that lies behind. Cape Spear is a place both for thinking, and for not thinking. It is a place to simply be. I don't recall seeing another soul that morning, though that could be faulty memory. The sun warmed us, the breeze calmed us, and the rocks we stood upon gave us strength.

We left after a time, and drove around to Fort Amherst, the harbor-protecting fortress that we had seen countless times from the elevated vantage point on Signal Hill, but had never visited. It looked different close up, at eye level — more worn. But the coastline… what a view that offered. We stood, breathed the sea air, and took more pictures. By the time the morning was almost done we had what we needed. Wind-blown hair, lungs filled with salt air, and the strength of the rock to carry us through the days ahead.

Life intruded as soon as we found ourselves back in the city and cell phone range. A call from my office in Ontario — an HR issue to resolve. I found a spot to pull off the road to talk, part of me wondering at the absurdity of dealing with such things at this particular time. Then I dropped Kenneth back at the hotel before driving to my mother's house. She wasn't alone; an old friend had come to see her… someone she had worked with years ago. The name I knew, though I have forgotten it now; the person I had only met once or twice before. I sat and listened, answered questions, remained silent during the observations about how much I had aged since the last time she'd seen me, when I was in university.

I stayed the afternoon, but before I left my mother insisted on showing me again the nurse's uniform hanging in what had been my closet, all the required pieces of clothing — now including the navy blue cape — organized neatly under the clear plastic coverings. The box with shoes and stockings, and the RN's cap, with its proud black band, sitting in its own plastic wrap, on the shelf.

Monday night, while my mother packed her hospital bags and talked to her sisters and friends on the phone, Kenneth and I worked in our hotel room. Perhaps we should have been with her at the house, but we weren't and I do not believe she wanted us there. She needed to sit in the chair she always occupied for evening telephone conversations, and talk as she always did with the people to whom she meant so much.

And I needed to be working with my son, so that in the morning, she and I both would be ready for the journey to the operating room.

Day 12

Tuesday, May 16

My wake-up call came around 5:00 a.m.; my mother's pick-up time was 6:30.

She was already waiting at the back door when I pulled into the driveway. She stood there, small suitcase by her feet and purse over her shoulder, with all the doors and windows closed behind her except the final one — a glass storm door — that she stepped through as I stopped the car and got out.

I wouldn't get to see her one last time in the kitchen, or in her chair in the living room, or putting the final touches on her make-up in her bedroom. If there were goodbyes for her to say, she had already said them. If there were images for me to preserve, they would have to exist already in my memories.

My mother had spent the majority of her life in hospitals, but it only occurs to me now, years after that particular day, that I had not previously taken her to hospital for some illness of her own. Maybe a medical appointment or two over the years, but she had infrequently been a patient in my presence.

We checked her in and I sat with her in the long rectangular room where those destined for surgery wait for their name to be called. In my memory the walls are cold and green, and the room harsh and metal. I don't think it was actually like that, but it's how I perceived this place.

My mother had completed her nursing training at this same

hospital — St. Clare's Mercy Hospital. After she'd been forced to stop working in Emergency (the area she loved best) because of the gastric hemorrhage she suffered when I was five-years-old, she'd become a nursing instructor, and everywhere in the building were nurses who at one point had been her students. The majority of them had called her 'Mom'; the care she showed them earned her that honour, and it is no exaggeration to say she was widely adored.

Because of this, I knew without a doubt that she would have the best possible care — these former students would repay her kindnesses and prove that they had learned well from her.

My dearest friend Hayes, who we'd visited briefly on Saturday, now worked in the Operating Room and was on duty that day. She came to see us while we waited. She wouldn't be in my mother's surgery, but would check on her as often as she could and provide me with updates whenever possible. For me, she was a lifeline.

When they came to wheel my mother away, we were waiting at the farthest end of the room from the doors through which patients exited, and I watched from there until she was out of sight. Then I clutched her bags and mine, walked to another, smaller rectangular waiting room, and sat in one of the wooden-armed, leather chairs. Eventually I pulled out pages I had brought with me to edit. They were a familiar weight on my lap, a familiar job to occupy some of my thoughts. The mechanical pencil in my hand was a comfort.

My brother Rik stopped by after he dropped his daughters at school. I have always been quieter than either of my brothers, so Rik contributed more to our conversation than I did. This was not unusual; every so often my mother used to remind me of an image she held of me in her mind. I was still young enough to be in a playpen, and on this particular day, I was wearing little red plaid pants and a white sweater. As was apparently my habit, I was observing what was going on with great intent, but saying nothing. My mother thought: *Poor little thing, how's she ever going to get on in the world if she never says a word?*

We used to laugh about that later, once I'd grown. I'd tell her: *Of course I didn't talk much. Between you, Steve, Rik and all our visitors, how was I supposed to get a word in edgewise?* The reality, though, was that I was more like my father in that regard. We tend towards quiet — listen more than we talk.

My Aunt Sheila came from her home in Ferryland, the historic outport on the Southern Shore where the fourteen Morry children in my mother's family had grown up, and joined us in the waiting room early in the day.

Sheila, the youngest of the seven sisters, is strength and beauty and laughter. She's a wildly entertaining storyteller, and blessed with what we used to call the 'Morry gift of gab.' She'd lived in Labrador for much of my life so I'd only met her briefly when she came to St. John's for visits, and didn't really have any chance to get to know her until the last weeks of my father's life. She'd come to visit my mother when she happened to be in town. She stayed for many days when she realized what was happening, saving us then with her stories and her laughter. She stayed with me that day too, so I would not be alone — saving me again with her stories and her laughter and her strength.

Time moves all too slowly in these waiting rooms, and moves slower still once the hands of the clock move past the time you were told you could expect the surgery to be over. Sometime in the early afternoon, Hayes came to tell us that my mother was in the recovery room, but they needed to keep her there longer. Something about difficulties they hadn't anticipated.

The next time she came it was to let us know my mother was being moved to the Intensive Care Unit, instead of a regular room as had been the original plan, and would have been the norm. The exact reason is blurry now, but there had been complications, and they needed to monitor her.

I still had my mother's small suitcase and purse with me, but since she wouldn't need them that evening, Sheila and I took them to the car before she left to head home. Sheila, I recall, wouldn't let me carry anything, because I'd had surgery just a few weeks before.

The rest of the day was spent waiting. Checking in with Kenneth and Peter back at home in Ontario. With Steve in BC. And waiting. Waiting outside the ICU for the doctor to come and tell me what had happened, what he had found, what to expect. Waiting for Hayes because she was my link to the nurses inside ICU.

Waiting for a doctor who didn't come. Waiting for Hayes, who always did. Waiting for news.

At some point I got a muffin from the hospital cafeteria — I hadn't eaten all day and needed to. Finally, sometime after 8 p.m., when I learned the doctor had, in fact, left the hospital and wouldn't be coming to see me, I departed too. On shaky legs and an empty stomach.

The image of my mother being wheeled away in her chair etched firmly in my mind.

Day 13
Wednesday, May 17

My memories of May 17th are divided into three distinct parts: a morning visit to Intensive Care so a grandson could see his grandmother; a surreal afternoon settling my mother into a private room on the sixth floor of St. Clare's Mercy Hospital; and an evening defined by a piece of carrot cake.

I'll start with the third: the carrot cake, and the kindness it reflected — a kindness that still reaches deep inside, and fills my eyes with tears. The definition, for me, of friendship.

I'd eaten virtually nothing for two days — hadn't wanted to. But at some point in the late afternoon I started to feel some semblance of appetite return and I began wishing for carrot cake. I said as much to Hayes when she somehow managed another visit to my mother's room. *The only thing I really want is a piece of carrot cake,* I told her.

I shouldn't have been surprised when the phone rang about forty-five minutes after I got back to the hotel room that evening. I shouldn't have been surprised that it was Hayes. She was downstairs, and needed the room number. She'd gone home after her long shift (a shift interrupted by trips to check on my mother and me) and had gotten her husband Bruce (Saint Bruce, she rightfully calls him) to drive her back into town from their home outside the city so she could buy carrot cake and bring it to my downtown hotel. The process must have added at least an hour and a half to her already long day.

I cried after the door closed behind her, standing there with the cake in my hands as she headed home for the second time that evening, to make dinner for her family. Or, I should say, for *the rest* of her family.

This was Newfoundland. And this was Hayes, the best friend anyone could ever ask for.

Rewind about six or seven hours. My mother had been released from ICU, and she would need her bags and everything in them — or so I thought. While the nurses settled her into her bed, I retrieved the bags from the car, my step lighter than it had been the previous day.

When I saw her for the first time after the surgery, her frailty was still a surprise, and the oxygen tube was disturbing. I hung her clothes in the room's closet — she wouldn't be able to wear any of them at that point, but maybe tomorrow. Her prayer-a-day book and stargazer lily card found a place on a small shelf inset into the wall. She couldn't really see them from her vantage point, but they were there for her anyway. Or maybe for the visitors.

Nurses, in my mother's day, wore outfits like the one she wanted to be buried in — spotless white uniforms, hats with the black band that marked their status as RNs, white stockings and shoes that were meticulously cared for. The nurses who tended her after her surgery wore the garments of the mid-2000s: smocks with pants and sneaker-like shoes — all colors, nothing uniform-like about them. She cooperated with her caregivers, was polite, but when they left the room she would comment sadly about their shoes and lack of uniforms.

Visitors, expecting a much more robust Mary, began flooding in. Most stayed just a short time when they realized rest was what she most needed. Some stayed a long time, sitting quietly in case she needed anything. We were relieved, because she was out of ICU and surely that meant she was improving.

Rewind further, back to the late morning. At that point we didn't know how long my mother would be in Intensive Care, but Kenneth and I were scheduled to return to Ontario the following day, so this would likely be the best opportunity for him to see her before he left. And seeing her was necessary, in case she wasn't able to come for his graduation in June after all.

I suspect if we'd been able to ask, my mother would have told us she didn't want Kenneth to visit her, especially in ICU. The image of her in bed, with oxygen tubes and surrounded by all manner of monitoring devices, is not the picture she would want to leave her grandson. She would fear, I think, that this sort of mental image would override all the others in his memory.

But it was a visit that needed to happen, which is something she would have also understood.

Kenneth found the hospital was quite different than the gleaming marvels of future technology he included in his novels at the time. In the futures he imagined, the ICU's sense of weariness is replaced by hope and energy — the knowledge that any malady might be overcome by the wisdom of doctors like Elandra Caine. This ICU was different. The carefully-erected barrier (he calls it an 'airlock') that separated it from the rest of the hospital. The hand sanitizer stations. The monitoring devices, the nearby nurses, and the oxygen… these are what he remembers.

He doesn't remember how long we stood by the bed — not long, I suspect — or what we said — just a little, if anything. He was aware that this might be the last time he saw his grandmother, and he knew her fate was out of his hands.

We were three generations there in the ICU — in a place none of us wanted to be.

Day 14
Thursday, May 18

Fog, in Newfoundland, has a particular character. There have been times in my life when it has felt intentional, almost sentient — as if it has come when it is needed, to wrap a soft blanket around me, protect me while I worked inside myself to find a way through some harsh reality.

On Thursday, May 18th, fog infused everything… a light fog at first, then a thicker, denser, heavier fog that caused the world to pause.

Kenneth and I were scheduled to fly out mid-afternoon. Steve was coming in the evening, so I had no worries that my mother would lack for the company and care she needed. Indeed, as a doctor he would know what questions to ask and what signs or symptoms to look for — things I didn't know. And his presence would bring her happiness, if anything could.

We packed early in the morning, a light fog blurring the view of Signal Hill from our window. Then I visited my mother in the hospital, a final visit before my flight. When I had left the night before, the nurses had expected she would be improved in the morning, so my step was again a bit light when I walked down the hall to her room.

But she was not improved, really. Not worse, but not better. Still weak, and tired, and the oxygen was still required. They were monitoring some fluid build-up in one of her lungs, which years prior had been damaged by tuberculosis. This was not abnormal, they told me — it was expected to clear.

And Steve would be there in less than twelve hours.

By the time we reached the airport, the fog had gotten thicker. We sat at our departure gate, Kenneth and I, wondering if the flight would actually be able to leave. Wondering if the fog was telling us that we should be staying — that to leave now was to somehow desert my mother when she needed us most. We talked about that — should we go back through security and ask to reschedule the flight?

But I knew, in the place I've learned to never question, that I was supposed to at least try to get Kenneth home that day, and I'm as certain about that now as I was then. I also knew I had to get home as well — had to escape St. John's that day, if it was at all possible, even if it meant I had to come back.

So we sat and waited, positioned in front of a wall of windows through which only the faintest outline of a plane was visible beneath the heavy shroud of fog. Waited through the first flight delay, then the second. Waited until late in the afternoon when the fog slipped back beyond the horizon and told us it was time to leave.

For now.

Day 15
Friday, May 19

I went to my office on Friday, May 19th. I needed normality. I needed to think about something that wasn't related to illness, and didn't involve hospitals. Between my surgery and my mother's, I'd been away from my desk for weeks. I needed, on so many levels, to be there.

On my way home from work, I stopped at a store that I wandered through some days for no other purpose than to decompress. I was still there when Steve called me, to give me the latest update and tell me he needed me to come back to Newfoundland.

Steve and I had talked frequently throughout the day. My mother's condition had not improved or even stabilized in the twenty-four hours since Kenneth and I had boarded the plane in St. John's. Indeed, the fluid build-up in her lungs had gotten worse throughout the night and was an escalating concern, as was her dependence on oxygen and her decreasing strength and lucidity. Pneumonia, they had decided. Apparently, the tuberculosis-damaged lung was much weaker than anyone in the family would ever have realized.

As I stood in an aisle by the picture frames and listened to Steve's voice, I learned she required more constant monitoring and care than was available in her regular room. With his encouragement, they were returning her to the ICU.

While I was relieved to know that she would be receiving the attention she needed, I was entirely aware of what the need for constant monitoring and care meant. I was also beginning to realize, just as we all were, that the tuberculosis she had survived as a young woman had been far more damaging than any of us had realized. Whether she was aware of that, whether she concealed that truth for her entire life, I will never know. Whether we should have predicted the danger ourselves, I cannot say. Perhaps we can be forgiven for never having guessed that my active, vibrant mother had lived the majority of her life on anything less than two lungs with full capacity.

But even had we known she'd been left with a lung ill-equipped to deal with the stress it was now enduring, there would have been no choice but to proceed with the surgery.

Steve believed that if the deterioration in her current condition continued, it would proceed rapidly, so we had very little time. As a family, we needed to decide what our mother had meant when she'd told Rik she never wanted to be on life support.

I had boarded a plane just over twenty-four hours earlier... brought Kenneth home... hugged and commiserated with cancer-fighting Atlas... held Peter through the night... gone to my office and done normal things for about eight hours... then stopped at a favorite store on the way home to look at picture frames and journals and housewares.

One regular day of respite, to partially restore the balance of my life... but now I headed home to update Peter and Kenneth, call my boss, book another flight, and pack another suitcase.

A suitcase filled with what-if clothes.

Day 16
Saturday, May 20

Now everything speeds up; at the same time it slows down.

Hayes picked me up at the airport mid-afternoon on Saturday. I almost had more luggage than her blue hatchback could accommodate — uncertain as I was of the length of my trip and the circumstances I would face, my packing had been, for want of a better word, thorough.

We stopped quickly at my mother's house so I could drop off my suitcase and garment bag — leave them unopened in my childhood bedroom. Then it was on to the hospital where we would have the first of too few family conferences about my mother's treatment options.

When I'd boarded the plane in the morning, I knew my mother's condition was continuing to deteriorate. Rik had said she'd told him that she didn't want to be kept alive on machines. *No life support,* her words had been. I can imagine her saying them. I can hear the tone she would have used and picture the look on her face as easily as if I had been present to witness the instructions.

But did that mean she wouldn't have wanted assistance while receiving treatment that could help with the pneumonia and give her time to heal? What exactly did 'life support' mean and at what point did the 'no life support' directive kick in? Could she possibly want us to just let her go, without trying to save her?

So many families are forced to ask themselves these questions. I wish that there were easier answers, but there are not.

I can't recall who else was there that day when Hayes and I reached the hospital. I remember only my two brothers, Hayes — who we asked to please stay, she was family too — and the female doctor who came to speak with us.

You never want to hear the words you inevitably hear in these rooms with doctors who are so practiced in their deliveries. The words trying to prepare you for things that make no sense and outcomes that can't possible be real. Outcomes they would know were wrong if only they knew your mother. The same mother who had already told her daughter exactly what clothes she wanted to be buried in.

The doctor's concern was clinical and legitimate: what if we managed to deal with the immediate danger? What if antibiotics helped address the pneumonia? There was still the cancer to deal with. The possibility of chemo seemed remote at best; based on my mother's age and her general physical condition, she likely wouldn't survive it. So why prolong the inevitable? Our mother wasn't a young woman.

I thought: *How can you think of our mother as old? You don't know her. You don't know how much she has done, how much she still has to do, how vibrant she has always been, the struggles she has overcome in her lifetime, the battles she has won, the difference she has made in this very hospital, the lives she has helped save... You don't know her. And if there's any chance at all that she can beat the odds, shouldn't we at least give her the chance? How can we sit in this room and give up on someone who never gave up on anyone else?*

We didn't have to make the decision right then, at least. Things weren't critical that afternoon. But they were heading in that direction, and when they reached a certain point, the choice before us would be whether to intubate — to ease the strain on her lungs so that the antibiotics would have time to work. We had hours, maybe a whole day, before the decision would need to be made.

That afternoon I made the first of many trips into the surreal world of the ICU. Through the outer, then inner doors — Kenneth's 'airlock' — then a right turn to take me to my mother's bed. She recognized me, knew I had come to visit, but she wasn't surprised to see me. I don't think she realized that I had flown home two days before, and was now back again, less than forty-eight hours later.

We spoke, but not about anything of significance. Silently, I learned to understand the readings on the monitor over her bed, so I would know what to look for in the vigil that would follow.

When we eventually left the hospital that evening, Steve, Hayes, and I went to a downtown restaurant for dinner. Of all the things I could remember, I remember the underground parking. I don't remember the food. I don't remember the conversation.

Then Steve and I went back to the house we had grown up in — me to my old bedroom, him to the one right beside it that he'd shared with Rik before moving to his own room in the basement. The furniture in his room was different than it had been — it was furniture we had given her when we first left Newfoundland. The furniture in my room was the same, a minor detail that was almost a metaphor for the very moment in time we found ourselves trapped within.

He slept — he felt a distinct comfort in being home.

I didn't — I couldn't even get under the covers of the tiny twin bed that had been my refuge for years. The small bedside lamp stayed on all night. The house, without either my mother or my father, was haunted by grief, beset by hollow horror.

My room, with my mother's casket clothes hanging in the closet, was a place I couldn't bear to be.

Day 17
Sunday, May 21

May 20th, 2006 was the last night I would ever spend in my parents' home, though I don't think I realized that when I called the hotel on Sunday morning.

If there was guilt at running away — for that's what it felt like I was doing — it was sufficiently overshadowed by my acceptance that I was incapable of staying.

The hotel welcomed me back, gave me a room with a view of St. John's Harbour and Signal Hill. When I could eat, a hot turkey sandwich with dressing, fries and gravy that has yet to be matched, was delivered on a tray to my room. I was also with family, literally: Aunt Sheila's daughter Nikki worked at the front desk, and one of the gifts of this time was the small chance it afforded us to get to know one another as we never had growing up. Her hugs and smiles were lifelines. Her friends and colleagues made this place a sanctuary.

This was not just for me; the hospitality and caring of Newfoundlanders is legendary. I believe it's founded in their innate generosity combined with an understanding of loss that's etched into their souls as deeply as the lines carved into the island's many cliffs.

The hotel was very near the hospital — they were, respectively, at the bottom and top of one of the famously steep hills of downtown St. John's. I simply needed to make a right turn out of the hotel's underground lot, head up that twisty hill and through one set of lights, then turn left onto the small lane outside the hospital's main entrance, park, and take an elevator to the fifth floor to be near my mother.

The waiting area was outside the outer doors to ICU, tucked at the end of a hall for some privacy, and it was mostly full that afternoon. People were arriving now as news spread, many driving hours to reach the hospital. Even though they could see my mother for only a few brief minutes, they didn't just visit her bedside and leave. They waited with us — aunts and uncles and cousins and friends, many of whom I had not seen in years, and Steve had not seen even longer.

We intubated that evening after another doctor-family conference. We had decided that an interim measure designed to ease the stress on my mother's system so that she had a chance to rally wasn't life support, per se. Every breath had been taking more and more effort, and none of them were giving her sufficient oxygen. Any chance that the antibiotics could work was being undermined by that struggle, and the related impact on kidneys and other systems was growing critical.

She knew and understood the plan: intubate, ease the pressure on her system, and give the drugs a chance to do their job. For how long, we didn't know. What the ultimate result would be, we didn't know. But at least we had hope.

When Mary Louise Barron looked up at me from her bed that day and said *remember, I will be with you always,* I should have realized that she didn't believe she would wake up. But it wasn't until later that it truly registered, and I came to understand that this was perhaps why she hadn't argued against the assisted breathing in the first place.

As evening moved to night, the sense of relief at the ease to her struggle was welcome. Hayes and I still kept vigil in the waiting area, checking regularly for updates to make sure all was well. Talking. Popping back into the room from time to time to watch the numbers on the monitors. Settling back in the waiting area again. Talking some more. By the time I returned to the hotel that night, my mother was resting peacefully, and with the lights of the harbor twinkling outside my window, I slept.

My mother would have hated, I know, to be remembered as she appeared on those days and nights in her hospital bed. But there is no worry in that regard. Because Mom, know that even now I cannot actually picture you in that bed, still wearing a hospital robe, supported by tubes and wires and all manner of machinery. There is not a single mental image of you from that time. Instead, I picture you in the long winter-white and black plaid coat you sewed, the one you always wore with the collar up... with black slacks, black turtleneck and stylish black leather shoes. Or the moss green boiled wool coat and black hat we bought on your first trip to Waterloo. Or your blue jeans, white collared shirt, and gray sweater for cold days at Bellevue. Or your white nurse's uniform and spotless white shoes.

And always, your eyes are happy and you are smiling.

Day 18
Monday, May 22

For reasons that are painfully obvious, Intensive Care Units don't have strict visiting hours. When I left the hospital on Sunday night, the nurses suggested an 11:00 arrival on Monday morning, unless we received a call suggesting we were needed sooner.

The telephone didn't ring through the night — my mother had been peaceful, her vitals improving. Monday felt lighter for that reason. After checking in at the appointed hour and sitting with her for awhile, I resumed my post in the waiting area. At regular intervals I'd make the trip through first the outer, then the inner doors, to sit or stand by her bedside. Heavily sedated as she was, she didn't know I was there, and talking wouldn't have been possible even if she did. Intubation is not conducive to conversation. But I was there anyway, my head tilted up and my eyes locked on the main monitor as I gained comfort from the numbers, and prayed the positive trend would continue.

There are sounds in an ICU you think you'll never forget. You take them with you when you leave in the evening and you hear them in your dreams all through the night. But time has taught me that after a period they do in fact dim, their meaning begins to fade, and eventually they grow silent.

I knew every nuance that day, however. People continued to visit, popping in to stand briefly at the end or side of her bed, keeping me company when I was in the waiting area, saying their own prayers. Sheila, Laura, Ursula, Flo, Esther, Mary Rogers, Betty, Jack, Kelly — aunts, uncles, cousins, my mother's friends, and Hayes of course, whenever she could.

I don't know what I ate that day. I don't know if I managed to do any editing while I sat in the waiting area, though I did bring it with me — a black leather knapsack always filled but rarely opened. What was most important was that by the time the skies had darkened and I was leaving again, the woman in the bed with the machines and assistive technologies appeared to be rallying.

As I walk this particular lane of memories, it is hard to feel again the lightness I allowed myself to feel that night. In retrospect, I know it was really nothing more than an illusion... the sun breaking briefly through the clouds, giving us a ray of hope that the skies would clear.

Which, of course, they wouldn't.

Day 19

Tuesday, May 23

My brother Steve celebrates his birthday four days before mine each year, on May 23rd.

When we returned on Tuesday morning at the appointed hour, we weren't expecting to be told my mother had improved sufficiently that the doctor thought she should be removed from the intubator. But that was the news and recommendation that awaited us.

We sat outside while the intubation process was reversed less than forty-eight hours after it had been initiated — surprised but not unhappy that it was happening so quickly.

I was on the other side of the bed when Steve leaned in to ask my mother if she knew what day it was and to thank her for his birthday gift — for rallying. I listened when he told her that just as they'd left the hospital together after he'd been born some fifty years prior, they were going to leave the hospital together again soon. I watched when she nodded back.

There will always be a question in my mind as to whether or not my mother would have survived if she had remained intubated. Would she have been able to gain more strength, or would she have become too dependent on the assistance — gotten to the stage that it would indeed have become actual life support? Also, if she had survived the post-operative ordeal, would she have been strong enough to fight the cancer? But the questions are pointless, because questions like those have no answers.

The one thing I do know is that my mother would never have allowed herself to die on Steve's birthday. She could not have shadowed the celebration of his birth with the anniversary of her death — she adored him too much, loved him too deeply.

Once my mother was breathing again on her own, the vigil of her vital signs once more became my focus. She was hoarse when they removed the tube from her throat, and still exhausted, but more lucid and aware than she had been since my return on Saturday.

I stationed myself again in the waiting area, kept company by aunts, uncles, cousins, my mother's friends, and Hayes. I returned to her bedside at times of my choosing, or when she happened to ask for one of her children. I left the hospital only for the time required to join my brothers for the birthday dinner Rik had arranged for Steve that evening.

There are parts of that day I can hardly bear to remember, yet they remain impossible to forget. All that really mattered, as the minutes of May 23rd ticked by, was what was happening to my mother physically, mentally, and emotionally. As she told me when she and I were alone and she felt strong enough to speak, she actually hadn't expected to wake up, and couldn't believe she was going to live.

Her questions to me were incredulous: *I'm getting better? I'm going to live?*

Maybe I should have answered yes to both, but I didn't. Instead I told her only what I knew to be the truth: that her oxygen levels and all her vitals had improved much over the past couple of days... that she was stronger than she had been... that everyone hoped and prayed the positive trend would continue.

And all we could do was wait to see what the overnight hours, and the next day, would bring.

Day 20
Wednesday, May 24

Based on the pace of my mother's deterioration after the intubation was removed, I suspect the date on her obituary would indeed have been May 23rd if we hadn't given the antibiotics time to fight the post-op pneumonia.

As morning moved to afternoon on Wednesday, May 24th, the advances made on Sunday night and Monday began to steadily reverse. It was as though a large ball of snow had been pushed up a hill, with every indication being that it would reach the top and stabilize. But it didn't make it. Instead, not so near to the top, it began to slide backwards, and then began rolling back down, gaining more speed with every inch.

For Steve, this was one of the hardest things of all. His life is helping people live, but he had been powerless to help his father, and now again was powerless to help his mother.

By mid-afternoon family conferences were again being called, and Steve and Rik summoned back to the hospital to discuss alternatives. There was nothing to be gained by intubation; if it hadn't worked the first time, it would not work the second. This time, any intervention would truly be life support — something she had herself now made clear to the doctor and nurses she did not want, would not permit.

We would not re-intubate, unless she specifically and lucidly requested that we do so, which wasn't going to happen. A face mask?

If she allowed it, yes, but otherwise no. Just an oxygen tube for as long as she was willing.

My mother took her fate into her own hands that afternoon, fueled by a refusal to live the kind of life she knew she would have if she survived. She would undoubtedly need oxygen on an ongoing basis. Chemotherapy, if she was strong enough to have it, would take a terrible toll. Her independence would be gone. Her dignity. Chances were she would not be able to see to her own needs; people — relatives, friends or caregivers — would have to come to the house to help her.

She could not, would not, impact the lives of her family and friends that way. She could not, would not, live like that. There would be no more intubation, despite her again weakening state.

It's OK Mom, we weren't going to force it on you, I thought as I again sat by her bed.

She just wanted to go home to die, she told my aunts that same day. She was so angry with us, they thought, for trying to keep her alive. It broke their hearts, and mine.

I'm sorry Mom, but we had to give you a fighting chance. I know you never expected to live — the uniform in my closet, all pressed and ready for the funeral home was a clear enough message — but there was a chance you would rally. And can't you see we never could have lived with ourselves if we'd just let you go? Can't you see we had to try?

And as for taking you home to die, you were too weak to return to Penetanguishene. But St. Clare's was in some ways as much your home... with all the years you spent there... all the nurses who called you Mom. If you couldn't be in the bed you shared with my father for more than forty years, at least you could still be surrounded by love, in a place you loved as well. A place where you took away pain, saved lives, and taught others to do the same. A place where you did your life's work.

The snowball that had been moving upwards with such hope was rolling back down the hill. It was unclear how long it would continue on this downward path, but there was no longer any doubt about its destination.

Day 21
Thursday, May 25

When we arrived at the hospital on the morning of May 25th, my mother was determined and in complete control. By this I do not mean she was physically stronger; in that regard her condition had reverted to where it would have been had we not intubated on Sunday night — grown worse in fact.

But it was as if her physical and mental capacities were inversely proportional to one another — the more she lost on the physical side, the more she seemed to gain in mental strength. This was not really a surprise to those of us who knew her best, and had witnessed her mental strength while growing up, then especially during the years of my father's illness.

She had already made her wishes known to the doctor and medical staff: she would accept no additional support on that or future days, beyond what was required to ensure she could see and speak with the people to whom she wanted to say goodbye. After that, there was to be no interference. The time had come to let her go.

We talked to her, Steve and I — asked if she knew what her instructions meant, needing to be sure of her certainty and lucidity. That confirmed, we left her bedside temporarily to make the telephone calls to people she most wanted to see. Because while it was possible she would linger, rally even, there was only a miniscule chance that she would be with us by the time the sun set.

I still have a small card I made to carry in my wallet on that second trip in May 2006 — one with the home and cell numbers for Sheila, Flo, Esther, Hayes, and others. I don't remember which calls we made directly, though there were only a few. The system, never formalized but still flawless, ensured that the moment a handful of people knew, the news would spread to all the others.

Our waiting area was moved inside the outer doors of the ICU to a room that had soft seats and gentle lighting. This was a place meant to offer comfort for families during the final hours. I would describe it in more detail if I could, but I can't. That's all I remember.

Soon the room was full, then overfull with people spilling out into the hall. Aunts, uncles, cousins, and friends funneled in one or two at a time to say hello, and then goodbye. No one tried to really control the flow. There was no longer any need for rest periods.

This was the morning when I asked my mother whether there was a sign I should look for, and told my aunts that there would be one — but I would only tell them what it was after I saw it.

By midday, my mother had been moved to a private room within ICU, the place where stays were to be short-term. The few belongings that had been in the drawer of her bedside table had been transferred to an identical unit there, and the machinery was all the same. But there were walls for privacy instead of curtains, and an extra chair or two.

I moved back and forth from my mother's side to the waiting room, not surprised by all the people who had come, only by the speed with which they arrived. Even my mother's family doctor, who had so quickly arranged the appointment with the specialist just twenty-one days before, came for a lunchtime visit. She wanted to tell me personally that the results of my mother's regular mammogram had arrived that morning. On any other day the news would have been chilling: the cancer, it seems, had not been isolated in my mother's abdomen after all.

Of course it hadn't, I thought.

The sound of my mother's labored breathing was the memory that haunted me most for months after her death, but I can no longer hear the ragged, struggling sounds. Thankfully, those echoes have faded. I sat alone at the foot of her bed for brief intervals, not wanting to be there, but not wanting to be anywhere else. Moving to her side to hold her hand from time to time. Leaving when someone arrived for a private moment.

Everyone I spoke with who visited my mom that day left with a message just for them. The conversations were brief — her voice was so raspy, her breathing increasingly labored — but still she managed, during her final hours, to say the things the people who meant so much to her needed to hear.

Still she managed to find the strength to be the woman who I would always remember as my mother.

By about 3:00 p.m. the stream of visitors had ended, and I was alone again at the foot of the bed. Sometime soon after the nurse who checked on her vitals looked in my direction.

Your brothers should be here, she told me.

I didn't react at first, unable to immediately process the implications. Then I suddenly realized hours had been reduced to minutes.

I can't remember if I asked the nurse if she could go to the waiting room to get Steve and Rik, or if I went. My next clear memory is of all three siblings in the room, and the nurse asking my mother if she wanted oxygen.

Will it make it easier, my mother asked, *easier to breathe?*

Yes, it will help, the nurse responded.

No, my mother insisted. *NO. NO. NO.*

She had said her goodbyes. Her children were with her. Her husband, her parents, and so many others awaited her. She would not linger; and she would leave entirely on her own terms.

It was really only minutes then, even if it seemed longer. Steve held her hand and spoke words only she would be able to hear. Each side and the foot of the bed guarded by a son or daughter listening for the next breath, watching the numbers on the monitor fall.

Then her anguished breathing finally stopped.

You miss a last breath because you don't realize it is indeed the final one until after there are no more. Her heart still beat for a brief spell after that, but not long. And the numbers on the screen didn't all fall to zero right away. Things weren't instantaneous like you see on television. But she was gone.

Obviously and finally gone, after just twenty-one days in May.

Strong, determined, and with help from no one.

Her children standing next to her.

From the small drawer unit by her bed, I gathered the items that would need to go home, or back to the people who had brought them for her, then made sure the nurses knew what had to go with her to the morgue. I went to the outer waiting room and called home to tell Peter and Kenneth that she had died, and my office to tell my boss, Arthur. Then I sat there with Hayes and Esther, literally not knowing what to do or where to go until my best friend took me in hand, guided me out of the hospital, and accompanied me to my mother's house. We had to ensure everything was organized for the following day.

Of course, I didn't stay the night in that place. Before darkness fell I was back in the sanctuary of my hotel, with my view of the Narrows.

Peter would be on a flight the following day. The clothes I would need for the wake and funeral were already hanging in the closet of the hotel, the clothes my mother would need in my childhood bedroom.

In that moment, there was nothing to do. And so I stood in the middle of the room and wept, standing until I could no longer stand, crying until there were no tears left.

Then I got up again and walked to the desk, with my mother's strength and example to sustain me, and sat at my laptop to write her obituary.

BARRON, Mary L. (nee Morry), R.N. — Passed peacefully on Thursday, May 25, 2006 at St. Clare's Mercy Hospital, Mary Barron, age 77 years, after a brief battle with cancer. Predeceased by her husband Richard J. in 1994. Left with loving memories her son Steve and daughter-in-law Glenna of Anmore, BC; her son Rik and daughter-in-law Sarah and granddaughters: Mae and Rose of St. John's; her daughter Jacqui Tam and son-in-law Peter and grandson Kenneth of Waterloo, ON. Also left to mourn brother Jack (Margaret), Bishop's Falls; sisters: Ursula Kieley, Laura Morry-Williams, Sheila Morry (Aubrey Paul) all of Ferryland; Margaret Bulko (Joe) of Maryland, USA; brothers-in-law and sisters-in-law and their families: Pat and Vonnie Barron of Alberta, Lawrence and Jo Barron of Mount Pearl, Marg Barron of Prince Edward Island, Jim and Flo Barron of St. John's, Theresa and Bill Janes, Cole Hr., NS; as well as countless nieces, nephews and numerous close friends and nursing colleagues. Resting at Carnell's Funeral Home, 329 Freshwater Road on Saturday and Sunday from 2-4 and 7-9 p.m. Mass of Christian Burial will take place on Monday, May 29, 2006 at 1:30 p.m. from St. Pius X Parish with interment to follow at Holy Sepulchre Cemetery. Flowers gratefully accepted or donations in Mary's memory may be made to the Dr. H. Bliss Murphy Cancer Care Foundation or St. Clare's Mercy Hospital. To send a message of condolence or to sign the memorial guest book, please visit www.carnells.com.

The level of strength and courage with which you lived your life amazed and touched everyone you knew. The strength and courage you displayed in these last weeks and in your last hour astounded even those of us who knew you so very well. You were a remarkable woman, and loving wife, mother, daughter, sister, aunt, friend and nurse. We will miss you, we will love you, and we will celebrate you forever. (Published 05/27/06)

Epilogue

On the Monday we buried my mother, her coffin was escorted into the church by an honour guard of nurses, and guided to its place in front of the altar by her son-in-law, Peter, brother Jack, three nephews, Vincent, Peter and Pat, and dear friend Mario.

As I knelt in the front-row pew after Holy Communion, Peter at my side, the nurses slowed so very slightly to touch my hand as they walked past. Of course these nurses would understand the incredible power of their gentle touches. Of course they would also know how important it was that any goodbye to my mother include them — she had organized so many such guards herself over the years, it was only fitting that she be honoured in the same manner.

Our dear Penetanguishene neighbor, Nora, who'd been my piano teacher when I was little, was the organist. My cousins Wynn-Ann, Lynn, Todd, and Nikki, and Rik's wife Sarah, all played a role in the service. The beautiful voices of cousin Margaret, Aunt Lillian's daughter, and her own daughter Anna, filled the church with *On Eagles Wings*. And as her casket left the church, it was accompanied by Rik's instrumental *Hand in Hand*.

Steve and I had chosen her casket together. It was wooden, with beautiful rose etchings. I knew instantly it was the correct one. The certainty I felt the moment I saw it didn't surprise me. Steve knew instantly as well, but was startled by the physical jolt that went through him. It was disconcerting, but powerful, and not a sensation he'd expected or previously experienced, he explained to me later.

I just smiled. *That was Mom making sure you knew this was the one she wanted,* I told him.

The traditional Newfoundland wake had been held on Saturday and Sunday, the room constantly packed with people. I was usually the first person visitors had approached at the funeral home. *You have to be Jacqui,* they'd say. *You look so much like your mother did at your age.*

Many of the people who'd taken the time to come to the wake attended the funeral as well, filling the parking lot and the church. My mother had feared the church wouldn't be full — we'd talked about that at our last lunch too. I'd reassured her then, and now I imagined her looking down and being content at the sight below her.

I met many of these people again outside the church in the parking lot. Thanked them for coming. There were hugs, memories, smiles, tears, and a lingering disbelief that it would take all of us a while to shake, if we ever truly did. And goodbyes. So many of these people I would not see again for a very long time. Some I would not see ever.

We lowered my mother into her place next to my father, then returned for the post-funeral gathering to the house where I'd grown up. The place I'd fled from days before. Aunts, uncles, cousins, the dearest of friends — they were all there, with food and drink, laughter and stories, and moments when everything would just suddenly grow quiet.

When Peter and I left to head back to the hotel and pack — we were flying out the next morning — I thought I'd be back in the summer, to help empty and ready the house for sale. But I never did go back... never stepped through the back door again. Maybe I couldn't.

Maybe the truth is that I didn't need to.

My mother was no longer there, and never would be again.

But her courage and her strength, her determination and her dedication, her style and her class, and all the lessons she had taught me, these would be with me always.

Afterword

In the ten years that passed between my mother's death and the release of this memoir — *Twenty-One Days in May* — I approached each day with the certainty that both my mother and father remain with me always. My mother's red and white roses, and my father's stargazer lilies, appear when I most need them. The examples my parents set and the lessons they taught guide every aspect of my life, both in terms of how I live it and what I try to accomplish.

And to a large degree, I will always see and judge myself through my mother's eyes, and be the better for it.